Theatre as Voyeurism

Theatre as Voyeurism
The Pleasures of Watching

Edited by

George Rodosthenous
University of Leeds, UK

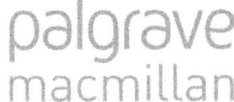

Selection, introduction and editorial matter © George Rodosthenous 2015
Chapters © their individual authors

All rights reserved. No reproduction, copy or transmission of this
publication may be made without written permission.

No portion of this publication may be reproduced, copied or transmitted
save with written permission or in accordance with the provisions of the
Copyright, Designs and Patents Act 1988, or under the terms of any licence
permitting limited copying issued by the Copyright Licensing Agency,
Saffron House, 6–10 Kirby Street, London EC1N 8TS.

Any person who does any unauthorized act in relation to this publication
may be liable to criminal prosecution and civil claims for damages.

The authors have asserted their rights to be identified as the authors of
this work in accordance with the Copyright, Designs and Patents Act 1988.

First published 2015 by
PALGRAVE MACMILLAN

Palgrave Macmillan in the UK is an imprint of Macmillan Publishers Limited,
registered in England, company number 785998, of Houndmills, Basingstoke,
Hampshire RG21 6XS.

Palgrave Macmillan in the US is a division of St Martin's Press LLC,
175 Fifth Avenue, New York, NY 10010.

Palgrave Macmillan is the global academic imprint of the above companies and
has companies and representatives throughout the world.

Palgrave® and Macmillan® are registered trademarks in the United States,
the United Kingdom, Europe and other countries.

ISBN 978–1–137–47880–1

This book is printed on paper suitable for recycling and made from fully
managed and sustained forest sources. Logging, pulping and manufacturing
processes are expected to conform to the environmental regulations of the
country of origin.

A catalogue record for this book is available from the British Library.

Library of Congress Cataloging-in-Publication Data

Theatre as voyeurism : the pleasures of watching / [edited by] George
Rodosthenous, University of Leeds, UK.
  pages cm
Summary: "*Theatre as Voyeurism* redefines the notion of voyeurism as an 'exchange' between performers and audience members in contemporary theatre and performance. Pleasure (erotic and/or aesthetic) is here privileged as a crucial factor in the way meaning is produced in the encounter with a theatrical work. George Rodosthenous has drawn together an intriguing selection of authors and the ten chapters make a significant contribution to the overarching critical project of assessing the value of approaching theatre through – and as – voyeurism. The authors focus on a range of case studies including specific theatre artists such as Jan Fabre, Romeo Castellucci, Ann Liv Young, Olivier Dubois and Punchdrunk. This edited volume is therefore relevant to prospective readers interested in various aspects of visual experience in the theatre today"—Provided by publisher.
  ISBN 978–1–137–47880–1 (hardback)
  1. Theater audiences—Psychology. 2. Voyeurism. I. Rodosthenous, George, 1973–
  PN1590.A9T475 2015
  792.01—dc23   2015001214

Typeset by MPS Limited, Chennai, India.

Contents

List of Illustrations	vii
Acknowledgements	viii
Notes on Contributors	x

Introduction: Staring at the Forbidden: Legitimizing Voyeurism *George Rodosthenous*	1

Part I Voyeurism and Directing the Gaze

1 Always Looking Back at the Voyeur: Jan Fabre's Extreme Acts on Stage *Laurens De Vos*	29
2 The Dramaturgies of the Gaze: Strategies of Vision and Optical Revelations in the Theatre of Romeo Castellucci and Socìetas Raffaello Sanzio *Eleni Papalexiou*	50

Part II Voyeurism in Space

3 Intimacy, Immersion and the Desire to Touch: The Voyeur Within *David Shearing*	71
4 In Between the Visible and the Hidden: Modalities of Seeing in Site-Specific Performance *William McEvoy*	88

Part III Voyeurism and Acts of Watching

5 The Pleasure of Looking Behind Curtains: Naked Bodies from Titian to Fabre and LeRoy *Luk Van den Dries*	111
6 Baring All on Stage: Active Encounters with Voyeurism, Performance Aesthetics and 'Absorbed Acts of Seeing' *Fiona Bannon*	128

Part IV Voyeurism and Exhibiting the Body

7 Thinking Critical/Looking Sexy: A Naked
   Male Body in Performance   147
   Daniël Ploeger

8 Viewing the Pornographic Theatre: Explicit Voyeurism,
   Artaud and Ann Liv Young's *Cinderella*   166
   Aaron C. Thomas

Part V Voyeurism and Naked Bodies

9 'Music for the Eyes' in *Hair*: Tracing the History of the
   Naked Singing Body on Stage   187
   Tim Stephenson

10 *Outlying Islands* as Theatre of Voyeurism: Ornithologists,
   Naked Bodies and the 'Pleasure of Peeping'   211
   George Rodosthenous

Index   226

List of Illustrations

Cover: *Inside* (2011) by Dimitris Papaioannou
(Photo: Rene Habermacher)

Intro. 1 *Inside* (2011) by Dimitris Papaioannou (Photo: Rene Habermacher)	2
Intro. 2 *Inside* (2011) by Dimitris Papaioannou (Photo: Marilena Stafylidou)	3
Intro. 3 *Inside* (2011) by Dimitris Papaioannou (Photo: Marilena Stafylidou)	4
1.1 *I am Blood* by Jan Fabre (Photo: Wonge Bergmann)	32
1.2 *I am Blood* by Jan Fabre (Photo: Wonge Bergmann)	34
1.3 *I am Blood* by Jan Fabre (Photo: Wonge Bergmann)	36
1.4 *I am Blood* by Jan Fabre (Photo: Wonge Bergmann)	37
1.5 *I am Blood* by Jan Fabre (Photo: Wonge Bergmann)	38
1.6 *I am Blood* by Jan Fabre (Photo: Wonge Bergmann)	40
1.7 *History of Tears* by Jan Fabre (Photo: Wonge Bergmann)	41
1.8 *History of Tears* by Jan Fabre (Photo: Wonge Bergmann)	47
3.1 Concentric bubbles of spatial distance	81
3.2 The unification of sensory engagement via spatial proxemics	81
3.3 Directional spectatorships	85
5.1 *Promethean Landscape II* by Jan Fabre (Photo: Wonge Bergmann)	119
5.2 *Low Pieces* by Xavier LeRoy (Photo: Xavier LeRoy)	120
5.3 *History of Tears* by Jan Fabre (Photo: Wonge Bergmann)	121
7.1 *SUIT* (2009–10) by Daniël Ploeger (Photo: Giel Louws)	153
7.2 Sphincter muscle contraction pattern registered in an experimental subject during masturbation and orgasm (Bohlen, Held and Sanderson 1980), used in *ELECTRODE*	158
7.3 *ELECTRODE* performance by Daniël Ploeger in Ostrava, Czech Republic, August 2011 (Photo: OCNM Archive / Martin Popelář)	159

Acknowledgements

My interest in Theatre as Voyeurism has been forming since my appointment at the School of Performance and Cultural Industries of the University of Leeds in 2002. This book project started in 2006 with my work on David Greig's *Outlying Islands*, which I saw at the Edinburgh Festival in 2002.

I would like to thank Paula Kennedy for believing in this project from the first day I shared my thoughts with her in 2006 and her invaluable support and determination to enable me to publish this book.

Also many thanks to Peter Cary and the editorial team at Palgrave Macmillan for all their help and guidance towards the final steps of the process, the anonymous readers for their constructive feedback and insightful suggestions, and our copy-editor Monica Kendall for her hard work. I am grateful to all the contributors of the volume for their excellent contributions and patience in working together to ensure the smooth publication of this volume.

Special thanks to Professors Jonathan Pitches, Mick Wallis and Chris Baugh for reading drafts of my initial book proposal and chapter on *Outlying Islands*, Susan Daniels, Dr Kara McKechnie, Dr Anna Fenemore, Dr Tony Gardner, Dr Philip Kiszely, Scott Palmer, David Shearing and my mentor Arthur Pritchard for the fruitful discussions on the matter and constant encouragement, all my colleagues and students at the School of Performance and Cultural Industries, and the School's Research Committee for granting me a semester of Study Leave to complete the editing of this volume.

I also need to thank Dr Demetris Zavros, Angela Hadjipanteli, Georgea Solomontos, Varnavas Kyriazis, Marina Maleni, Lea Maleni, Tom Colley, Scott Harris, Ashley Scott Layton, Michael Fentiman, Katerina Papadakou, Sam Newton, Jordan Taylor, Michalis Christodoulou, Stergios Mavrikis, Kitsa Kyriacou, Lauren Garnham, Lucy Loader, Nathaniel Hall, Riccardo Meneghini, Todd Cijunelis, Soula Loucaidou, Kyriacos Karseras, George Z. Georgiou, Anastasia Georgiou, Barney George, Konstantinos Rigos, Michael Measter and all the performers and designers I worked with over the years for their emotional support and development of my directorial practice.

Special thanks go to the members of the TAPRA Performance and the Body group for their feedback on my chapter on *Outlying Islands*, as well as David Greig for the interview on his compositional processes. Also to Andrew Wyllie, Peter Thomson, Simon Trussler and Dimitris Papaioannou for their help and co-operation.

I owe a lot of gratitude to the photographers Rene Habermacher, Marilena Stafylidou, Wonge Bergmann, Giel Louws, Martin Popelář and Xavier LeRoy who gave me permission to include their wonderful photographs in the volume, as well as all the actors and performers portrayed in them.

I would like to mention especially Dr Duška Radosavljević who has been a persistent and critical sounding board to all my ideas and thoughts about theatre ever since we met. Duška has been, and still is, an unshakable inspirational soul mate and a remarkable academic who has been supporting and enlightening my academic work for nearly two decades.

I would like to thank my sister Marina Rodosthenous for her encouragement and my brother Nektarios Rodosthenous for his assistance in my Introduction. And finally my mother Aphrodite and my late father Andreas who are jointly responsible for my education, upbringing and interest in theatre.

Notes on Contributors

Fiona Bannon is Senior Lecturer in Dance in the School of Performance and Cultural Industries at the University of Leeds, UK. Fiona is founder of Architects of the Invisible, a collective that explores improvisation as collaborative practice in performance. She is Chair of DanceHE, a representative body for dance education and research in higher education. Current research includes the preparation of a manuscript-investigating collaboration as aesthetico-ethical practice in *Performance and Dance* and forthcoming chapters exploring dance, identity and mental health, ethics and improvisation, and exploring relations through motion.

Laurens De Vos is Assistant Professor in Theatre Studies at the University of Amsterdam, Holland. He obtained his PhD in English drama from Ghent University, Belgium. He has written articles and books on several playwrights such as Sarah Kane, Tom Stoppard, Mark Ravenhill and Samuel Beckett and on the legacy of Antonin Artaud in contemporary theatre. His current research is focused on processes of looking and visuality in the theatre.

William McEvoy is Lecturer in Drama and English at the University of Sussex, UK. He has published essays on site-specific theatre, contemporary British and European directors, and the theatre theory of Hélène Cixous. He is currently working on contemporary British and Irish playwrights and on the writer–director relationship in recent UK theatre. He currently reviews for *The Stage* newspaper and was formerly chair of *The Stage* awards for Acting Excellence and lead reviewer for *The Stage* at the Edinburgh Festival.

Eleni (Elena) Papalexiou is a lecturer at the Department of Theatre Studies, University of the Peloponnese, Nafplion, Greece. She has a PhD from the Université de la Sorbonne – Paris IV (Centre de Recherche sur l'Histoire du Théâtre). She is the author of *Greek Tragedy on the Modern Stage* (2005, in French) and *Romeo Castellucci/Socìetas Raffaello Sanzio: When the Words Turn to Matter* (2009, in Greek). She has also written several papers and articles about the modern stage. She was the main researcher of the Research Project 'Archivio' (University of Crete, 2012–13) and is now participating as a member of the main research team in the large-scale Research Project 'Arch: Archival Research and Cultural

Heritage-Aristeia II' (University of Athens, 2014–15), both concerning the theatre archive of Romeo Castellucci and Socìetas Raffaello Sanzio.

Daniël Ploeger holds a PhD from the University of Sussex, UK, and is currently Senior Lecturer and Course Leader Performance Arts at The Royal Central School of Speech and Drama, University of London. He is also Principal Investigator of an AHRC-funded arts-science project on digital performance and the politics of electronic waste.

George Rodosthenous is Associate Professor in Theatre Directing at the School of Performance and Cultural Industries of the University of Leeds, UK. He is the Artistic Director of the theatre company Altitude North and also works as a freelance composer/director for the theatre. His research interests are 'the body in performance', 'refining improvisational techniques and compositional practices for performance', 'devising pieces with live musical soundscapes as interdisciplinary process', 'director as coach', 'updating Greek tragedy' and 'the British musical'. He is currently editing *Contemporary Approaches to Greek Tragedy: Auteurship and Directorial Visions* (forthcoming) and *The Disney Musical on Stage and Screen: Critical Approaches from 'Snow White' to 'Frozen'* (forthcoming).

David Shearing is a performance artist and academic working across art forms. He has exhibited at various festivals in the UK and presented work internationally. He is Research Associate in Scenography at the University of Leeds (School of Performance and Cultural Industries) where he is conducting research into 'Audience Immersion and the Experience of Scenography'. His interests span a number of fields, including the integration of hi and low technologies within performance, sound spatialization, environmental design, found spaces, immersive practices and video projection. In 2013 David's immersive project 'and it all comes down to this ...' won the World Stage Design award for Best Installation design. www.davidshearing.com.

Tim Stephenson is Senior Lecturer in Creative and Cultural Industries (Cultural Analysis) at the University of Leeds, UK. Teaching and research are focused on the theory and practice of cultural management across the arts disciplines and the socio-political analysis of the performing arts. Tim trained as a professional musician (percussionist and composer) and maintains an active musical career alongside his academic career.

Aaron C. Thomas is Visiting Lecturer in the Department of Theater, Dartmouth College, USA. He has taught in both the School of Theatre at Florida State University and the Department of Theater at Dartmouth College. His most recent essay 'The Queen's Cell: Fortune and Men's Eyes and the New Prison Drama' was published in *Theatre Survey*, 55:2.

Luk Van den Dries is Professor of Theatre Studies at the University of Antwerp, Belgium, and freelance dramaturg. Together with Louise Chardon he founded the theatre company AndWhatBesidesDeath. He has written extensively on Flemish theatre and is the author of *Corpus Jan Fabre* (2006).

Introduction: Staring at the Forbidden: Legitimizing Voyeurism

George Rodosthenous

In Euripides' *The Bacchae* (405 BC), Pentheus is regarded as one of the first voyeurs on the theatrical stage. When the god Dionysus offers him the opportunity to observe – hidden – the orgiastic activities of the Bacchants in the mountains, Pentheus accepts, even if he has to deny his muscular masculinity and dress up as a woman in order to blend in and remain unnoticed. Pentheus' desire to watch the women in the mountains dancing and singing in ecstasy does not bode well for him as, in the end, he is killed and decapitated by his own mother; his guiltless visual pleasure is punished with extreme death.

In the myth of Salome (and in particular Wilde's 1891 version), Salome dances the 'Dance of the Seven Veils' for Herod. In return for this, she asks for the head of John the Baptist to satisfy her mother's thirst for revenge. Since then, theatre audiences have been watching forbidden acts of sexual encounters, disrobing and (accidental) nudity. The presence of stage nudity is now a regular feature in European productions, while elsewhere it becomes a powerful directorial tool for the director/auteur to provoke, scandalize, get noticed, outrage, titillate and excite the unsuspecting and, at times, conservative audiences by converting them to complicit voyeurs.

There are, of course, productions that are now notorious because of their use of nudity, which has become instrumental to the marketing, promotion and indeed commercial success of the work. Whether we are examining the stripping scene in *Calendar Girls* (2008)[1] or *The Full Monty* (2000), the first sexual encounter in *Equus* (1973), *The Graduate* (2000) or *Outlying Islands* (2002), the shower scenes in *Take Me Out* (2002), 'the scene before the Intermission' in *Hair* (1967), the rape scene in *Lulu* (1895) and *The Romans in Britain* (1980), the flashes of flesh in *Privates on Parade* (1977), *The Judas Kiss* (1998) and *The Pass* (2014), the sexual

2 Staring at the Forbidden

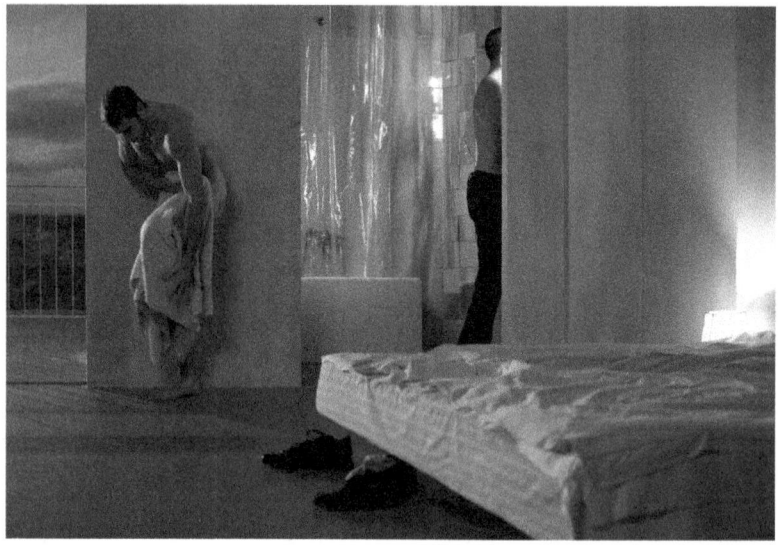

Figure Intro. 1 *Inside* (2011) by Dimitris Papaioannou (Photo: Rene Habermacher)

athletics in *The Blue Room* (1998) or the entire (adult) musicals *Oh! Calcutta!* (1969) and *Naked Boys Singing* (1998), these works carry the seed which unfolds voyeuristic feelings within the audience. Contemporary theatre artists such as Calixto Bieito, Jan Fabre, Romeo Castellucci, Xavier LeRoy, Konstantinos Rigos and Dimitris Papaioannou[2] have pushed the boundaries of what is acceptable to watch on stage through their experimental and, at times, controversial performances.

In Papaioannou's six-hour performance installation *Inside* (2011) in Pallas Theatre, Athens, the audience were invited to drift in and out of the space, select their viewing angle and watch a group of performers undress, lie in bed, take a shower, eat, stand on their balcony and get immersed in a range of everyday activities. Papaioannou grants his audiences permission to watch these repetitive daily rituals, as if through a keyhole, and allows them to look at the 'inside' of an Athenian flat with as much intensity as they wish. He presents them with a series of raw, lyrical, poetic, everyday vignettes and transforms the audience into a 'photographer' who can choose their angle of viewing. The work allows the viewer to direct their gaze inside the action, touch the bodies of the performers with their look and opt to go in or out of the 'performative' space. The audience's invasion of the space is not exposed, but the

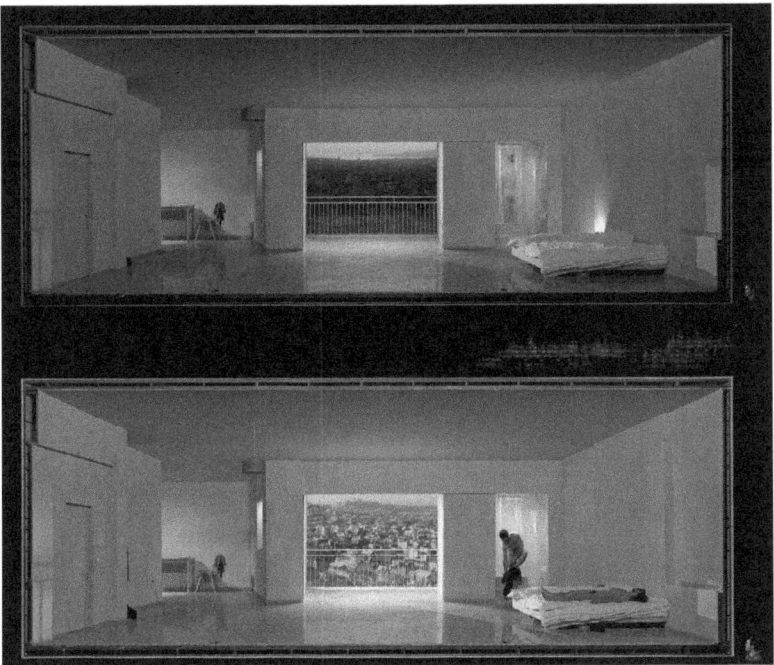

Figure Intro. 2 *Inside* (2011) by Dimitris Papaioannou (Photo: Marilena Stafylidou)

solipsism of the performers on stage is coupled with the loneliness of their actions.

In the same way that a Bach fugue draws us in and enables us to see the musical interconnections and thematic development, *Inside* places us in the forbidden area of watching explicitly acts which are private and hidden through repetition and variation of the movement material. Our voyeurism is encouraged and liberated from any feelings of guilt or anxiety. This 'theatre as voyeurism' experience reminds us of the daily mini-performances we perform, unnoticed, and how these are now presented as mock-documentary programmes and reality television such as *Big Brother* (Endemol UK, 2000–present) and exposed by choice through websites such as *cam4.com*.

This volume will discuss the suggestion that theatre is a voyeuristic exchange between the performer and the audience, where the performer (the object of the audience's gaze) and the audience (the voyeur of this exchange) are placed in a legalized and safe environment for that interaction. Voyeurism, getting access to forbidden visual imagery, is

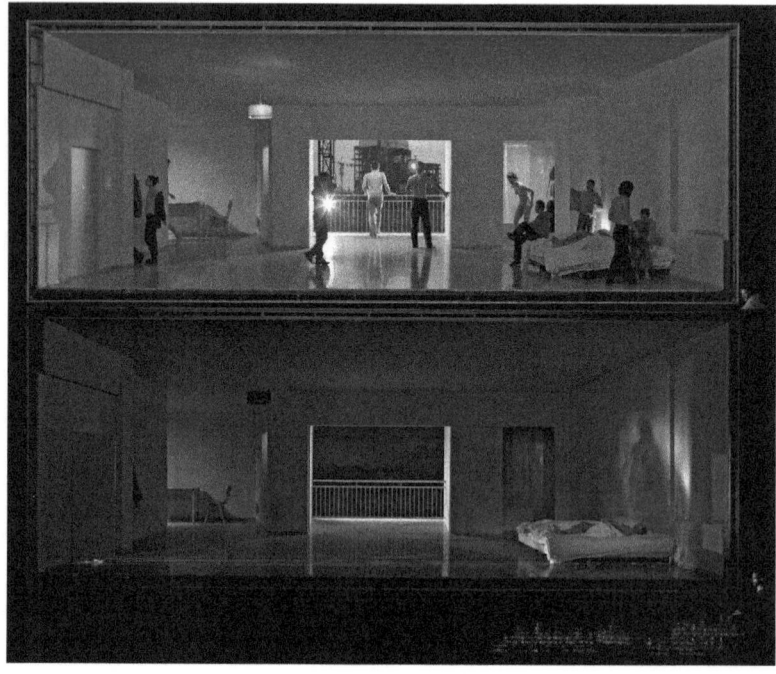

Figure Intro. 3 *Inside* (2011) by Dimitris Papaioannou (Photo: Marilena Stafylidou)

often used to imply a morally dubious position, but this book offers an alternative perspective and aims to redefine the term.

Definitions of the forbidden

Due to a non-consensual agreement and ever-changing attempts to clinically define voyeurism, its definition has been amended and updated many times in medical encyclopaedias. Spencer R. Smith's detailed 'Voyeurism: a review of the literature' (1976) provides Benjamin Karpman's 1954 definition where voyeurism is described as a 'pathological indulgence in looking at some form of nudity as a source of gratification in place of the normal sex act' (Karpman in Smith 1976: 585).

Kaplan and Krueger in Laws and O'Donohue's *Sexual Deviance* (1997) give a detailed list of terms used to describe the condition which includes John Money's (1996) definition as 'a paraphilia of the solicitational allurative type in which sexualerotic arousal and facilitation or attainment of orgasm are responsive to, and dependent upon, the risk of being discovered while covertly watching a stranger disrobing or engaging in sexual activity' (Money in Kaplan and Krueger in Laws and O'Donohue 1997: 297–8). They also add a list of variations of terms which includes 'peepers', 'inspectionalism', 'mixoscopia', 'scoptolagnia', 'scopophilia', 'scoptophilia', 'troilism' and 'pictophilia' (1997: 298). And in particular:

1. Scoptolagnia: Sexuoerotic gratification produced by watching people engaging in sexual activity.
2. Scopophilia: The sexual need to watch others undress.
3. Scoptophilia: Excessive interest in looking at genitals or sex acts as a sexual stimulus [...] and sexual gratification which depends upon watching others engaging in sexual activity.
4. Troilism (or tiolism): A paraphilia wherein there is a dependence on observing one's partner on hire or loan to a third person while engaging in sexual activities, including sexual intercourse with that person [...] Troilism differs from voyeurism in that the person being observed is not a stranger.
5. Pictophilia: Dependence upon viewing obscene or pornographic pictures or video tapes.

Jonathan Metzl updates the literature review in his comprehensive 'From scopophilia to *Survivor*: a brief history of voyeurism' and suggests that voyeurism is an 'act of aversion' (2004: 415). By referring to the psychoanalyst Otto Fenichel, he associates voyeurism with short-lived gratification and the castration anxiety. Fenichel proposes that '[t]he fact that no sight can actually bring about the reassurance for which patients are striving (forces) voyeurs to look again and again, and to see more and more, with an ever increasing intensity' (1945: 347–8).

Irvin Yalom discusses the elements of aggression and forbiddenness in voyeurism and suggests that 'there may be countless "voyeurs" who never come to our attention and spend their lives unmolesting and unmolested in the world of the burlesque theater, pornography, stag films, and beauty contest' (1960: 305). He identifies the pleasure from seeing as 'removal of unpleasure' (1960: 306) and confirms that some 'voyeurs who observe scenes of sexual intercourse seem to participate in the act by identifying with one of the participants' (1960: 307). This associative relationship can be also seen in the audience members connecting with what they see on stage (either by empathy or by direct association). They might, like voyeurs, get (sexual) excitement or a heightened state by watching something that is generally regarded as 'forbidden' (1960: 309). Other ways of describing voyeurism are 'irrepressible curiosity', a 'fascination' with the forbidden (1960: 310) or a 'pitiable caricature of curiosity' (1960: 311) because the practice of voyeurism, as a forbidden pleasure, lies within the 'doing of that which is prohibited' (1960: 318).

For the purposes of this book, I would like to divest the notion of voyeurism from the negative heritage bestowed on it by clinical psychoanalysis and propose a new definition here, which, in my view, addresses the phenomenon of voyeurism. It could be argued that the contemporary audience has been placed in the position of a voyeur not by an inherent pathology but by the nineteenth- and twentieth-century insistence on the 'fourth wall' in theatre.[3] Focusing on the notion of 'pleasure' rather than 'deviance', I am therefore proposing that voyeurism can be defined as an intense curiosity which generates a compulsive desire to observe people (un)aware in natural states or performed primal acts and leads to a heightening of pleasure for the viewer.

Redefining voyeurism in theatre

Clay Calvert in his insightful *Voyeur Nation* proposes four categories of 'mediated voyeurism': video verite voyeurism, reconstruction voyeurism, tell-all/show-all voyeurism and sexual voyeurism (2004: 4). In order to apply his methodology more explicitly on theatre, I would like to adapt this methodology and offer a series of 14 kinds of 'theatrical voyeurism'. These are provisional and there is slippage between and across the categories of experience.

1. **Accidental voyeurism** When, during a performance, the audience gains pleasure by observing an action on stage that was unplanned and s/he becomes a witness of that action. This might include wardrobe malfunction, lighting malfunction, a fall or a mistake on stage.
2. **Celebrity voyeurism** When the audience attends a performance simply to watch a celebrity disrobe on stage. When it was announced in 2000 that Kathleen Turner would appear naked in *The Graduate*, £90,000 worth of theatre tickets were sold in a single day. Other notable examples include Nicole Kidman in *The Blue Room* (directed by Sam Mendes, 1998), who was described by Charles Spencer of *The Telegraph* as 'pure theatrical Viagra' (1998), Daniel Radcliffe in *Equus* (directed by Thea Sharrock, 2007) and Daniel Sunjata in *Take Me Out* (directed by Joe Mantello, 2002). The celebrity's nudity

becomes the main (marketing) focus of the production. In the UK, there are even specific websites which provide full reports on the extent of stage nudity such as the http://partially-obstructed-view.blogspot.co.uk.

3. **Collective voyeurism** When the audience is sharing the performance experience with other audience members (hen-night parties watching *Naked Boys Singing*), as opposed to single-member audience experiences and one-to-one performances.
4. **Complicit voyeurism** When the audience is forced to observe a moment of violence involving nudity and humiliation and is unable to intervene (for example, the rape scene in *A Street Car Named Desire* [1947], or in the shower scene in *Take me Out*).
5. **Compulsive voyeurism** When audience members revisit repeatedly a specific production because of its nudity or sexual content. It might also take the form of filming the show during the performance in order to upload it later for repeated viewing.
6. **Emotional voyeurism** When the audience witnesses an intense scene where a character on stage removes all layers of protection and is left emotionally naked in the narrative (for example, King Lear's final speech).
7. **Explicit voyeurism** When the audience observes explicit sexual acts within the narrative (a strip show, Salome's 'Dance of the Seven Veils' in *Salome* [1891] or a sex show), or when technological devices are inserted inside the performers to present the inner workings of their organs (for example, Castellucci's *Julius Caesar* [1997]).
8. **Furtive voyeurism** When the audience sees a fleeting moment of the character's nudity where the character makes an attempt to hide the nudity (because of guilt, embarrassment or humiliation), but is still seen by the audience (for example, the shower scene in *Kes* [1976]).
9. **Implicit voyeurism** When the audience observes nudity which is either suggested behind gauze or is dimly lit and is more imagined than actually seen.
10. **Intellectual voyeurism** When the audience is a step ahead with the thinking of the characters and can see what will happen to the narrative or to the story ahead of the character (this can be the case in biographical dramas, for example *Piaf* [1978]).
11. **Intimate voyeurism** When the audience is in close proximity with the performer or in a one-to-one exchange (for example, *You Me Bum Bum Train* [2004] and Punchdrunk's *Sleep No More* [2011]).

12. **Naked voyeurism** When the audience is required to be naked in viewing the performance (for example, in the infamous *Naked Brunch* [2010] cabaret performance and its non-negotiable audience nudity http://edinburghfestival.list.co.uk/event/ 10003889-the-naked-brunch).
13. **Pathological voyeurism** When the voyeuristic activity becomes active and audience members are actually masturbating during a performance.
14. **Scopophilic voyeurism** When the audience has an excessive interest watching the performers in everyday (non-sexual) scenes, acts of violence and privacy.

As in the cases of traditional voyeurism, the theatrical voyeur 'seeks no contact with the observed individual' (Kaplan and Krueger in Laws and O'Donohue 1997: 297), and pleasure or 'gratification may be received from looking instead of participating' (1997: 298). This becomes more challenging in immersive and site-specific performances where the audience is placed within the narrative action (see chapters by Shearing and McEvoy in this volume) and has the opportunity to interact with the theatrical/performative action.

Contextualizing voyeurism

In this section, I will explore some of the historical arguments surrounding what it means to be a viewer and a voyeur within a theatrical framework. Through a contextualization of the historical debates on the audience–actor relationship, I will argue that the excitement of the exchange between voyeur and voyeur-ed which is increasingly present in popular cultural discourse (such as television and print media), is not as exciting as the thrill of being *complicit* in the 'forbidden' act of being nude in public (or being witness to this act), whilst paying for the privilege to do so. The academic literature is divided into three subsections: theatrical voyeurism, visuality and spectatorship, and the pleasure (and guilt) of looking.

Theatrical voyeurism

Patrice Pavis acknowledges the voyeuristic qualities of theatre in his definition of theatre as a 'visual art par excellence and an institutionalized space for voyeurism' (1998: 388). Robert Leach agrees, by stating that 'the situation licenses voyeurism: in the special circumstances of the theatre, in the privacy of the darkened auditorium, the individual may indulge in the "gaze", which is impossible in most social situations'

(2008: 176). Furthermore, Alan Read observes that theatre 'poaches on everyday life for its content, relationships, humour, surprise, shock, intimacy and voyeurism' (2004: 47). Kiki Gounaridou makes a fine analogy between theatre and entertainment by asserting that 'those who see this play [*What the Butler Saw*, 1969] in a theatre are already participating in a type of voyeurism. As entertainment, theatre itself is inherently group voyeurism on an artistic scale. Most people go to the theatre hoping to get a glimpse into a life that is not their own' (2011: 61–2).

Tori Haring-Smith analyses the historical schism in the evolution of the spectator–performer relationship, and the separation of their worlds, positing that, '[w]ith the use of electric light came the rise of the fourth wall that encases the audience [...] inside an impermeable box' (in Delgado and Svich 2002: 98). It is this paradigm shift in the presentation of Western theatre that instigated a change in the audience's role in the actor–spectator relationship. Haring-Smith notes how this plunging of the audience into darkness and the actors into light forced the actors to exist in a separate world, 'under the observation of paying audience members'. No longer were the audience and actors occupying the same space, the audience, in effect, 'had become voyeurs' (in Delgado and Svich 2002: 99).

Most theories regarding the spectator and voyeurism stem from cinematic disciplines. Laura Mulvey's contribution to film theory in 'Visual pleasure and narrative cinema' was instrumental in establishing the concept she coined as 'the male gaze'. She uses Sigmund Freud's psychoanalytic observations on scopophilia from his *Three Essays on Sexuality* to conclude that '[a]lthough the instinct is modified by other factors, in particular the constitution of the ego, it continues to exist as the erotic basis for pleasure in looking at another person as object. At the extreme, it can become fixated into a perversion, producing obsessive voyeurs and Peeping Toms, whose only sexual satisfaction can come from watching, in an active controlling sense, an objectified other' (1975: 8). Christian Metz goes a step further to compare the cinematic experience to the theatrical one by stating that 'cinematic voyeurism, *unauthorised* scopophilia, is from the outset more strongly established than that of the theatre' (1977: 63). In *The Imaginary Signifier* Metz provides a vital analysis of the passion of perceiving and makes some crucial references to the nature of the voyeur in relation to the space, object, the eye and the body (1977: 60) and defines the 'passion for Perceiving' (1977: 58) as a desire to see and hear (see Lacan's sexual drives or Freud's self-preservation drives).

Theatre academic Spyros Papaioannou indicates that '[m]ost accounts of theatrical voyeurism place the discussion within a feminist terrain, arguing for the de-traditionalization of conventional watching and the de-objectification of the image of women that used to be perceived as a passive "spectacle", available exclusively for male gazing (see Freedmand 1990; Carlson 2004, 186)' (2014: 170). When analysing the work of the company Punchdrunk, he adds that 'the act of voyeurism is somehow freed from its "deviant" manifestation as an ethically forbidden intrusion; on the contrary, it is encouraged, acquiring the potentials of stimulating theatrical engagement' (2014: 169).

In discussing Beckett's *Catastrophe*, Avra Sidiropoulou explains that the performers can flirt with the 'voyeuristic tendencies of the spectators, who, in turn, will be thrilled to discard with the limiting signifiers of the mise-en-scene in order to enjoy their unadulterated bodi-ness [...] In the end, the idea of *presence*, which, as Lehmann reminds us, nevertheless embodies representability, unmediated, uncensored, and unique, night after night of performance, cultivates and perpetuates theatre's communal and therapeutic mission, actuating shared, unrepeatable, sensual, and vital adventures' (2011: 124).

Visuality and spectatorship

In *Visuality in the Theatre: The Locus of Looking*, Maaike Bleeker dissects different ways of looking in theatre (through internal and external focalization, sexuality, consciousness) and links them to the creation of meaning in theatrical performance. She relates voyeurism with a certain kind of transcendence (2008: 132) and emphasizes that 'although some theatre traditions and theatre practices do exploit the voyeuristic pleasure of peeping through a keyhole into another world while remaining invisible in the dark, a wide range of other theatrical practices demonstrate that this is not a necessary characteristic of the theatre event, nor is it a necessary precondition for the intense experience referred to as "presence"' (2008: 133). Dominic Johnson in *Theatre and the Visual* juxtaposes voyeurism with fetishism and points out that '[p]erformance and visual culture can train the eye, and revise the values we ordinarily ascribe to objects of vision. These acts of looking are necessarily difficult, even costly in psychic sense, regardless of whether the effects they produce are pleasurable or painful. Demystification requires some level of complication of the ordinary processes of looking; it is less likely to arise when one engages in happy acts of looking' (2012: 52).

In *Modes of Spectating* Oddey and White argue that spectating goes beyond 'simply watching. It is about substituting a sensory, kinetic and cinematographic experience' (2009: 8). They differentiate the terms audience, spectator and watching, and state that the 'spectator wants to engage in a more active way, to play a significant part or role in the reception of the work' (2009: 9).

Schneider develops her own theory about viewing and being viewed and also expands it to an interesting parallel with the ritual. She reminds us that '[m]eaning "a place for viewing," the *theatron* provided a space for particular visual form [...] [it] is a man-made cave clearly marked "look but don't touch" [...] an a-tactile visuality' (Schneider 2000: 26). Intense looking can sometimes be elevated to 'touching' the object of desire, and Josephine Machon clarifies the definition of 'haptic touch' (Bouchard 2009; Marks 2000, 2002; Schneider 1997) by reminding us that 'sight can become tactile through looking and *looking again* at the sensual aesthetic of the work, which activates a sensory involvement akin to touch within this act of looking alone' (2013: 78).

Susan Bennett's extensive study on *Theatre Audiences: A Theory of Production and Reception* (1997) gives a detailed examination of that relationship and includes an analysis of the reader-response theory and semiotics, and also addresses the spectator's obsessions. However, it fails to acknowledge the voyeuristic aspect of that exchange. If, for example, we examine conventional dramatic texts that 'respect' and fully utilize the 'fourth wall' to expose personal dramas and secrets, we can see that the audience is there not to participate in but to witness the events. It is also apparent that the characters seem to be unaware of our gaze. Thus, Rebecca Schneider claims that as an audience, 'we achieve a facsimile, an almost but not quite "suspension of disbelief"' (2000: 24). In effect, we are very self-aware when we have become an audience/voyeurs of a dramatic performance but we are able to suspend this conscious thought and allow ourselves to *temporarily* believe that what we are witnessing is a real-life drama. It is this temporal state of consciousness which allows us to experience real emotion from something which is a fictional construct.

The pleasure (and guilt) of looking

Theatrical pleasure is the main theme of Anne Übersfeld's (1982) article 'The pleasure of the spectator'. She observes that theatrical pleasure is a collective experience, which is multiform, and does not involve a passive reception (1982: 128). She proposes that voyeurism resembles aspects of unrequited love. 'Seeing one's dreams without being able to touch them: such is the pleasure and frustration of stage representation' (1982: 135). In her analysis, it becomes clear that '[p]art of what can be called the fascinated voyeurism of theatre audiences comes from this mechanism of pleasure [...] the pleasure of seeing human relations in their most conflictive and passionate forms' (1982: 136). Übersfeld compares pleasure with desire and notes that

> if pleasure finds its fulfilment as sensual pleasure at the precise moment that the ever-increasing gap between the acting-out and the fiction, between the body and the character portrayed, disappears; if pleasure lies, then, in the ability of the spectator to relate to a presence, it is also blocked by taboos: the taboo against touching, even against seeing in close quarters, the taboo against seeing (knowing) with certainty. (1982: 138)

Her conclusion is rather pessimistic in proclaiming that '[t]he essential situation of the spectator is dissatisfaction, not only because he cannot possess the object of desire (and if he did, he would possess something other than what he desired), but because his intelligence itself is unable to bridge the gap' (1982: 138).

Daphna Ben Chaim, in her remarkable study *Distance in the Theatre: The Aesthetics of Audience Response* (1984), links the power of our imagination with the actual pleasure we derive and concludes that,

> [e]ven if the drama presents 'dying agonies' we take pleasure because we know, on some level of our consciousness, that the event is not real, and because we experience the freedom of our imagination, and, no doubt, on condition that it will produce a 'larger perspective' [...] The intensity of our imaginative engagement determines our pleasure. (Ben Chaim 1984: 76)

Simon Shepherd's intriguing *Theatre, Body and Pleasure* focuses on the body in performance and addresses theatre as 'a practice in which societies negotiate around bodily value and bodily order. In that negotiation theatre is not simply an art of bodies but an art of bodily possibility, an event where the limits of body are negotiated, fetishised, imagined somehow else' (2006: 10). The book includes a discussion of bodily value but does not make any explicit link to the voyeuristic pleasure in watching bodies perform. Further books on fetishism and performance are the graphic *The Explicit Body in Performance* by Rebecca Schneider (1997), dealing with feminist performance artists, queer theory and the postporn modernist movement, and Jacqueline Rose's *Sexuality in the Field of Vision* (1986), which dissects Freud's and Lacan's writings on sexuality. In doing so, she recognizes that 'one of the chief drives of an art which today addresses the presence of the sexual in representation – [is] to expose the fixed nature of sexual identity as a fantasy and, in the same gesture, to trouble, break up, or rupture the visual field before our eyes' (Rose 1986: 227–8).

The physical uninvolvement of the audience with the stage(d) action is synonymous with some of the characteristics of voyeurism. Leonard Blank writes that

> [t]he sexual excitement and tension [...] may be associated with aggressiveness and the forbidden. Voyeuristic conflict and pathology may be accentuated by mystery and taboo that promote *compulsive* looking [...] The voyeur achieves gratification in a complicated way. He looks at the forbidden, expresses aggression in his defiant behaviour, avoids any commitment to interpersonal intimacy, and, all the while, in his *passive* fantasy needs not surrender one iota of his ideals and imagined assertiveness. (1973: 24)

In some cases, plays of a voyeuristic nature could possibly induce some feelings of guilt in the audience as they become self-aware that they are complicit in the culturally shameful act of watching 'forbidden' pleasures on stage. Eric Bentley feels that this guilt is an important part of the theatrical experience:

> Perhaps if one took the guilt away, the dirty picture, so called, would lose much of its appeal, and perhaps if one took from theatre the element of voyeurism, the occasion would lose much of its appeal [...] Scholars call the modern stage the peepshow stage. The corollary is that this is a theatre for Peeping Toms [...] The pleasure of looking on is in itself an equivocal thing. It includes such delights as feeling one has committed the crime yet is able to escape the penalty [...] the pleasure of watching is continuous with the pleasure of peeping. (1991: 156–7)

Adam Alston develops further this idea of guilt and links it to the experience of immersive theatre. He notes that 'the pleasures of experience, even of experiences that may otherwise be defined as negative – anxiousness, fear, guilt, shame, embarrassment, etc. – may end up being felt as positive, stimulating, or challenging attributes of encountering an event' (2013: 130). Alston also believes that '[c]ommercial enterprise can consequently emerge to profit from pleasure-seeking [...] Where there is desire for the sexual, in any of its manifestations, there is usually an industry for it as well, no matter how niche' (2013: 136).

Voyeur with a ticket

The journalistic community has also contributed extensively to the discussion of the audience as voyeur by creating hype surrounding specific productions such as *The Blue Room, Equus, Take me Out, The Drowned Man* (2013), thus supporting the commercial part of this transaction. One of the most discussed companies in relation to voyeurism is, undeniably, Punchdrunk. Theatre critic Michael Billington writes on *The Drowned Man*: 'The shock came when the secretary, a seductive figure with a Louise Brooks hairdo, looked up from filing her nails to snog – in so far as one can someone wearing a mask – one of the male onlookers. That says a lot about a show in which voyeurism is as important as Woyzeck and which reminds us that the movies turn us all into guilty spectators of other people's lusts' (Billington 2013). On another immersive company's work, dreamthinkspeak, he mentions that *The Rest is Silence* (2012) 'turns us into voyeurs witnessing a story of murder, lust and madness with a furtive enjoyment'. Ben Brantley adds that '"[You Me] Bum Bum" [Train] puts you at the spotlighted center of a cast that can run into hundreds; "Malfi" underlines, in exasperating and tantalizing ways, your helplessness (and perhaps your guilt) as an anonymous, voyeuristic spectator' (Brantley 2010). For *Sleep No More*, he observes that it 'is, in short, a voyeur's delight, with all the creepy, shameful pleasures that entails' (Brantley 2011).

Charles Spencer, when reviewing the 2014 Royal Court production of *The Pass* (directed by John Tiffany), gives specific advice to the voyeurs in the audience by specifying that '[v]oyeurs will be pleased to learn that these two outstanding actors both look exceptionally buff in their underpants. Suddenly however the horseplay takes on a sexual tinge and, more surprisingly, an unexpected tenderness' (Spencer 2014). While Lyn Gardner notes that the actual theatrical space affects our relationship with voyeurism and, in particular, that '[i]ntimacy may be the key here. Theatre is so much about the act of looking in any case that to stare at people making love makes you feel even more like a voyeur or peeping Tom in the dark' (Gardner 2009). And in her review of Tiger Lilies' *Lulu* she proposes that 'the repetitive window imagery reminds us that we are all peeping toms, paying to look. It makes you as uncomfortable as hell, but you never turn your fascinated gaze away' (Gardner 2014). Dominic Maxwell of *The Times*, reviewing the 2014 Globe production of *The Duchess of Malfi* with Gemma Arterton at the newly built Sam Wanamaker Playhouse, remarks that she 'speaks Webster's blank verse with seductive ease. We are so close to her open flirting that we feel like voyeurs' (Maxwell 2014). Michael Longhurst, who directed *'Tis Pity She's a Whore* (1633) in the same theatre, discovered that as a director you have to '"[m]atch your ideas to the architecture." The dictum is especially pertinent in the Playhouse, which is "as close as we can get to the space the play was written for. You can feel the architecture webbed into it. The space is hugely voyeuristic, which is perfect for a play like this"' (Jays 2014).

In the USA, there is more resistance to showing nudity on stage and in particular '[g]ay or no, nobody really wants to see a limp, wet penis flopping around under bright theater lights if they don't have to. In *Take Me Out*, the audience is treated to many wet penises, but not even the big ones can add girth to a play that is inherently flaccid' (Westcoat Sanders 2005). In that specific production, the extended shower scenes expose the entire cast in the private act of communal showering. Barbara Hoffman indicates that '[i]t isn't the nudity Daniel Sunjata minds, or playing a gay baseball player – it's just, well, those on-stage showers. That, and the theatergoers who whip out their binoculars' (Hoffman 2003). Male nudity on stage still remains guarded territory in theatre. Jay Whitehead, a member of an all-male burlesque troupe, affirms that the '[m]ale anatomy, and penises in particular, are used in pop culture today for one or two reasons it seems: comedy and shock, and often both simultaneously. It is one of this generation's remaining taboos. It is a taboo that is often disarmed with dismissive laughter' (Whitehead 2014: 28).

Michael Billington makes a strong statement when it comes to his own views about nudity on stage and concludes by highlighting that '[w]hat we need to put an end to is the smirking voyeurism of a commercial theatre that whets our appetite with nudity and then swathes it in shadows. By all means, let's have nudity on stage. But at the same time, let us ensure that it is guiltless, open and unashamed rather than constantly going off, as it were, at half-cock' (Billington 2007).

Legitimizing the stare

The principal aim of this book is to propose that theatre is closely associated with the act of voyeurism. To link a popular and cathartic form of entertainment to an act that is often related with paraphilic behaviour, guilt and disturbance of privacy might seem perverse at first glance. But, as we will see unfolding in the chapters of this book, the two have more in common than first expected. Is it an innocent stare or an exploitative feat of the senses? Is voyeurism an active or a passive act?

The theatre is a legal place to exercise voyeurism. The voyeur seeks no active engagement with the performer, only with the spectacle. It is done on an intellectual level and the experience is a multi-sensory one. Theatre enables voyeurism and makes it an acceptable art form where the audience removes its forbidden attributes through collective viewing. Perhaps it all starts with the box office. The viewer *chooses* where to sit – how close they want to be to the experience of viewing. The box office functions as the facilitator of the voyeuristic exchange.

One could argue that in many ways theatre is not voyeurism. It is collective as opposed to solitary, one has to pay for the right to watch and it involves people 'pretending' to be experiencing live experiences. Sometimes the characters speak to the audience directly and this disrupts the contract of the 'secluded viewer'. But, in many other ways, watching theatre provides similar excitement and on some occasions it heightens the sexual interest of the viewer. There are certain elements in theatre that can upset the voyeuristic exchange between the performers and the audience. Very often, in order to disguise the discomfort of nudity, the writer or the director accompanies it with comedy: this is evident in the genre of the trouser-dropping comedies or the accidental drop of a towel which lightens the sexual tension of the suggestive imagery. This comedic approach is an attempt to extract any element of sexual pleasure in watching the performers naked, thus transforming the nudity into a fleeting moment of slapstick.

Addressing the audience is also problematic when we discuss voyeurism in theatre. Voyeurism implies a certain degree of passivity and non-contribution. Extreme and overt exhibitionism can hinder the elements of an unveiling which is observed accidentally or unwillingly. For Silverstein 'exhibitionism is a tendency to display one's abilities or to behave in such a way as to attract attention. When the risk of exposing one's abilities, or one's product, is met with respect and admiration, pride evolves and the capacity to continue risking exposure develops' (1996: 34). John Money asserts that exhibitionism and voyeurism are 'antipodes of one another, on the polarity of signal output and input, transmission and reception respectively. To exhibit is to transmit a solicitation, whereas to peep as a voyeur is to receive an alluring image' (1986: 78). Exhibitionism implies welcoming the gaze, while voyeurism does not need that extra element of additional performativity. It suffices to have a natural moment of 'being' or getting naked. Thus, strip shows with their emphasis on the agreement 'if you pay, you can watch' can also be another element that undermines the voyeuristic exchanges in the theatre. Still, voyeurism in theatre is not adversely affected by the financial exchange which happens at the beginning of the show.

The voyeuristic pleasure requires access to real bodies and body parts. Prosthetics can remove the sexual pleasure of observing these bodies and risks diminishing the interest of a voyeur. This might be a legal requirement in order to portray extreme sexual acts on stage as in La Fura dels Baus' production of *XXX* which caused 'hysteria in some quarters for its smashing of sexual taboos' (Billington 2003). Billington continues to report that

> [o]nly the most naive theatre-goer will assume any of this is for real: the stage is filled with prosthetic penises, forming a startling contrast to the actors' own dangling appendages. What the show, directed by Alex Olle, is actually offering is pastiche porn to release us from our presumed inhibitions and to ram home Sade's point that sexual pleasure pursued to its limits is spiritually liberating [...] And the only passage of real eroticism comes when the cast put their clothes back on, and for a brief moment become quite sexy. (2003)

Even though the director of *XXX* could have succeeded in placing his audience in the position of a voyeur, the prosthetics and 'pastiche porn' forced the audience to actually assume a meta-position in relation to the content, rather than remain in the position of 'a voyeur'. And, thus, Olle transcends the viewing of sexual material into a meta-theatrical device. Contrary to Billington's assertion, the relief of watching performers put their clothes back on insinuates a sense of disappointment which reveals a moment of erotic unfulfilment.

Voyeurism's ability to release satisfaction can go beyond an exploitative thirst for watching. It can be recontextualized as a need to connect, to explore and to understand. Undoubtedly, this spiritual liberation for the passive audience can become an active source of pleasure which can heighten the viewing experience and deliver a thrilling ride of emotions and insights.

The structure of the book

This collection of interrelated essays is arranged in a palindromic form which links the chapters together, but it can be read in any order by the reader. The chapters are coupled with clear thematic associations and benefit from their interconnection and inter-contextualization. The shape of the book allows for a conscious dialogue between the essays, with a constructive system of cross-referral and quotation. Divided into five parts, it covers a range of approaches to theatrical voyeurism under the thematic interconnections of 'Voyeurism and Directing the Gaze', 'Voyeurism in Space', 'Voyeurism and Acts of Watching', 'Voyeurism and Exhibiting the Body' and 'Voyeurism and Naked Bodies'.

Part I addresses the issue of the direction of the audience's gaze through either the dramaturgical devices of the performance or the shapes dictated by the director in order to lead its audience to 'read' the stage material in their own individual way. Part II is explicitly linked to a discussion of space as a theatrical and performative arena in which the spectacle unfolds, and how that space facilitates the unfolding of the action and enables voyeuristic activity. What follows, in Part II, is a central discussion of voyeurism as a specific act of watching, whether that might appear as a violation of privacy or as an 'absorbed act of seeing'. The penultimate Part looks at voyeurism from a performer's point of view, addressing processes of exhibiting the human body and creating explicit imagery which verges on the pornographic. It might be worth acknowledging that while most discussions on theatre begin with the text, this one concludes with investigations of voyeurism in text – which is also perhaps an unexpected angle on the topic itself. Thus, Part V provides some enticing insights into our interaction with naked bodies and how that interaction can spark voyeuristic impulses, behaviours and activities which trigger the audience's imaginations, giving specific examples from *Hair the Musical* and David Greig's *Outlying Islands*.

Laurens De Vos' chapter, 'Always Looking Back at the Voyeur: Jan Fabre's Extreme Acts on Stage', offers an analysis of Jan Fabre's work, and in particular *I am Blood*. In his introduction, De Vos gives a theoretical context by presenting Jean-Paul Sartre's theories from *Being and Nothingness* and Marcel Duchamp's *Etant donnés*. These are linked with critical rigour to Foucault's 'Panopticon' and its influence on Fabre's work. He explains how Fabre subverts the voyeur's gaze and comments further on the seclusion of the voyeur. Within his analysis, he addresses Artaud's influence on the work *I am Blood*, and provides a fascinating discussion of *jouissance* and Derrida's ideas of repetition and singular signs. In his closing remarks, De Vos states that 'the spectator's protective cocoon of secrecy and seclusion is torn apart, he is caught in his voyeuristic desires and all of a sudden again becomes aware of the gaze of the object looking back'.

The second chapter of the volume, 'The Dramaturgies of the Gaze: Strategies of Vision and Optical Revelations in the Theatre of Romeo Castellucci and Socìetas Raffaello Sanzio', by Eleni Papalexiou deals with some fundamental questions about the meaning of watching, and also the notion of being watched. She starts with the etymology of the word *theatron* and continues to formulate her own strategies in exploring the dramaturgy of the gaze. She explains how 'the gaze of the spectator penetrates into the human existence' and applies that to the work of Romeo Castellucci, and in particular *Julius Caesar*. Her second strategy expresses the idea of the 'third image', which focuses on the *Divine Comedy, Paradise*, and how the spectator fills the gap with the creative power of his imagination. She concludes her chapter with a reference to the unbearable 'violence of the gaze' and its relationship to the stage's function as a double mirror. Thus, she destabilizes the relationship between the watcher and the watched.

The next Part of the book deals with voyeurism in space, where David Shearing's contribution readdresses how we experience immersive performances, and in his chapter 'Intimacy, Immersion and the Desire to Touch: The Voyeur Within' he focuses on the *Electric Hotel* and Punchdrunk's *The Drowned Man: A Hollywood Fable*. His writing explores the use of sound in performance and how it creates aural intimacy. He considers Merleau-Ponty's account of phenomenology and asserts that 'to reduce voyeurism – or the act of looking – to a single sensory mode of engagement, such as site, neglects the synthesis of bodily engagement'. Shearing elaborates on intimate acoustic spaces and the writings of Pallasmaa, Holl and Bonenfant. The pleasure of watching is juxtaposed with hedonistic and narcissistic desire, and he explains how this leads to a desire of the audience to be touched. He concludes with his own account of his experience attending *The Drowned Man* and proposes that 'mask, spatial organization and headphones act as devices of concealment, creating spatial distances that reassert voyeurism within an expanding immersive and intimate context'.

William McEvoy articulates his approach to site-specific performance through Frisch Scarpetta and Kantor in his 'In Between the Visible and the Hidden: Modalities of Seeing in Site-Specific Performance'. The work of the theatre company Hydrocracker is contextualized and used to pose questions on viewing and critiquing site-specificity and the viewer. The ephemeral nature of performance raises additional issues on recording and repeating work of this kind, and McEvoy proposes 'a model of criticism based on engagement with disparate texts and different modes of writing'. He demonstrates how site-specificity changes the act of criticism, and how the idea of *emballage* can help us reconstruct the visual 'through memory, deduction or inference'. Within this context, he further concludes that '[i]t is a mode of theatre no longer dominated by the visual, but offering a more plural, phenomenological engagement of the senses and of memory; we move through the work [...] guessing at meanings, doubting our former epistemological certainties: a multi-sensory voyeurism'.

Part III explores voyeurism and acts of watching and features Luk Van den Dries' 'The Pleasure of Looking Behind Curtains: Naked Bodies from Titian to Fabre and LeRoy'. He begins his discussion by a vivid description of Titian's painting *Diana and Actaeon* and focuses on the look as an act of violence. He compares the complicity of looking with Bertolt Brecht's 'half-curtain' and the unveiling of what is hidden. Jan Fabre's work is scrutinized under the notions of tangible corporeality and obscenity, while the body's explosive plasticity is read as an 'alphabet of the muscles, the joints, the vertebrae, and the bones'. His account of LeRoy's *Low Pieces* addresses the spectators' own sensitivities, references and considerations. This seems to be in a similar line with Bannon's proposition that looking starts from the body and that we need to let one's glance become corporeal.

In Chapter 6, 'Baring All on Stage: Active Encounters with Voyeurism, Performance Aesthetics and "Absorbed Acts of Seeing"', Fiona Bannon engages with multi-sensory reactions to watching performance. She supports her arguments by focusing on the vulnerability of watching, relationality and the ethics of voyeurism. She challenges the notion of nudity on stage through the work of Clark and Toepfer, discussing voyeurism as 'an absorbed act of seeing'. Extending the implications of watching naked bodies, she discusses LeRoy's *Low Pieces*, Halprin's *Parades and Changes* and Dave St-Pierre's *Un peu de tendresse bordel de merde*.

Part IV shifts the focus to exhibiting the body. Chapter 7 is dedicated to the naked male body, and Chapter 8 to the explicit naked female body. Daniël Ploeger, in his 'Thinking Critical/Looking Sexy: A Naked Male Body in Performance', presents a conceptual approach to nakedness, which draws from research in psychology on the 'framed perception of naked bodies, and perspectives from performance and cultural studies'. He explores the work of Spencer Tunick, Marina Abramović and his own work *ELECTRODE*. He investigates tensions within his own work and critiques disciplines around the body and other normative body types. The performer provides four frames of nakedness borrowed by Eck (2001): the pornographic frame, the informational frame, the commodified frame and the art frame. In his conclusion, he addresses the conflict between these different frames, and traces audience responses to readings of his own naked body.

The eighth chapter deals with approaches to the naked exhibited body and the pornographic in theatre. Aaron C. Thomas considers the work of Ann Liv Young in 'Viewing the Pornographic Theatre: Explicit Voyeurism, Artaud and Ann Liv Young's *Cinderella*' and questions the 'value of the pornographic in the theatre' and 'what pornography itself might make possible'. He interrogates Walter Kendrick's important work on pornography *The Secret Museum* and invites the reader to imagine its pornographic utility. These theories are cast alongside Hunt's and Bataille's notions of gratuitousness and Artaud's views on the pornographic theatre. He places the body of the viewer within the centre of this critical framework and summarizes Grosz's proposal that this kind of theatre leads to a pleasure which is '*kathartic* – sexuality of release, orgasm, and ejaculation'. His discussion of *Cinderella* and its explicit pornographic content is linked to audience reception which can be 'deep anger, frustration, and horror, as well as embarrassed fascination and lingering unsettlement'. Thomas stresses the significance of pornographic theatre and points out that 'the most effective way for the theatre to defend itself from Artaud's accusation that it is nothing more than a brothel, offering only momentary excitement, is, paradoxically, to move even closer towards the pornographic'.

Part V includes two chapters on the relationship between voyeurism and naked bodies. Tim Stephenson, in '"Music for the Eyes" in *Hair*: Tracing the History of the Naked Singing Body on Stage', goes beyond the surface of viewing musical theatre as mere entertainment and counter-argues that they provide a subtextual re-enforcement of masculine hegemony and the sexualized objectification of women. He provides a historical overview with a useful linkage to nudity in (adult) musicals. Stephenson contends that *Hair* was evolutionary rather that revolutionary and, despite the use of male and female full-frontal nudity as protest, *Hair* only confirmed the inherent patriarchy of the time through exploiting and commercializing the voyeurism of the exposed naked singing body. With clear links to Pavis, Butler and Dyer, the author blends in issues of gender and representation and how these shape the audience's reception of these works. As a closing statement, he then provides an up-to-date evaluation of the genre's contribution to the contemporary creative industries that exploit the voyeuristic tendencies of their audiences and questions whether audiences flock to musicals for music or the 'music for the eyes'.

The final chapter of the volume is by George Rodosthenous and is entitled '*Outlying Islands* as Theatre of Voyeurism: Ornithologists, Naked Bodies and the "Pleasure of Peeping"'. David Greig's *Outlying Islands* is used as a case study for the exposition of this argument. Alongside the textual analysis, there are explicit links to Philip Howard's original Traverse Theatre Company production of *Outlying Islands* and its critical reception. The playwright's own suggestion that his protagonists are 'supposed to be there to watch birds, but really they watch each other' (Greig in Rimmer 2002) is recontextualized in relation to the presence of the audience watching the performers' bodies performing on stage. Issues such as nudity in theatre and homosociality in remote social environments, with their own possibilities of overt voyeurism (and exhibitionism), are also explored.

David Wiles in his *Theatre and Time* suggests a clear division between the visual and the aural in theatre. Analysing Stockhausen's 'quest for the nature of rhythm and its roots in the body', Wiles proposes that rhythm has the ability to 'join human beings whilst spectacle and the gaze tend to separate' (Wiles 2014: 66). If rhythm unites us and the gaze divides us – as audience members – because of personal circumstances, preferences, sexuality, cultural upbringing, tastes, then I propose that by emphasizing the visual aspect of the spectacle and looking at the theatre through the previously stigmatized prism of voyeurism can enable us to acknowledge and to articulate our response to observing the human body in action.

The presence of the binoculars in the Grand Circles and Balconies of the Victorian playhouses is a constant reminder that theatre is associated with voyeurism. The binoculars give the audience permission to spy, to come closer to the happenings on stage while remaining at a safe distance in the dark. It is, yet, another unspoken authorization to watch: a silent agreement licensing voyeurism. The ten chapters of *Theatre as Voyeurism: The Pleasures of Watching* provide their own fascinating observations on how theatre-going is indeed a communal activity which has overt and unambiguous links to the complex, but not uncommon, condition of voyeurism. Whether voyeurism offers 'spiritual liberation', 'a kind of transcendence', 'a removal of unpleasure' or simply a gratifying fulfilment of our intense curiosity, it heightens the viewing pleasure in the theatre. And by focusing on that pleasure of watching, we can find out more about ourselves, our identities and our fantasies.

Notes

1. I refer here to the stage versions not the films.
2. Dimitris Papaioannou is a Greek artist. He frequently uses the naked body in his performances in a sculptural way which resembles Greek statues, famous

paintings and works of art. Papaioannou directed the Opening and Closing Ceremonies of the Olympic Games in Athens in 2004. More information can be found at www.dimitrispapaioannou.com/en/profile.
3. Many thanks to Dr Duška Radosavljević for pointing out this perspective on the issue.

Bibliography

Alston, Adam (2013) 'Audience participation and neoliberal value: risk, agency and responsibility in immersive theatre', *Performance Research*, 18:2, 128–38.
Ben Chaim, Daphna (1984) *Distance in the Theatre: The Aesthetics of Audience Response* (Ann Arbor, MI: UMI Research Press).
Bennett, Susan (1997) *Theatre Audiences: A Theory of Production and Reception* (London: Routledge).
Bentley, Eric (1991) *The Life of the Drama* (New York: First Applause Printing).
Big Brother UK (2000–present) [TV Series] Endemol UK, Channel 4/Channel 5.
Billington, Michael (2003) 'XXX', *The Guardian*, 25 April, www.theguardian.com/stage/2003/apr/25/theatre.artsfeatures2 (accessed 30 October 2014).
Billington, Michael (2007) 'Taboo or not taboo', *The Guardian*, 15 February, www.theguardian.com/culture/2007/feb/15/michaelbillington.features11 (accessed 30 October 2014).
Billington, Michael (2012) 'The Rest is Silence – review', *The Guardian*, 7 May, www.theguardian.com/stage/2012/may/07/rest-is-silence-dreamthinkspeak-review (accessed 30 October 2014).
Billington, Michael (2013) 'The Drowned Man: A Hollywood Fable – review', *The Guardian*, 17 July, www.theguardian.com/stage/2013/jul/17/drowned-man-hollywood-fable-review (accessed 30 October 2014).
Blank, Leonard (1973) 'Nakedness and nudity: a Darwinian explanation for looking and showing behaviour', *Leonardo*, 6:1, 23–7.
Bleeker, Maaike (2008) *Visuality in the Theatre: The Locus of Looking* (Basingstoke: Palgrave Macmillan).
Bouchard, G. (2009) 'Haptic visuality: the dissective view in performance', in A. Oddey and C. White (eds), *Modes of Spectating* (London: Intellect).
Brantley, Ben (2010) 'Voyeur with a ticket', *The New York Times*, 11 August, www.nytimes.com/2010/08/15/theater/15notebook.html?pagewanted=all (accessed 30 October 2014).
Brantley, Ben (2011) 'Shakespeare slept here, albeit fitfully', *The New York Times*, 13 April, www.nytimes.com/2011/04/14/theater/reviews/sleep-no-more-is-a-macbeth-in-a-hotel-review.html?_r=1&adxnnl=1&pagewanted=all&adxnnlx=1392466721-pXFS3qIMtqLllg58yvdU2Q (accessed 30 October 2014).
Brantley, Ben (2013) 'Showing it all, revealing nothing', *The New York Times*, 13 April, www.nytimes.com/2013/06/09/theater/stage-nudity-becomes-ever-less-revealing.html?pagewanted=all (accessed 6 June 2013).
Calvert, Clay (2004) *Voyeur Nation: Media, Privacy, and Peering in Modern Culture* (Boulder, CO: Westview Press).
Delgado, Maria and Caridad Svich (eds) (2002) *Theatre in Crisis: Performance Manifestos for a New Century* (Manchester University Press).
Fenichel, Otto (1945) *The Psychoanalytic Theory of Neurosis* (New York: W.W. Norton).

Foucault, Michel (1977) *Discipline and Punish: The Birth of the Prison* (London: Penguin).
Gardner, Lyn (2009) 'Who needs onstage nudity? There's nothing like a sexy metaphor', *The Guardian*, 2 February, www.theguardian.com/stage/theatreblog/ 2009/feb/01/theatre (accessed 30 October 2014).
Gardner, Lyn (2014) 'Lulu: A Murder Ballad – review', *The Guardian*, 4 February, www.theguardian.com/stage/2014/feb/04/lulu-a-murder-ballad-opera-north-tiger-lillies-review (accessed 30 October 2014).
Gounaridou, Kiki (ed.) (2011) *Text and Presentation* (Jefferson, NC: McFarland).
Hoffman, Barbara (2003) 'Shiver his timber: Broadway's newest member has a ball in Take Me Out', *The New York Post*, 25 February, http://nypost.com/2003/02/25/shiver-his-timber-broadways-newest-member-has-a-ball-in-take-me-out/ (accessed 30 October 2014).
Jays, Davis (2014) 'Carnage by candelight', *The Guardian*, 24 October, www.theguardian.com/stage/2014/oct/24/michael-longhurst-tis-pity-shes-a-whore (accessed 30 October 2014).
Johnson, Dominic (2012) *Theatre and the Visual* (Basingstoke: Palgrave Macmillan).
Laws, Richard D. and William O'Donohue (eds) (1997) *Sexual Deviance: Theory, Assesssment, and Treatment* (New York: Guilford Publications).
Leach, Robert (2008) *Theatre Studies: The Basics* (Abingdon: Routledge).
Machon, Josephine (2013) *Immersive Theatres: Intimacy and Immediacy in Contemporary Performance* (Basingstoke: Palgrave Macmillan).
Marks, Laura (2000) *The Skin of the Film: Intercultural Cinema, Embodiment, and the Senses* (Durham, NC, and London: Duke University Press).
Marks, Laura (2002) *Touch: Sensuous Theory and Multisensory Media* (Minneapolis: University of Minnesota Press).
Maxwell, Dominic (2014) 'The Duchess of Malfi at the Sam Wanamaker Playhouse', *The Times*, 16 January, www.thetimes.co.uk/tto/arts/stage/theatre/article 3976691.ece?CMP=OTH-gnws-standard-2014_01_16 (accessed 30 October 2014).
McMillan, Joyce (2002) 'A question of value', *The Scotsman*, 5 August.
Metz, Christian (1977) *The Imaginary Signifier: Psychoanalysis and the Cinema* (Bloomington: Indiana University Press).
Metzl, Jonathan (2004) 'From scopophilia to *Survivor*: a brief history of voyeurism', *Textual Practice*, 18:3, 415–34.
Money, John (1986) *Lovemaps: Clinical Concepts of Sexual/Erotic Health and Pathology, Paraphilia, and Gender Transposition in Childhood, Adolescence, and Maturity* (New York: Irvington).
Mulvey, Laura (1975) 'Visual pleasure and narrative cinema', *Screen*, 16:3, 6–18.
Oddey, Alison and Christine White (2009) *Modes of Spectating* (Bristol: Intellect Books).
Papaioannou, Spyros (2014) 'Immersion, "smooth" spaces and critical voyeurism in the work of Punchdrunk', *Studies in Theatre and Performance*, 34:2, 160–74.
Pavis, Patrice (1998) *Dictionary of the Theatre: Terms, Concepts and Analysis* (University of Toronto Press).
Read, Alan (2004) *Theatre and Everyday Life: An Ethics of Performance* (London: Routledge).
Rimmer, Louise (2002) 'I'm shocked by what my plays end up saying', Interview with David Greig in *Scotland on Sunday*, 11 August.
Rose, Jacqueline (1986) *Sexuality in the Field of Vision* (London: Verso).

Schneider, Rebecca (1997) *The Explicit Body in Performance* (London: Routledge).
Schneider, Rebecca (2000) 'On taking the blind in hand', *Contemporary Theatre Review*, 10:3, 24–6.
Shepherd, Simon (2006) *Theatre, Body and Pleasure* (Abingdon: Routledge)
Sidiropoulou, Avra (2011) *Authoring Performance: The Director in Contemporary Theatre* (New York: Palgrave Macmillan).
Silverstein, J.L. (2007) 'Exhibitionism as countershame', *Sexual Addiction and Compulsivity*, 3:1, 33–42.
Smith, Spencer R. (1976) 'Voyeurism: a review of the literature', *Archives of Sexual Behavior*, 5, 585–608.
Spencer, Charles (1998) 'The Blue Room', *The Telegraph*, 23 September.
Spencer, Charles (2014) 'The Pass', *The Telegraph*, 17 January, www.telegraph.co.uk/culture/theatre/theatre-reviews/10580611/The-Pass-Royal-Court-Theatre-Upstairs-review.html (accessed 30 October 2014).
Übersfeld, Anne (1982) 'The pleasure of the spectator', *Modern Drama*, 25:1, 127–39.
Westcoat Sanders, Justin (2005) 'Take me out', *The Portland Mercury*, 2 June, www.portlandmercury.com/portland/take-me-out/Content?oid=33776 (accessed 30 October 2014).
Whitehead, Jay (2014) 'Are you staring at the size of my gimmick? Applying burlesque conventions to a different anatomy', *Canadian Theatre Review*, 158, 27–32.
Wiles, David (2014) *Theatre and Time* (Basingstoke: Palgrave Macmillan).
Yalom, I.D. (1960) 'Aggression and forbiddenness in voyeurism', *Archives of General Psychiatry*, 3, 305–19.

Part I
Voyeurism and Directing the Gaze

1
Always Looking Back at the Voyeur: Jan Fabre's Extreme Acts on Stage

Laurens De Vos

In *Three Essays on the Theory of Sexuality* Freud has identified scopophilia as the pleasure of looking (see Freud 1974 VII: 157). While actors and actresses are often said to secretly and unconsciously exult in a societally accepted form of exhibitionism, spectators take the role of voyeurs, indulging in different forms of scopophilia. It is worthwhile having a look at this comparison by outlining the contours of voyeurism, for even if this phenomenon unconsciously grounds the spectator's pleasure of looking in a more Aristotelian theatre tradition of plays with a dramatic narrative, performed on a stage separated by the so-called fourth wall from the spectators who are sitting in a dark auditorium, contemporary postdramatic theatre has changed the conditions of the relation between actors and audience inasmuch that a new contract may not follow the same rules.

In this chapter, I will look at the postdramatic theatre of Jan Fabre and trace in his performances the game he plays, as a director, with the audience's voyeuristic inclinations. I contend that while theatre is not fit to live up to the 'standards' of a fully voyeuristic situation, Fabre does address the voyeur in each spectator and then subverts this position. Fabre's most enticing and breathtaking performance so far is probably *Je suis sang* (*I am Blood*) (2001) and I tend to see it as the most sublime example that exceeds the well-ordered world of language and takes us to a mystical world in which the audience's look is directed towards and away from their phantasms. Therefore, in this chapter, I will mainly focus on this production in order to situate Fabre's theatre work, and refer to other performances where they may further illuminate my analysis.

Duchamp and the seclusion of the voyeur

What exactly is voyeurism? Surely, it must be something other than a person watching another person, nor can it find its *habitat* in the mutual consensus to look at each other. One of the more illuminating descriptions of voyeurism is given by Jean-Paul Sartre, who, in his *Being and Nothingness*, situates voyeurism in the image of a man looking through a keyhole. 'I am alone and on the level of a non-thetic self-consciousness' (Sartre 2003: 283). One of the finest illustrations of the principle of voyeurism in modern art is Marcel Duchamp's *Etant donnés*, which he began shortly after the publication of Sartre's *Being and Nothingness*, and which was exposed to the public only after the artist's death in 1968. It shows a wooden wall with several holes through which visitors can peep, behind which they will discover a nude, partly hidden, reclining woman in a landscape, her legs spread and her vulva exposed to the voyeur, or rather almost offered, as it is the most foregrounded point. In her left hand she holds up a gas lamp.

If we consider Duchamp's *Etant donnés* and Sartre's peephole anecdote as prototypical for the voyeur's activity, what primarily seems to be necessary for the voyeuristic act to succeed is a certain degree of seclusion. 'I am alone', Sartre writes, and the keyhole, just big enough for my eye/my I, ascertains this condition. Furthermore, the image of the keyhole presupposes the notion of secretion. This secretive aspect is definitely bound up with the gaze as a means to exercise power over someone. I indulge in the knowledge of seeing without being seen, of being the master having full control over the slave.

Although intricately connected with the feeling of power, this mode of seeing is different, then, from the 'Panopticon' composition. Michel Foucault's discussion of this architectural structure in *Discipline and Punish* illuminates the ingenuity of this surveillance system in a prison. From a central tower with wide windows around which a peripheric building is divided into separate cells, each and every prisoner at each and every moment realizes that he might be watched by the supervisor in the tower, even if he is not. The fact is that he can never be sure when he is being kept an eye on, and when not, for Venetian blinds cover the windows of the tower, allowing the guard to look out and preventing the inmates from looking in. 'The Panopticon is a machine for dissociating the see/being seen dyad: in the peripheric ring, one is totally seen, without ever seeing; in the central tower, one sees everything without ever being seen' (Foucault 1995: 202–3).

Foucault describes this optical relation having recourse to the metaphor of the theatre. Indeed, it is tempting to compare the watching supervisor in the tower with the spectator in a theatre auditorium, and the inmates in their cells with the performers knowing that someone is looking at them. 'They are like so many cages, so many small theatres, in which each actor is alone, perfectly individualized and constantly visible' (Foucault 1995: 200). And yet, the comparison hides from view similar objections to ascribing to the theatre spectator voyeuristic motives. What is crucial, after all, in the field of visibility that Foucault has revealed in the panopticon structure is the hierarchical difference between the all-seeing supervisor as the subject within this field and the inmate as the object of the seeing activity, captive of the look of the other. However, these roles do not apply to the theatre. To claim that actors find themselves subjected to the look of the spectators is obviously true, but it misses the whole point of what theatre is about, and that is the mutual exchange of energy between the auditorium and the stage, between the spectator and the performer. In other words, the former's look is always cast back by the gaze of the object being looked at. Subjectivity can only emerge in the scopic field if my look is returned and thus acknowledges my own presence. Additionally, contemporary theatre increasingly interacts with the audience, acknowledging this interrelationship as an intricate part of the theatrical experience. Productions in which the fourth wall comes out unscathed are becoming very rare indeed. Last but not least, theatre has always been a social activity where people attend a production not merely for artistic or aesthetic reasons, but to make an impression themselves as well. Watching a play without being seen by others for a lot of people would be much less fun. Therefore, the assumption that the audience is nothing more than a witness does not seem to stand the test.

Therefore, unlike the supervisor in his tower, who is far from the counterpart of the spectator in a theatre, the audience share a clearer parallel with the inmates in the cells precisely in *their mutual knowledge that they are being watched*. This is why the theatre cannot be called a voyeuristic structure as we have defined it drawing upon the examples given by Sartre and Duchamp. After all, the voyeur's goal is to see without being seen, and in this sense, it is the solitary supervisor whose shoe would fit. Voyeurism cannot be separated from its secretive nature, for due to the voyeur's absorption into the object being looked at his self-awareness disappears and makes room for a certain transcendence: 'there is no self to inhabit my consciousness, nothing therefore to which I can refer my acts in order to qualify them' (Sartre 2003: 283). Sartre connects self-awareness with the feeling of being the object of the Other's gaze: 'I see *myself* because *somebody* sees me' (2003: 284). This idea will later be confirmed by Jacques Lacan, who in *The Four Fundamental Concepts of Psychoanalysis* claims that one's look is always returned; one cannot look without being looked at. Lacan, therefore, situates the manifestation of the loss of the self in the scopic field, as the subject is determined by the external source of the gaze of the Other. However, this loss and the implementation of the lack allow one to become a subject in the first place, capable of self-reflection. This fits in with Sartre's statement that one can only see when being seen.

During voyeuristic acts, which necessitate the complete absence of the 'Other' and the seclusion of the watcher, this process of self-reflection is suspended. Contrary to the 'normal' scopic register in which the gaze is always returned, this scheme is momentarily deconstructed into a one-way direction of looking, offering the certainty to the voyeur that the object of his look is completely unaware of his look. This is why Sartre also speaks of the often neglected ambiguity of keyholes and the like through which the voyeur looks; these serve as 'both instruments and obstacles' (Sartre 2003: 283).

In this sense, then, the darkened auditorium of the theatre, concomitant with the fourth wall (not coincidentally, the terminology

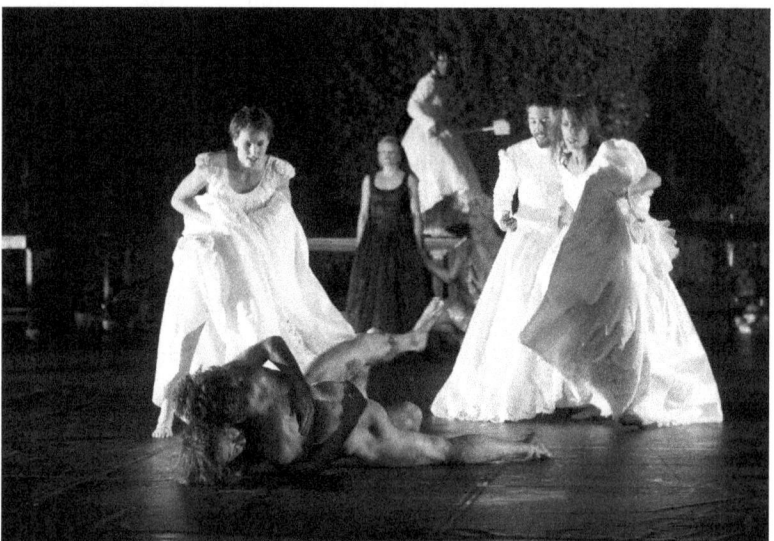

Figure 1.1 *I am Blood* by Jan Fabre (Photo: Wonge Bergmann)

alludes to the same peeping inclination as a door's keyhole), provides an admirable attempt to reconstruct an imaginary transparent wall that can be considered an instrumentalized obstacle, although, for reasons I have outlined in the previous paragraphs, it can never entirely live up to the standards of seclusion and transcendence that voyeurism necessitates.

In this perspective, in the voyeuristic act of looking the human lack is temporarily bracketed in the phantasm of the suspension of desire. The voyeur wants to blend into the scene he is watching in which he recognizes the fulfilment of his desire. Strictly speaking, therefore, the looking subject, marked by a sense of self-awareness through the scopic exchange, stops being a subject in the voyeuristic act but rather becomes the object due to a lack of self-recognition.

Je suis sang: transcendence ...

The Flemish theatre maker, sculptor, drawer and video artist Jan Fabre has been working on an impressive oeuvre that constitutes a universe that draws on the ambiguity between seeing and being seen and the issue of how to deal with being a divided subject, in which also the audience is compromised. In what follows, I will map out how Fabre questions the notion of the divided subject, representing his performances as laboratories where the search for the self is being examined.

From the onset *I am Blood* emphasizes the incantatory nature of language, as what is happening on stage is directed by the leading actress as a kind of sorceress or shaman, wearing a black wedding dress and walking in circles around her world with a book on her head. During the performance she recites – hissing like a snake – solemn verses in Latin. Her litany consists of fragments borrowed from the twelfth-century mystic Hildegard von Bingen, the thirteenth-century Franciscan Jacopo da Milano and the Bible. Moreover, towards the end of the production, in a final act of becoming liquid, one after another she mentions the different veins with their Latin names that she is about to cut. The apparently endless and repetitive list shifts the emphasis from the signification of the words to their sounds, thus altering the state of mind of the audience and making them participants in a ritual.

Obviously, in creating this kind of ritualistic tableau, Fabre is indebted to Antonin Artaud. The combination of an incomprehensible stream of words with a physically exhausting performance that explores the limits of the body is the essence of his Theatre of Cruelty. While Artaud has recourse to all kind of neologisms that are meaningless as much

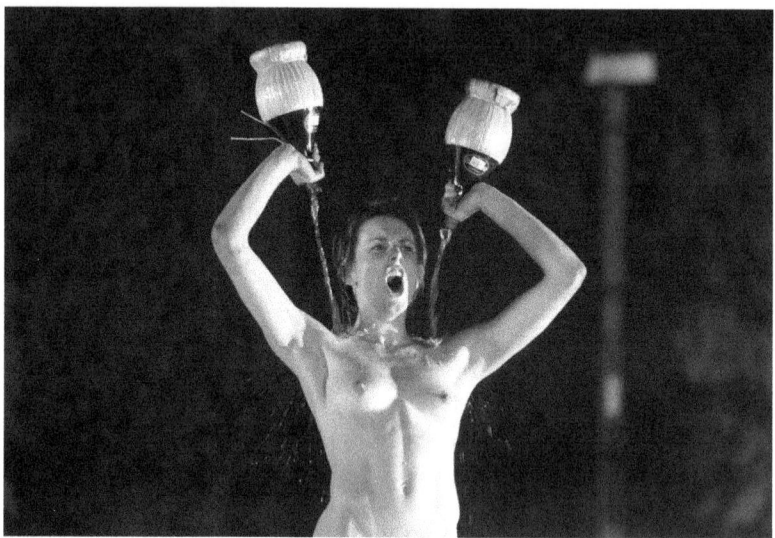

Figure 1.2 *I am Blood* by Jan Fabre (Photo: Wonge Bergmann)

as poly-interpretable, Fabre uses Latin declamations which fulfil the same role. Both build up their performances with animalistic howls, screams and yelling. Words that are recognized as belonging to a human language (often Fabre's texts are made up of several languages, as, for instance, in his 2009 production *Orgy of Tolerance*, where English was larded with fragments in Dutch, French and Croatian) lose their significance. The DNA of language is disentangled and isolated in separate strings, the combination of which becomes, therefore, unreadable. About one of Fabre's early works, *The Interview that Dies*, Emil Hrvatin writes: 'Communication has shifted to the level of elementary materials of the discourse, to the level of the words where communication between characters is no longer possible' (Hrvatin 1994: 133). It is a conclusion that holds true for Fabre's other work too, testifying to a strong thematic perpetuation in his work.

Like Artaud, Fabre wants to liberate man from the linguistic carcass in which he is imprisoned. This is where the much used metaphor of the beetle fits in: it has to throw off its shell and expose the moist and fleshy body within. The body is the central site where the suffocating and restrictive limits of language can be bypassed. By eliminating the organization of the body as part of a structuring system of other bodies in a coded society, Artaud as well as Fabre try to find 'a body without organs'. Organs, after all, are a body's grammar. As they control the digestive system, they are responsible for the corporeal organization. Analogous to the way the organs in a body need externally administered food to digest, the mind, functioning metaphorically like the stomach, absorbs external linguistic elements to shape words and sentences. We are fed with words and grammar and secrete the same substance moulded in one or another shape. Nailing us down within the law of creation, organs, just like words, bring the flux of forces to an end, a stream that ultimately dries up in comprehensible preconceptions and solidifying forms. Without function or organs, the body can liberate itself from all automatisms and obtain the freedom to establish a new world of chaos. Hence, he must get rid of all bodily organizational principles and corporeal fluids (see De Vos 2011: 44). Likewise, corporeal purification is a recurrent motif in Fabre's performances.

The body is subject to a perpetual expulsion; in *De Keizer van het verlies* (*The Emperor of Loss*) (1996) a clown is carrying his heart in a plastic bag, and in *As Long as the World Needs a Warrior's Soul* (2000) urine, excrement and gall juices of both human beings and animals are hung up in jars. *I am Blood* and *History of Tears* (2005), in which not only tears but urine and sweat are examined, continue this series of performances in which Fabre (almost like a medieval chirurgeon) cuts open the body to study its fluids and let them run free. In *I am Blood*, a Christ figure with a crown of thorns appears on stage. He represents the law to which we are subjected, the totem that – as Freud has reminded us – prevents us from breaching the incest taboo, thus installing the first and most principal step towards civilization. Not coincidentally, in celebrating the Holy Communion, Christ offers to the community his body and his blood to be consumed, a holy ritual by which we channel and restrict our hidden desires.

A body without organs is a deranged body, a body purified by the plague, as Artaud proclaims in a much quoted fragment from *The Theatre and its Double*: 'Like the plague, theatre is a crisis resolved either by death or cure. The plague is a superior disease because it is an absolute crisis after which there is nothing left except death or drastic purification' (Artaud 1999 IV: 20). The body of blood that emerges in Fabre's performance has overcome its own limits; after the metamorphosis man has become whole again. He is no longer subject to the human lack. The French title of his production allows Fabre to pun on the ambiguity of the homophony of *sang* and *sans*. After the attack on my being human, on my bodily restrictions, and after having shed off my shell, I can finally be, without lack, without organ-ization – an emperor

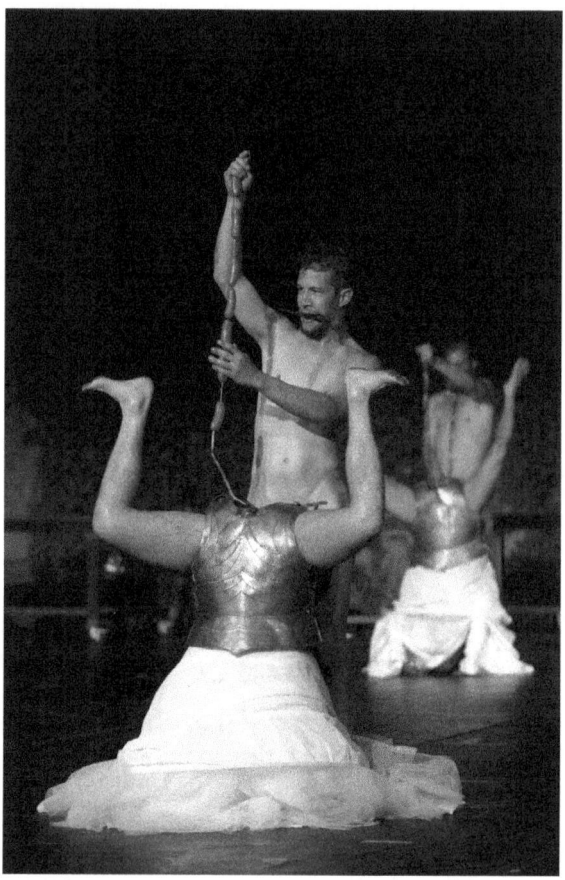

Figure 1.3 *I am Blood* by Jan Fabre (Photo: Wonge Bergmann)

without loss. After the metamorphosis, I will return to a pre-linguistic stage in which I have not yet been caged by language. Unless I can wallow in a stream of blood (*je suis sang*), I have to cope with the frustration of my existence as a flawed being, perpetually being burdened with the human lack (*je suis sans*).

Throughout his career, whether it is as a theatre maker, sculptor or drawer, Fabre has always been preoccupied with the human lack, preventing man access to the world of the real. This runs parallel to Lacan's notion of the symbolic castration and the irrevocable loss of which the phallus is the first signifier, which is the onset of the participation in the dimension of linguistic signifiers (the beetle's shell; the actor's body) and

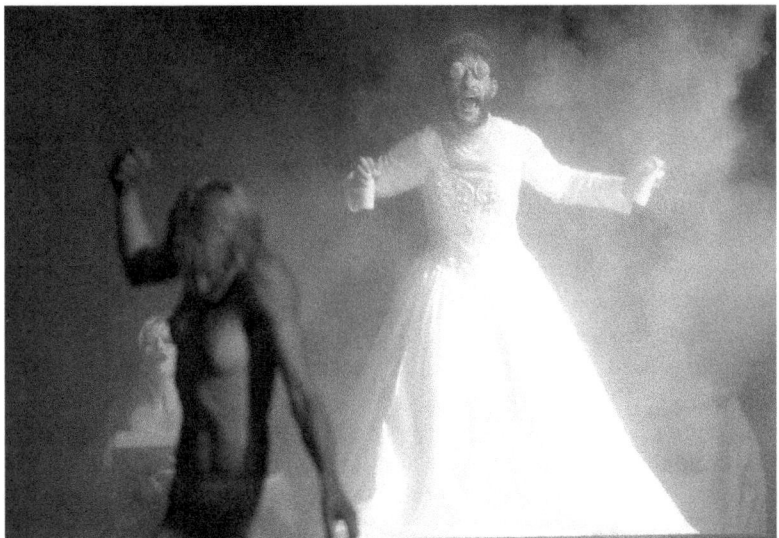

Figure 1.4 *I am Blood* by Jan Fabre (Photo: Wonge Bergmann)

the end of the impossible enjoyment of the real. Although the pre-oedipal stage of the real is a logical antecedent to the oedipal, symbolic stage, it is actually the latter that engenders the real in retrospect (in a different terminology, Freud refers to the same phenomenon as an effect that is *nachträglich*). The order of the symbolic, therefore, has both engendered and murdered the real. Since one can only exist thanks to the symbolic castration, it turns out that man will necessarily be alienated from himself. The human lack is quintessential to man's existence as a human being.

One could easily maintain – and rightly so – that all art, along with science and religion, is a persevering though equally fruitless attempt to undo the human lack and find the wholeness of the pre-oedipal stage again. In fact, most if not all human activities aspire to obtain this. And yet, Fabre unravels the dynamics of the ambition to create a body reborn as a unity with itself and the surrounding world. His characters listen to the lack deep down in themselves. *I am Blood* shows chirurgeons sticking glasses on two women's naked bodies in order to listen to the gurgling of the blood, the dull beating of the heart. The body is turned inside out. Thus, Fabre wants to unchain the deepest drives of man. To liberate man from the corporeal yoke, the body needs to flow out entirely in blood. We need to be prepared to hurt ourselves, to torture ourselves, as is exemplified by the naked figure of St Sebastian, pressing between arms and chest a series of arrows. We abandon the formal organization of skeleton and organs and embrace the new fluid body that is unburdened by the societal and religious taboos that are often centred on blood. In the very first scene of the production, on both sides of the stage, hooded figures, as if they were monks, sit on a table, and scrub it as if chased by the devil. It seems like an act of purification, in order to cleanse the blood that has not been spilled yet. This obsession with purification recurs later in the production, when several characters like madmen start rubbing between their legs in an attempt to erase the human stain.

Dionysus too makes his entry in Fabre's play. From the very beginning of the play, a corpulent man, naked but for a bright red tanga, crawls over the scene. His nipples are painted red as blood. Permanently present on the stage, he enjoys a big cigar or indulges in naked breasts. Towards the end, the sorceress announces the dissection of his body, incision after incision. In an incantatory rhythm she recites all veins in Latin; the anatomical dissection becomes an act of undressing, till nothing remains but blood. 'I empty myself / I free myself / I liberate myself.' This ritual results in a body of blood. Naked bodies dance frantically to live rock music and pour wine over themselves. It is a scene reminiscent

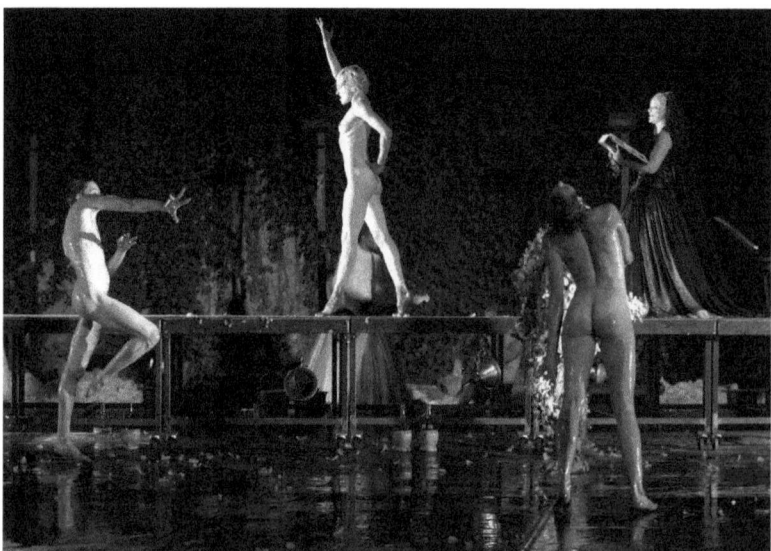

Figure 1.5 *I am Blood* by Jan Fabre (Photo: Wonge Bergmann)

of an image in Fabre's 1991 production *Sweet Temptations*, in which an orgy of sex and violence is celebrated to Iggy Pop's 'Lust for Life' by masked figures. And in so many productions – it is safe to say that it has become Fabre's hallmark – humans become animals: chased bulls, howling dogs and turkeys in *I am Blood*; barking dogs in *As Long as the World Needs a Warrior's Soul* (2000) – to give but a few examples of seemingly never-ending variations on this theme. Humans becoming animals, humans becoming saints; it is the theatrical illustration of Friedrich Nietzsche's Dionysian intoxication, an exaltation that encompasses a perpetual metamorphosis as another interpretation of his idea of the eternal return (see Nietzsche 1985: 117–19 and Vande Veire 2002: 141).

They return to the aforementioned pre-oedipal stage from which the subject with its human lack has retreated. In staging these primal phantasms Fabre forces the spectator in the role of voyeur who transcends his self-consciousness in view of the apparent erasure of the human lack. The voyeur is aghast at the sight of the Dionysian flux that seems to stem from a stage prior to the symbolic castration, and forgets about his own subjectivity while watching these primal scenes. Since man can only approach the feeling of being a non-divided being in sexuality in an ever failing attempt, the body is Fabre's most important device. If not naked, a lot of the time, his figures very often engage in some sort of sexual intercourse or masturbation. It need not be said that the sight of a flawless scene without castration in voyeurism will, in most cases, be encountered in a sexually charged activity behind the keyhole.

On stage, Fabre's figures realize the audience's hidden desires and fears at the same time: the rejection of the implementation of the law and the two principal taboos that Freud distinguished in *Totem and Taboo*: the prohibition to murder the father and the obligation of exogamy. According to Freud, the inscription of these taboos marked the beginning of civilization. However, liberated from all restrictions, Fabre's de-subjectified characters celebrate their newly gained freedom. Blood, we hear in the production, 'is no alarm signal, it is a transformation', in order to reach 'a final destination for the fluid body / a place where it can live on eternally'. At this final stage, the body is no longer an object that fits in the utilitarian dynamics. 'No one will buy my body / I am blood [...] No one will have my body sin / I am blood' until the very last line: 'No one will have my body bleed / for I am blood'. Liquefying the body in order to immortalize it is a theme that finds in *I am Blood* definitely a culmination point, but on which Fabre varies in earlier and later work, such as *Quando l'uomo principale è una donna* (2004); in this dance solo, dancer Lisbeth Gruwez slides and crawls over the stage that has been

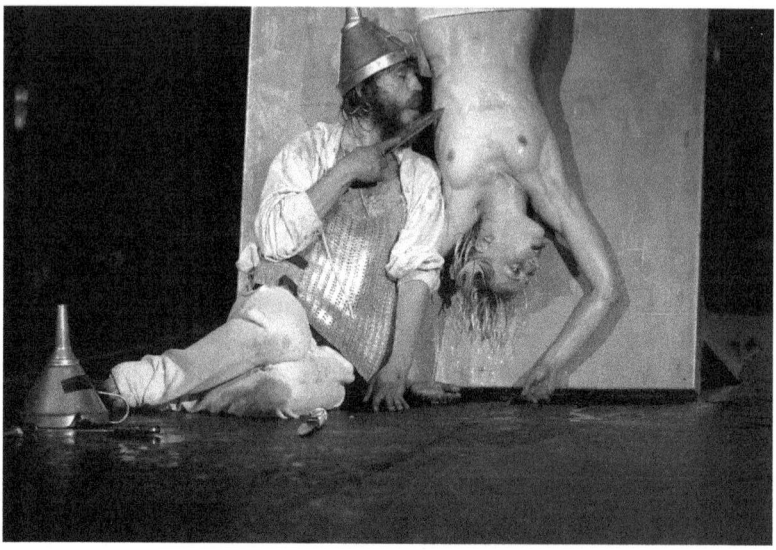

Figure 1.6 *I am Blood* by Jan Fabre (Photo: Wonge Bergmann)

poured over with olive oil. In a liquid homogeneous mass she almost melts together with her environment; an ambition that we recognize not only as Fabre's, but also as one of Artaud's main preoccupations. Artaud's theatre was to bring on the stage a performance based on 'a physical gesture that could annihilate death, society and the organs of the body, to create a body in constant movement' (Barber 1993: 146). Rather than to *have* a body, at this final stage one should have undone the initial crime of dispossession and *be* a body. His plea for an eternal body is not altogether different from what Fabre's characters proclaim:

> man has known immortality. The only, the real! The corporeal immortality. The eternal duration of the body, of the same man in the same body, through the times without stop and space forever unfathomable [...] Man was immortally created, and this is no holy story, this is the story of the truth [...] The magic was to continue. To perpetually continue. (Artaud 1968: 92)

Jan Fabre's *tableaux vivants* do not chronologically narrate a story. Through associations, metaphors and allegories they rather evoke an atmosphere in which past and present merge into an eternal

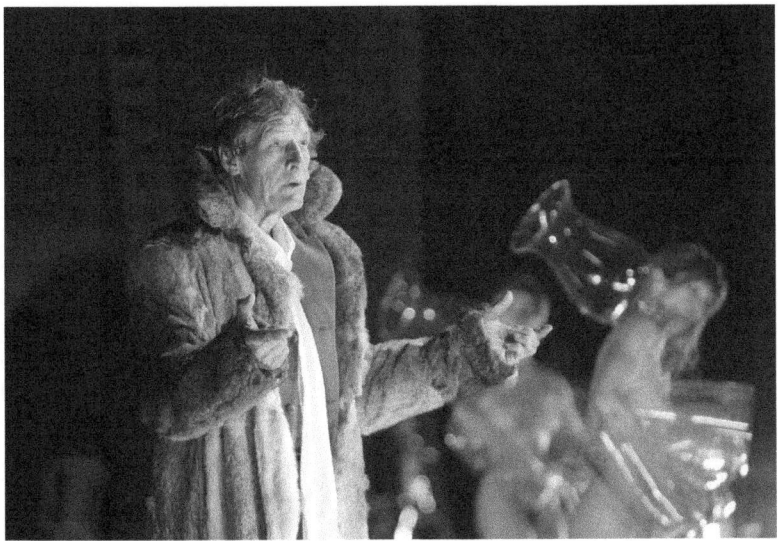

Figure 1.7 History of Tears by Jan Fabre (Photo: Wonge Bergmann)

timelessness. They are dream sequences, emerging from an otherworldly space and submerging us into our subconscious; sequences in which 'we can recognize day residue, but nevertheless seem to have originated in another world' (De Brabandere 1997: 33). Neither are the characters on stage psychologically carved. Again, having recourse to Artaud probably comes closest to a description of Fabre's dream-like characters. They are moving, a-historic hieroglyphics. As he repeatedly stresses in *The Theatre and its Double*, Artaud's adherence to the use of hieroglyphics allows a direct communication without the intermediary function of arbitrary words. These hieroglyphic actors mark a departure from the European psychological and textual theatre, as they do not enter into rational dialogue. Dream-like images and hieroglyphics speak for themselves; they do not need to be interpreted or translated. A beautiful illustration of this idea is the image of the aforementioned figure of Dionysus who is seated on his knees on the long train of a woman's wedding dress. Pressing a long sword in her back, he pushes her forward. While the stage is occupied by several other characters, she elegantly and solemnly moves from the right to the left at the back. The sublime unveils the ultimate image that erases all antagonisms – the appearance of an image that subverts the fundamentals of language that is literally unpronounceable.

... deconstructed: a failed encounter with *jouissance*

However, although they share the same dream, Artaud differentiates from Fabre in his steadfast belief in the singularity of such an act, and it is here that Fabre smashes the voyeur's phantasm and brings his de-subjectified transcendence back to earth. The moment a gesture, an act or a word would be repeated, Artaud states, it would be endowed with meaning and integrated in the symbolic web of signifiers. Repetition does not only place what is repeated on the axis of time, it also brings along death as it kills the pre-symbolic origin, which is, then, deprived of its absolute singularity. 'Let us [...] acknowledge that what has already been said no longer needs saying; that an expression twice used is of no value since it does not have two lives. Once spoken, all speech is dead and is only active as it is spoken. Once a form is used it has no more use, bidding man find another form, and theatre is the only place in the world where a gesture, once made, is never repeated in the same way' (Artaud 1999 IV: 57). In one of his essays on Artaud, Jacques Derrida points out that Artaud's challenge to theatre to find fully singular signs that cannot possibly be repeated does not stand a chance:

> For there is no word, nor in general a sign, which is not constituted by the possibility of repeating itself. A sign which does not repeat itself, which is not already divided by repetition in its 'first time,' is not a sign. (Derrida 2001: 310)

The singular nature of the Theatre of Cruelty, then, can never be obtained. 'It is still to be born' (Derrida 2001: 293); it is continually being born, on the verge of originating. Artaud's theatre entails a permanent promise, yet its eternal becoming will never end in affirmation, for this would immediately put an end to the singularity it hopes to find. The time of the Theatre of Cruelty, therefore, is the eternal future.

A child of his time, Fabre is well aware of this eternal promise, of the Sisyphus-like nature of this enterprise. He belongs to a generation that is permeated with the ideas of Lacan and Derrida, and that is, hence, convinced of the infeasibility of overcoming the symbolic castration and of grabbing the sublime of unity. However, Fabre deliberately wants to play Sisyphus, and to go and seek for the Holy Grail. Doubtlessly, it is no coincidence that one of his videos directly refers to this mythological figure; in *The Problem* we see Jan Fabre along with two German philosophers, Dietmar Kamper (who would die shortly afterwards) and Peter Sloterdijk. All three dressed in a tuxedo, a black coat and a white scarf, they ponder about the world, about life and death, meanwhile pushing forward a huge earth ball. They not only philosophize literally in front of their world, they also climb their balls and play with them. In addition, they are scarabs – by far the most recurrent creature in Fabre's work – inch per inch pushing up the dung ball they have made themselves.

Thus, although Fabre is strongly indebted to the ideas of Artaud, he is anti-Artaudian in his more postmodernist stance of revealing the emptiness behind what we tend to capitalize as the Truth. Because his actors are devoid of every kind of realism and occupy another world, they fulfil the role of symbols rather than of psychological characters. 'The actors have become symbols that cover up the empty space of the play' (Hrvatin 1994: 143). The ostentatious presentation of the symbolic function of the images reveals their veiling force. They are merely symbols for something that cannot be represented. So is his *Flemish Warrior*, a hollow sculpture of a hare made up of the greenish shells of beetles where there is nothing underneath the scarabs' hollow shells. The performance, then, and in extension life itself, boils down to a 'joyful tomfoolery', with reference to Fabre's 1988 video performance *The Scheldt*, in which the camera registers a sloop in which Fabre one after another launches the glass-blown, neon-blue words 'Hé – wat – een – plezierige – zottigheid!' (Hey what a joyful tomfoolery!). Here again, Fabre demonstrates how futile man and life is. He is but a dot on a big river, and on this passageway to death, the only thing he can aim for is to have a little bit of fun while trying to leave something behind, well aware that he can hardly be seen from the river's banks and that nobody will notice what he is doing. What we see in this video performance, then, is the erection of a gravestone for Icarus, who tried to reach the sun in vain; almost no one has seen him fall into the water, and our ways to commemorate him are futile – made of fragile glass that is waiting to be swallowed by the sea. And yet, it is worthwhile to do it, with grandeur and style.

Fabre's characters indulge in this commemorative ritual, knowing that they will never succeed. But ever so vigorously, they begin again, over and over again. In this respect, there is an outspoken Beckettian aspect to them. The actors continuously repeat their actions, often till they are physically exhausted. *De macht der theaterlijke dwaasheden* (*The Power of Theatrical Madness*) (1984) staged actors repeating endlessly the same ballet exercises. In his 1991 production *Zij was en zij is, zelfs* (*She Was and She Is, Even*), Els Deceukelier, wearing a wedding dress, repeats over and over 'once more / once more / once more'. A similar procedure is used almost 20 years later in *Orgy of Tolerance*, featuring a bunch of women and men who cannot stop masturbating.

Rather than triggering one's desire, this eternal repetition leads the spectator to boredom and indifference. While he has been led to his innermost phantasms and desires by means of the scenic hieroglyphics of Fabre's tableaux, the never-ending repetition to which some actions are subjugated brings home to the audience that the ultimate object of desire is not only impossible to reach, it does not exist either. Behind the world of signifiers and 'glowing icons' – the title of a 1997 production in which Fabre staged characters taken from fairy tales, TV and showbiz whose entry into the realm of myths has emptied them of any significant meaning – lies literally nothing. The exhaustion that results from a seemingly never-ending repetition confronts us with the quintessential core of what desire consists in – that it is directed onto nothing. What lies beyond the territory of the symbolic order cannot be represented. It is the outside that harbours the ultimate truth unstained by deformed and disabled signifiers, which serve as the falsifying medium that never succeeds in exactly expressing the signified. Its formless nature prevents the truth from ever being translated in representative form, thus construing a deceitful façade hiding the real of the signified from view. Hence, beyond the symbolic order lies a black hole of nothingness, the unbridgeable gap of madness and death, an abyss yawning to swallow the subject into some Bermuda triangle. Desire, then, is unveiled as a perpetuum mobile that has as its object something that is in fact nothing. Try as we may to look for a theological sense, the essence will always remain an illusion (that needs to be cherished though).

Fabre's characters are subjugated to a Sadean will to perpetually start all over again till the point that the repetition becomes a dynamics in itself, without aim or perspective included. It is a gratuitous *'Encore!'* that exists only for its own sake. 'There is nothing left to celebrate, certainly no analysis of desire. There is emptiness, boredom, idleness, meaningless locomotion, and gradually, as the show continues, the erotic meaning of the 'once more' disappears and is replaced with a worrisome repetition of something from which meaning has withdrawn for good' (Hertmans 2002: 49). This *'Encore!'* is the immediate consequence of what Lacan calls the dynamics of *jouissance*. It should not surprise that Lacan situates this *jouissance* on a corporeal level and hence speaks of a *'jouissance* of the body'. *'Encore'* is always *'en corps'*.

The pursuit of *jouissance*, then, is an attempt to annihilate the lack in the 'Other' and comes down, clearly, to a path towards death. *'Jouissance* is an enjoyment, but an enjoyment that does not know how to stop, that does not know any limits, the only aim of which it is to be repeated. *Jouissance* is an enjoyment in pain' (Schokker and Schokker 2000: 137). Its demand on the subject *'Encore!'* sounds increasingly louder and peremptory. *'Encore!'* is the imperative that drives *jouissance*.

However, the body cannot possibly survive the blows of *jouissance*, which explains why Fabre tires his actors on stage out till the verge of collapsing. The limits of what the body can take are transgressed in the face of the perverse *'Encore'* game. Hence, Fabre's characters can be nothing but bodies. If they are subject to *jouissance*, there is no other way than to disrupt them of rationality and psychology, and take them back to a mythical and a-historic world that is dominated by utter chaos:

> In short, the problem is that the body is not made to the measure of enjoyment. There is no enjoyment but the enjoyment of the body, yet if the body is to be equal to the task (or duty) of *jouissance*, the limits of the body have to be 'transcended'. Pleasure – that is, the limit of suffering that a body can still endure – is thus an obstacle to enjoyment. Sade's answer to the impossibility of surpassing this limit is fantasy, the fantasy of infinite suffering: the victims are tortured endlessly, beyond all boundaries of imagination, yet they go on living and suffering, and even become more and more beautiful, or more and more 'holy'. (Zupançiç 2000: 80–1)

In these repetitive sexual acts of copulating and masturbating bodies, Fabre confronts the audience with their own voyeuristic tendencies. What is being shown in these scenes, after all, is not the phantasm representing the erasure of the human lack, but the very impossibility of this idea. The voyeur's look through the keyhole is cast back upon himself, the tables have been turned on him as he has become the object in the scopic field himself. The exhaustion of sexuality performed by naked bodies transgresses and thus shatters the audience's phantasm, bringing them back to their flawed state of being a subject.

Fabre's staging of sexual bodies is not altogether different from Slavoj Žižek's analysis of pornography in *Looking Awry*. The psychoanalytic idea that the look of the subject is always returned by the gaze of the object being looked at is eliminated in pornography. 'Instead of being on the side of the viewed object, the gaze falls into ourselves, the spectators, which is why the image we see on the screen contains no spot, no sublime-mysterious point from which it gazes at us' (Žižek 1991: 110). Thus, pornography is always a failed encounter with the object-gaze in the other. By trespassing the limit of showing everything, it goes too far, and misses the point from which the object gazes at us that confirms our status as divided subjects. Instead, Žižek notes, it is not the porn actors but the spectators of pornography who are degraded to the position of object.

Pornography confronts us with the impossibility of ever reconciling the subject with his desire. What seems attractive at first sight, appears to be a vulgar, depressive scene. 'The unattainable/forbidden object approached but never reached by the "normal" love story – the sexual act – exists only as concealed, indicated, "faked". As soon as we "show it" its charm is dispelled, we have "gone too far". Instead of the sublime Thing, we are stuck with vulgar, groaning fornication' (Žižek 1991: 110). A similar procedure can be witnessed in Fabre's work, who deliberately reveals as illusory the spectator's voyeuristic phantasms by the repetitive copulative and masturbatory acts, ad nauseam. At this point the spectator is awakened from his de-subjectified position and cast back on his status as a subject marked by an insurmountable lack.

Thus, on the one hand through the direct, Artaudian staging of mythical figures appealing to the audience's most fundamental and primal desires, phantasms and fears, the spectator is caught as a voyeur looking in the mirror on stage at his own mixed emotions. He is captivated by the secret wish to continue on the path of *jouissance*, of transgressing the Law and trespassing on territory that would free us from our human lack. This makes Fabre's tableaux, coming from the garden from which we were expelled, so intriguing and enticing. It also renders an uncanny feeling to his productions. Uncanny, because it brings home something that 'ought to have remained secret and hidden' (Freud 1955 XVII: 225). And yet, through endless repetition Fabre reaches a point where fascination turns into indifference and lack of interest. At this point he reveals the illusion of the image. In staging actions being repeated till both actors and audience are tired out, Fabre succeeds in revealing the emptiness behind any claim for fullness that he equally stages as a dream-like trajectory taking along the spectator in his hidden desires and fears.

Precisely in his postmodernist worldview he differs from Artaud, who strongly held on to the belief in the possibility of an original creative process that could escape the principles of a coded and obligatory system. Fabre has abandoned this illusion and stresses in all his work the utopia of a journey that lies beyond the unspeakable. To the audience it hits home that their phantasms and fears that are being shown on stage will not result in a catharsis, but in the revelation of emptiness. The illusion that Fabre's theatre creates not only points at the illusion

Laurens De Vos 47

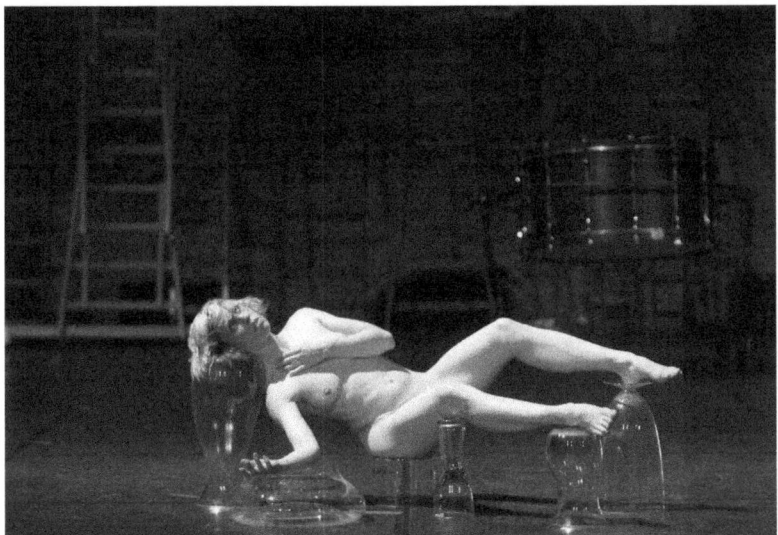

Figure 1.8 History of Tears by Jan Fabre (Photo: Wonge Bergmann)

of theatre itself, but at the similarities between the fiction of theatre and life. Life is as much a game as theatre is, though both are deadly serious.

In fact, already in the opening scene of *I am Blood* we are reminded of this adage. Standing high up on a gallery against the back wall warriors wearing suits of armour soon hastily and with clanging sounds descend via an iron fire escape and occupy the stage for a stamping choreography. Meanwhile, left and right on heavy, iron tables several figures are playing jacks – apparently for high stakes. As spectators, we are witnessing a very tough gambling game; we have to choose – we cannot have our cake and eat it. And our ultimate drive, to have it both ways, is doomed to be chained in its eternal return.

Moreover, Fabre's frequent use of armour also refers to the shells of scarabs. Just as the skeleton of beetles refers to something that was once present, and now covers up emptiness, the knights' suits of armour bear the marks of human presence, yet in fact they hide bodies without subject, without identity, without individuality. Aware of the impossibility of the Artaudian ideal, Fabre is living proof that, these days, the 'Theatre of Cruelty' cannot be realized on stage. Only the body flowing out in blood can bring salvation, but there is a reason why the subtitle of *I am Blood* reads 'A medieval fairy tale'. The show remains an unreal story, and the subversion of any claims to its high stakes and its alleged realness comes from both medieval chirurgeons who appear as mirroring figures at both sides of the sorceress. In a very ceremonial way they are dressed in green clothes reminiscent of a surgeon's. However, the alchemical-like funnel that is placed upside down on their heads immediately subverts their role and places them in a medieval world that is reminiscent of the paintings of Hieronymus Bosch. They are charlatans, excelling in the make-believe world that is theatre. The ultimate metamorphosis is a dream that we can only reach through our imagination, but that will never come true. Man can only hold on to new attempts: once more, once more, once more.

Conclusion

In Fabre's performances the voyeur's look is not allowed to remain fixated on its object. His transcendence as part of his phantasms is only sanctioned in order to disclose the illusion of these phantasms. What is being looked at does not remain silent, it becomes a speaking subject looking back at the spectator and thus confronting him with the desire of the Other.

I began this chapter with a reference to Marcel Duchamp's installation *Etant donnés*. Precisely this work served as the inspiration for Fabre's 2004 production with the same name. Els Deceukelier plays the enigmatic naked woman with the gas lamp, yet in contrast to Duchamp's installation, in which the nude is nothing more than the product of the spectator's look and imagination, she starts speaking, thus presenting herself as a subject with her own desire. As a result, the spectator's protective cocoon of secrecy and seclusion is torn apart, he is caught in his voyeuristic desires and all of a sudden again becomes aware of the gaze of the object looking back. This process crystallizes in his homage to Duchamp but is inherent in all of Fabre's work.

Bibliography

Artaud, Antonin (1968) 'Il y a dans la magie ...', *Tel Quel*, XXXV, 90–5.
Artaud, Antonin (1999) *Collected Works*, vols I–IV (London: John Calder).
Barber, Stephen (1993) *Antonin Artaud. Blows and Bombs* (London: Faber & Faber).
De Brabandere, Adri (1997) *Jan Fabre* (Brussels: Vlaams Theater Instituut).
Derrida, Jacques (2001) *Writing and Difference* (London: Routledge).
De Vos, Laurens (2011) *Cruelty and Desire in the Modern Theater: Antonin Artaud, Sarah Kane and Samuel Beckett* (Madison, NJ: Fairleigh Dickinson University Press).
Foucault, Michel (1995) *Discipline and Punish: The Birth of the Prison* (New York: Vintage Books).

Freud, Sigmund (1953–74) *The Standard Edition of the Complete Psychological Works*, trans. James Strachey, 24 vols (London: The Hogarth Press).
Hertmans, Stefan (2002) *Engel van de metamorphose. Over het werk van Jan Fabre* (Amsterdam: Meulenhoff).
Hrvatin, Emil (1994) *Herhaling, Waanzin, Discipline. Het Theaterwerk van Jan Fabre* (Amsterdam: International Theatre and Film Books).
Lacan, Jacques (2001) 'On a question preliminary to any possible treatment of psychosis', in *Ecrits: A Selection*, trans. Alan Sheridan (London: Routledge), 198–249.
Nietzsche, Friedrich (1985) *Götzendämmerung* (Frankfurt am Main: Insel Verlag).
Sartre, Jean-Paul (2003) *Being and Nothingness* (London: Routledge).
Schokker, Johan and Tim Schokker (2000) *Extimiteit. Jacques Lacans terugkeer naar Freud* (Amsterdam: Boom).
Vande Veire, Frank (2002) *Als in een donkere spiegel* (Amsterdam: SUN).
Verhaeghe, Paul (2009) *Over normaliteit en andere afwijkingen* (Leuven: Acco).
Žižek, Slavoj (1991) *Looking Awry: An Introduction to Jacques Lacan through Popular Culture* (Cambridge, MA: The MIT Press).
Zupančič, Alenka (2000) *Ethics of the Real: Kant, Lacan* (London: Verso).

2
The Dramaturgies of the Gaze: Strategies of Vision and Optical Revelations in the Theatre of Romeo Castellucci and Socìetas Raffaello Sanzio

Eleni Papalexiou

Theatre from its very inception was created of voyeuristic material. Aristotle in his *Poetics*, the first theoretical text written on theatre, refers to the pleasure enjoyed by the viewers «τὰς εἰκόνας ὁρῶντες» (as they watch likenesses) (Aristotle 1448b). The etymology of the word «θέατρον» (theatre) leads us to the term «θέα» (view), meaning look, contemplation, while *theatron* is «ὁ τόπος ἐν ᾧ θεᾶται τις», signifying the place where someone both watches and is being watched.[1] This reference to the origins of the theatre is not coincidental. In ancient Greek drama the role of the spectator and the power of the gaze were of primary importance, in the same manner as in the theatre of Romeo Castellucci and his artistic company Socìetas Raffaello Sanzio, on which this chapter focuses. Posing the question 'what is the meaning of watching?', Romeo Castellucci advocates a dramaturgy of the gaze, attempting to activate the ability of watching, as well as being watched.[2]

To realize the significance of the above question, the role of the spectator in the modern age of images and information must be better understood; we are spectators and, at the same time, viewing objects of a continuous voyeuristic spectacle, prisoners of repetitive meaningless images projected in live streaming that invade our consciousness and steal our very being. As French philosopher Guy Debord pointed out in his renowned essay *The Society of the Spectacle*:

> The spectator's alienation from and submission to the contemplated object (which is the outcome of his unthinking activity) works like this: the more he contemplates, the less he lives; the more readily

he recognizes his own needs in the images of need proposed by the dominant system, the less he understands his own existence and his own desires. The spectacle's externality with respect to the acting subject is demonstrated by the fact that the individual's own gestures are no longer his own, but rather those of someone else who represents them to him. The spectator feels at home nowhere, for the spectacle is everywhere. (1995: 23)

The theatre of Socìetas Raffaello Sanzio is opposed to the dominant world of communication; it belongs to the world of revelation and insight, allowing us to see images that emanate from the inner areas of our existence. According to Romeo Castellucci, the theatre should serve as a switch in this flow of unambiguous images (see R. Castellucci 2013: 19). He seeks to subjugate the spectator's gaze in amazement, inventing a dramaturgy that reveals the deepest meaning of the onstage image.

Romeo Castellucci's dramaturgies of the gaze will be examined here under three aspects: firstly, we will explore how the gaze of the spectator penetrates into hidden areas of human existence; secondly, we will analyse the concept of the 'third image', a forbidden stage image that, although not visible to the spectators, is apparent in their imagination; lastly we will study the archetypical relationship of θεᾶσθαι (watching and being watched) through stage devices that operate as a double mirror, making us, the viewers, the object of viewing.

Voyeurism against verbalism: from the rhetoric of the speech to the rhetoric of the body

In *Julius Caesar*, a production in 1997,[3] an actor, interpreting the role of a mysterious '...vskij' (referring to the Russian emblematic stage director Konstantin Stanislavsky), introduces a medical instrument, an endoscope, into his nose in order to enable us to travel inside his body. This scene is projected in front of the audience on a large screen. The use of the endoscope allows the spectators – as if through a keyhole – to penetrate inside the body of the actor and observe the topography of the larynx, its muscles and the mucous membranes which produce the words.

In this exploration of the throat, the spectators do not only see the inside of the body, but also another image taking form, the female genitalia,[4] evoked by the shape of the vocal cords. Thus, there is a kind of obscenity involved in being a witness to such a scene: the close-up of the larynx, which dilates and contracts, and the simultaneous gargling, is almost pornographic – an image rich in allusions, which, according to Castellucci, contains also an ironic commentary on the apparently virile rhetoric power of politicians (2001c: 277). In a very original way, this invention of the stage director allows us, voyeur-like, to see for once a private aspect of the actor, which is not external, but internal. Consequently, the insertion of the endoscope into the throat is a rhetorical gesture, which literally shows the carnal birth of speech, as well as the inner world of the actor (Papalexiou 2012: 78–9).

This special and surprising dramaturgy is based on a more general theorization of the dramatic art by the director. Romeo Castellucci radically objects to the theories of Stanislavsky, according to which the actor must arouse the emotions of the spectator. Socìetas Raffaello Sanzio challenges the traditional schools of acting, which are based on the psychological approach to the theatrical role, and on the element of mimesis. Its members criticize the classical theatrical tradition, as they believe that it deprives the actor of spontaneity and his/her potential to improvise, thus transforming him/her into a sort of marionette who responds to the manipulations of its master, the poet. Consequently, the creativity of the actor is limited to an endless practice in the production of words. Moreover, Romeo Castellucci rejects the intellectual technique of the actor, which is limited to the muscular effort needed to conceal a series of tiny and inevitable grammatical errors: when the actor speaks on stage, the word just uttered loses its power from the very attempt of verbal production (2001d: 87).

The *logorrhoea*, that is the verbal diarrhoea of the actor, and the traditional acting methods have been in the gun sight of the Socìetas since the mid-1980s and their production of *I Miserabili*. With this performance the troupe invaded into the core of the art of acting – that is, the traditional diptych 'speech and movement' – breaking with the theatre practice of their time.[5] In this production the audience watched a standing herald who remained motionless and speechless throughout the duration of the show. With this concept, the Socìetas expressed opposition to the domination of speech, since speech catalyses every effort by the spectator to 'hear' the original language of the performance. The spectacle also posed questions concerning the role of the actor, who in this case was on the stage as a spectator of himself, abandoning any preexisting theatrical language, since he is the one who brings the authentic language on his own body. Claudia Castellucci explains:

> there is a Herald, the Great Ignoramus who knows nothing and doesn't want to know anything. As a maximum expression of behavior, the

Herald lives between the stage and the theatre pit, mediating between the two areas with writings in extra-temporal languages.

He is not involved in the play, yet he is more a part of it than anyone else, because he discloses the play's character of pure reality. His total refusal to utter a single word marks the resulting trauma of the calendars and vocabularies, primary offshoots of the law and real obstacles for *I Miserabili*. (1992: 60)

The moment when the actor freezes on stage is recorded by the Socìetas as the 'Herald's paralysis'. This apparent immobility places the body as organic matter in the centre of the scene. The body then becomes the symbol of voicelessness, immobilization and invariance, contrasting with the empire of speech, which requires a constant renovation. 'Like the static origin of a whirlpool, the Herald concentrates the dynamics of the entire phenomenon in his paralysis' (1992: 62).

The opposition of Socìetas Raffaello Sanzio to the incessant flow of speech by the actor clearly appears again in *Julius Caesar*, in the famous monologue of Mark Anthony. Romeo Castellucci remarks:

> Anthony's speech to the rostra of the Roman Forum: here is the masterpiece of rhetorical hypocrisy. That is, the nucleus of dramatic art. The 'exterior line' indicated by Stanislavskij, totally deprived of the 'interior' one.[6]

In Castellucci's performance, Anthony was played by Dalmazio Masini, an actor with a tracheotomy. When appearing on stage, his 'uncommon' body, a body marked by illness, made the spectators feel surprised and uncomfortable. A person with a handicap on stage often causes numerous reactions related to ethics: voyeurism, exhibitionism, manipulation, exploitation, provocation. In contrast to conventional theatre, Castellucci does not see a sick, deformed or 'ab-normal' body as a pathological predicament; his motive for the actor's choice is purely dramaturgic. In his own words:

> In my collaboration with actors 'beyond norms', as it is called, I was with people who were fully aware of what they were doing. I always explained to them that their presence results from the very requirements of the drama. I abhor the use of people with disabilities in the modern theatre to visualize some pathogenicity, or to satisfy the voyeuristic curiosity of the bourgeois. I worked with bodies wounded by life experience, focusing always on the dramatic necessity of the stage. (Castellucci in Papalexiou 2009: 109–10)

Thus, the actor, or rather this body, was selected as an authentic dramatic material, in order to protest against the incessant flow of political speech.

Ready to start his monologue, Anthony was presented standing on a pedestal on which the Latin word *ars* was inscribed, referring to the art of persuasion as an organ of political propaganda. Then the voice of the actor transformed into the exact opposite of speech. In this scene the spectators witnessed the heroic encounter of an internal battle. The hoarse and distorted voice of Anthony resisted the corrupt speech, enunciated by the self-same Anthony. Through that castrated voice, almost reduced to silence by the actor, who himself was only capable of uttering some kind of gargling noises, the titanic combat of the voice against the word was taking place. The imprisoned and reprimanded voice expressed anger and indignation, because, at the same time, it succumbed to the charms of speech. In this *mise-en-scène*, it was this voice that the spectators were meant to hear, not Anthony's broken speech. As Claudia Castellucci underlines:

> Rhetoric is the prevalence of the form which pulls the force of the content. It is the dress of the word which, here, sounds out even its origin: the voice, the phonic emission. And it does so without mercy.[7]

> Therefore the voice can act as a means of liberation and resurrection of speech. (R. Castellucci 2001b: 80)

The rhetoric of the word gave way to the rhetoric of the body, the latter becoming the vector of authentic speech.[8]

The third image: in between seen and unseen

In our everyday life, we are bombarded by a stream of misleading images modelled by the media, relayed in art and vice versa, in a perpetual self-reflective process; this mirror of hypnotic allusions forms our way of seeing as spectators. In the antipodes of this condition, theatre has to invent an alternative language of communication. A series of questions can be formulated here: How can our gaze penetrate the surface of fake and embellished images? How to look at the horrible and inhumane, in other words the non-representable? How is it possible for the spectator to see the 'real image'? For Romeo Castellucci, the representation is a procedure of optical revelation, in which the non-transparency, the non-direct visibility, the blurriness holds a key role; as for the truth, it remains always hidden. He remarks:

> Being against the truth, this is what theatre is. Art poses problems but does not solve them, it is a question and not a key. Certainly the relationship with the truth ceases to be present on the stage, but hidden, covert. The stage does not hide any secrets, however it makes us see the slipping of the truth. (2008b: 36–7)

The outcome of truth in the theatre is not directly visible; it is for this very reason that means and devices that hide the truth by creating illusion are often seen on Romeo Castellucci's set: masks, filters, coatings, fuzzy windows, steam, curtains, etc. What is absolutely striking is the feeling that each element combined with others still has its rightful place in a creative process that stems from the initial concept and especially the dramaturgy of performance (Papalexiou 2009: 25–6).

In 1985, with the production *Santa Sofia – Teatro Khmer*,[9] Socìetas Raffaello Sanzio declared a 'holy war' against the false images that dominate art and are promoted by the mass media. In the homonymous *manifesto*, Claudia Castellucci, adopting terms stemming from a vocabulary both religious and military, addressed herself to the 'future follower of the non-existent', declaring the birth of the theatre of a 'new religion'. The Basilica of St Sophia became the symbol of the Socìetas' crusade against images.[10] The emblematic church of Constantinople, after the fall of the Byzantine Empire, was deprived of its rich illustrations by the Ottomans. Its frescoes and mosaics were gradually covered with a thick mustard-yellow layer and then four giant green medallions with verses from the Quran were added to the interior of the building. These four discs now stand still as masks covering old Byzantine representations. Starting from a religious symbol, Socìetas Raffaello Sanzio declared its own iconoclasm, praising a 'theatre that refuses representation'.[11] Adopting the Platonic conception which condemned the art of imitation and representation (*Respublica* 3.394–6 and 10.604–6), the first action of the Socìetas was to destroy everything that existed before, wishing to break with the image of the world that had shaped our perception of reality. Each image, then, must be torn down, allowing us to experience 'the unique fundamental reality: the anti-cosmic Unreal, the entireness of the unthinkable things' (C. Castellucci 2001: 288).

The realistic image is a contradiction in itself, since its mission is to represent something that we customarily see as real. So, to enable the viewer to conceive reality, each acquired image must be crushed. However, it should be noted that iconoclasm for the Sociètas does not imply non-figurative theatre, but a theatre where new representations will flow. 'What existed before no longer exists; this is iconoclasm' (C. Castellucci 2001: 288).

In his attempt to invent a new theatrical language and communication, Romeo Castellucci explores the etymology and history of words. Every word and every concept that he chooses travels through a long history through the centuries. According to him, even a title should involve a resonance and be treated as a musical theme. It must sound loud and clear like brass, lucid (C. Castellucci 2001: 272). And when the title sounds correctly in the ear of the artist, there follows the stage of classification, in which the issue of philological elaboration is associated with the etymology. One must discover the roots of the word 'to be able to cut them' (2001: 272). The word is somehow a key, which opens a path through the brain of the artist. He can then see images that do not belong only to him, but to everyone, ecumenical images:

> The ecumenical has the power to remove the artist from the centre and make him disappear behind his work. For this reason, my creations do not actually belong to me at all. I bid them farewell, as I watch them move away. The spectacles belong to everybody, as the body of a prostitute offered to whoever spends a penny. (R. Castellucci 2008a: 19)

The power of images in the theatre of Romeo Castellucci stems from the fact that the myths involved can be analysed at many different levels, also providing a strict structure. Thanks to their archetypal form, these images mark the viewer indelibly and affect him in an automatic manner, as they are based on an existing context: they are somehow lurking in the darkness of our brain. According to the art historian Aby Warburg, there is a river of images that runs through the history of mankind. Like a re-emerging subconscious, these images reappear regularly on various occasions. It is 'an intense drama of heterogeneous time taking body together' (Didi-Huberman 2002).[12]

Behind these images, the artist must fade, become permeable, transparent and invisible. The performance does not belong to him but to the spectators who will create their own images. Romeo Castellucci invokes the creative power of the spectator, as his spectacles require the active participation of the audience. His work develops through the entire temporal dimension – not only in terms of performance, but mainly thanks to the spectator's contribution, well after the end of it.

Regarding this issue, Romeo Castellucci evokes the Mysteries of Eleusis, the celebrated religious rites of ancient Greece, and particularly the notion of ἐποπτεία (*epopteia*). The *epopteia* was the second degree of initiation into the mysteries, but the ritual of its practices was and remains occult. During the *epopteia*, the initiates were supposed to be witnessing a revelation, an epiphany (from the verb φαίνω [phainō] = make something appear, become evident). The candidates for initiation should therefore see the hidden things, which cannot be described with words. For Romeo Castellucci, the *epopteia* can be seen as a poetic power of the gaze that has the ability to create the object represented (Papalexiou forthcoming).

The third part of the *Divine Comedy*, *Paradise*,[13] presented by Romeo Castellucci in the form of an installation, is a striking example of the effort required by the viewer. The poetic trilogy of Dante ends with a mystical vision in which language reaches its limits. It is a journey in the dark, which leads to the light. At the end of his journey, in paradise, Dante sees a light, but it is a light that blinds anyone who is trying to face it. So he is unable to see paradise with his mortal eyes, and so everything is transformed into a dark night. Naturally, the light that Dante seeks throughout his journey is not, in fact, a natural but a spiritual light.

In the installation of Romeo Castellucci, the visitor is first immersed in an extremely bright room then s/he is led to a second space, which is very dark and is accessed by crossing a gap – in this case it is a simple round black hole. Traversing this obscure passage is like stepping into the pupil of an eye. Thanks to the sound produced by the water, the visitor obtains a sense of depth and the third dimension. We are immersed in a soundscape that allows us to feel the presence of the liquid element, a sense that evokes the memory of amniotic fluid. It resembles a passage to life and consequently to death. It is a painful process similar to childbirth. This is one of many interpretations to which this almost aniconic experience can lead.

Inside the dark room, we begin gradually to perceive the torso of a man planted into the black wall, while at the same time high-falling water flows into a lake. The image that inspired Romeo Castellucci is *The Nigger of the 'Narcissus'* by Joseph Conrad. In this short novel, *Narcissus* is the name of a ship floundering in a terrible storm. At the moment of absolute risk, a black sailor disappears and later his companions discover him wedged inside the hull of the ship. Nobody can pull him out of this trap.

'This is a painting by Bacon', explains Gilles Deleuze, referring to this image of the sailor of *Narcissus* (2002: 23). He associates it with Francis Bacon's work *Triptych May–June 1973*,[14] where a man tries to hold on to a washbasin, futilely resisting to the drag of a black hole swallowing him into the drain. We see here the mirror effect which frequently appears in the theatre of Castellucci: each work is a mirror of the previous, from mirror to mirror, from image to image, from performance to performance; travelling in time. Starting from the work of Dante, we meet that of Joseph Conrad, then that of Bacon, and finally end up with that of Romeo Castellucci.

In the second part of the *Divine Comedy*, *Purgatory*,[15] we witness yet another example of the appeal to the creative power of the spectator. However, in this scene the audience is faced with an empty stage, no actors or action. In the previous scene we see the everyday life of a family: the mother, who is preparing the meal, the little son, who is playing in his room, the father, who returns from a business trip. Everything takes place in a naturalistic setting, to an almost routine rhythm. This routine is interrupted by the rape of the child. Although nothing is visible, we can hear the cries of the victim of torture.

Romeo Castellucci has incorporated one of the basic rules of Greek tragedy: the violent act may not be seen on stage. Violence is mentioned but it is totally prohibited as spectacle. Indeed, in Greek tragedy, the viewer learns the terrible events via a messenger or preceptor. So in *Purgatory*, violence is banned: the screams of the child are barely audible to the audience while all they see is an empty set. The spectator is invited to 'fill the gap' with his creative power, to conjure up a personal intellectual space that belongs to him exclusively (Papalexiou 2012: 83).

This is what Romeo Castellucci calls the 'third image' (see Papalexiou forthcoming); this designation is inspired from the field of music where the third harmonic is a fundamental parameter of acoustics. If the musical composition is naturally based on the phenomenon of frequencies, in the theatrical compositions of Castellucci, a similar principle is applied to the images. His theatrical work is built in line with the assumption of the 'third image', a concept that involves the spectator as a developing agent of the show, as a maker of images, by himself and for himself. The empty stage opens a keyhole in the mind of the spectator, when the reality is rejected as too harsh and non-representable. Nevertheless, the part of the performance involving the rape of a child provoked violent reactions by some spectators who shouted and abandoned the theatre. The 'scene', although invisible, was unbearable for them. The spectators could not suffer the view of what they did not see. The entire incident was played in the darkroom of their brain.

As the realistic representation of violent scenes in the theatre seems unattainable, the decision of a stage director to represent the rape of a child or genocide is usually limited to verbal narration – a practice known from ancient Greek tragedy. The narrative, however, as cruel and brutal as it is, proves often weak and insufficient to communicate the horror. So if the narrative of a genocide belongs to the 'excessive form' (Sarrazac 1999: 36) of theatrical diegesis, the staging of the methodical extermination of people in concentration camps belongs to excessive form of theatrical performance and is possibly non-representable.

The second part of Castellucci's production *Genesi: From the Museum of Sleep*,[16] entitled 'Auschwitz', concerns the systematic murder of children in concentration camps. To present the tragic events that took place in Auschwitz, Castellucci did not select either the verbal narrative or the representation. To stage this topic, he includes it in the 'Museum of Sleep', as if it were a dream, in which everything, initially immobilized in formalin, suddenly seems to be released. The source of the artistic inspiration and the concept of the performance has been the pattern 'dream within a dream' by Primo Levi. The Italian writer recalled the painful experiences of Auschwitz and described the stories of children who violently lost their childhood (Levi 1965).

On the stage of *Genesi*, barbarism is hidden: we see six little children, dressed as bunnies, apparently sprung from the world of *Alice in Wonderland*, playing carefree, in blissful ignorance of what is to come. Another area bordered by white curtains represents a clinical laboratory, where human lives are sacrificed 'in the name of science'. Human organs fall from above.

> These are my lungs which were taken away from me in 1857
> This is my liver which was taken away from me in 1903
> This is my womb, with the ovaries, which was taken away
>   from me in 1938
> This is my heart which was taken away from me in 1944.
>   (Socìetas 1999: 25)

Then a single voice is heard, that of Antonin Artaud: 'I'm not crazy, I'm not delirious, I do not exist' (Papalexiou 2009: 62–4). Juxtaposing poetry to barbarism, the artist evokes the ideas of Artaud and his poetic formula of the 'body without organs' (1974: 287). The body without organs is a liberated body, an eternal body, without beginning or end, nor birth and death. References to Lewis Carroll fantasy world operate here as an inverse mirror, reflecting another universe away from the concentration camps, or, to use the words of Claudia Castellucci, a world of 'inverted reality' (2001: 301-2).

Eye to eye: the unbearable violence of the gaze

Romeo Castellucci often reminds us that a show becomes important when it is looking at the viewer. It is like a circular flow, an alternating current, as well as a curtain that opens in front of both the spectator and the spectacle (Papalexiou forthcoming). We become voyeurs but also subjects to voyeurism. In his performances, the spectators are often placed in a violent face-to-face relationship with themselves.

In Castellucci's theatre, optical waves penetrate the stage and the pit. We are being monitored by cameras, as in *The Minister's Black Veil*,[17] we are having our picture taken as in *M.#10-Marseilles* or *Hell*,[18] windows and mirrors reflect our idols (*Hell*), animal eyes are fixed on us (*R.#7-Roma*),[19] children's gazes enervate us (*Br.#4-Bruxelles*).[20] Even the patient and piercing look of Jesus, as depicted in the enormous backdrop of *On the Concept of the Face Regarding the Son of God*,[21] is directed to the actors on stage, but also to us, the spectators.

In the above-mentioned performance, as in *Purgatory*, we initially face a realistic setting. An aged man, the father, watches TV seated on his white couch, while his son is preparing his medicines for him. The dialogue between the two men is simple, ordinary and trivial. The only element breaking the realism is the imposing, enormous, dominating picture of Christ at the back of the set. It is a work by the Renaissance master Antonello da Messina. The figure of Christ constitutes the distinguished face and body of the entire history of Western art. The face of Christ overwhelms us and draws us in his own orbit, absorbing our minds through space and time. The temporality, therefore, is conceived as a relative term. Faced with an image renowned and relentless, we travel to the core of Western civilization, discovering at the same time an individual time, that of our personal history (Papalexiou 2011: 67).

In Castellucci's performance the audience faces the gaze of Christ and vice versa. Thus, the spectators direct their gaze, but, simultaneously, they are also the subject of another's gaze. As indicated by the title of the performance, the entire dramatic structure and stage concept are organized around the face, but especially around the eyes of Christ.

Jean-Luc Nancy's view on this kind of 'dramaturgy', associated with the visual dimension of theatre, is very pertinent:

> The face may emerge from the shadows; it can also, in the middle of a stage, rather carry forward this dark side that is at the centre of gaze: in any case, the issue is *obviously* that of a circle toward an opening, an orbit toward a hole. Something revolves around the eyes: the organized structure of a painting around a figure is not sufficient; it must still be organized around the eyes – about his/her vision or his/her clairvoyance. What is he/she looking at, what should he/she see or watch? This is of course the heart of the matter. (2000: 17–18)

Romeo Castellucci submits us to the gaze of Christ, who is looking down on us blissfully, majestically, imperatively, interweaving the roles of subject and object in the performance: we are looking at his portrait, yet we are devastated by his look. We are face to face. To see that you are being watched raises the issue of the given power of the gaze, which reverses the traditional roles (actor/spectator) of a conventional theatrical performance.

> When a figure manages to reach a spectator with precision, it gives to the latter the sensation of being an object. Subject and object fuse but without confusion. Activity and passivity become one and the same. The figure is planted in the spectator, giving the latter the sensation of being taken on before she can take it all in. (C. Castellucci 2007: 181)

In complete rupture with the dominant face of Christ, we are still watching in the foreground this old man with his son. After this monotonous scene of everyday routine we suddenly hear the weeping of the father, together with sounds indicating the expulsion of organic matter from his anus. The father defecates and his excrement turns into the basic dramatic matter of the show that overflows from his nappies and spots the white sterile environment. The son patiently and uncomplainingly takes care of his father. We are witnessing a taboo private scene as well as an endless martyrdom to which the father submits his son. The impurities soon over-flood the scene, rendering impossible the purgation of the hero. 'Thus the scatological dimension surpasses the realism and the situation becomes metaphysical. We pass from scatology to eschatology and are transferred to a metaphorical dimension of the performance' (R. Castellucci 2011b: 3).

The body is humiliated because of the desire to live, in juxtaposition to the body of Christ, which was elevated to the skies, abandoning its flesh and its intolerable excretions. Watching the performance, we cannot help but recall Antonin Artaud and his words 'La où ça sent la merde ça sent l'être' (2004: 1644). We are confronted with an unbearable scene that shows the fragile and private side of human existence. The drama of the actor unfolds in a bipolar plan: under the look of the spectators and of Christ as well. The actors are placed under our gaze like martyrs that must bear the weight of their art, as He suffered the burden of the cross. The body of Jesus Christ is transubstantiated in that of the actors who stand on the stage to be sacrificed, to become objects of *theasis*, victims of our gaze. The Son of God embodies the most dramatic role, wearing the mask of a human man. This is the material depiction of an immaterial existence, for the visible side of the invisible: 'He that hath seen me, has seen the Father' (John 14:9).

In this scene Romeo Castellucci raises the fundamental problem of the actor which is exposure (see R. Castellucci 2001a: 133). In his eyes, the actor is a μάρτυς (martys), meaning both the one exposed deliberately to the subjective violence of the gaze of others and the one obliged to represent the violence of the world with objectivity (R. Castellucci in Debrinay-Rizos 2000: 99). The stage will eventually be his limit and its measure will be the pain caused by exposing his body to the gaze of others. In other words, we see and feel a body that dares to express a risky contact with the viewer. Romeo Castellucci identifies the carnal power of theatre with the uniqueness of a tamed violence:

> The body-figure impinges on the hard surface of the gaze, like a hammer on the glass [...] The actor is this 'Angel of the odd', who, abandoning the backstage of orgies, 'enters' the stage, rupturing the density of history. He smashes the syntax, focusing on the accuracy of the body and regulates reason with the inhuman ferocity of radical myth. (R. Castelluci 2001c: 88)

In the next scene of *On the Concept of the Face Regarding the Son of God*, Romeo Castellucci attempts to turn the most innocent yet the most violent gaze to the audience, which is that of the children. The world of children and the violence perpetrated on them by adults is frequently present in the theatre of Socìetas Raffaello Sanzio. For instance, in *Genesi* with the children-guinea pigs of Auschwitz, in the episode A.#02-Avignon[22] of *Tragedia Endogonidia*, and in the scene where Rembrandt's *Anatomy Lesson* takes place with a child victim. Also in *Hell* we see little children, enclosed in an enormous glass cube, later covered by a black cloth.

The presence of children invokes a double substance. They are both victims and judges because of their innocence. The basic question posed in *On the Concept of the Face Regarding the Son of God* as much as in *Purgatorio* concerns the error of the Creator. How does the Creator turn his creation into a victim? According to the Christian view, no one has the right to judge their fellow man, or rather the Son of God, since no one is sinless. 'He who is sinless among you, let him cast the first stone' (John 8:7). Who could then judge God? A child possesses no life experience, therefore it is beyond any judgment. In the Bible, children are also referred to as lambs. Therefore they are the only ones entitled to judge God. In *On the Concept of the Face Regarding the Son of God* one child, and afterwards others, enter on the stage and start throwing grenades at the face of the Christ. The children condemn their idol, renouncing the picture of the person that Western culture has imposed on them, refusing to sacrifice themselves in order to purify humanity from sin, a mission that Christ had undertaken himself as the Lamb of God: 'Look at the lamb of God who takes away the sin from the world' (John 1:29).

The children after the act of stoning turn their gaze one by one towards the spectators. So, when the children appear on stage, the superficial tension of fiction is rejected, followed by the revelation of the power of the gaze. The look of the children is burning us, piercing us. Their eyes function as a mirror of the voyeuristic gaze of our violence. We kill with our eyes, but this look is killing us. We watch, yet we are being watched, a concept that evokes the visual dimension of theatre or the dramatic side of painting, hence Diego Velázquez's *Las Meniñas*, where 'We are You'. Claudia Castellucci explains:

> The greatest artists always held up not so much the internal relation between the various elements of vision, but rather the estuary of gazes that emanate in and from a picture as in the optical and physic density of gazes in Velasquez's *Las Meniñas*. The great painters and the great sculptors have always considered the theatre of their works; they have always thought about the dramaturgy. (C. Castellucci 2007: 181)

The voyeuristic violence forced by the spectator is reflected in Romeo Castellucci's creation of *Schwanengesang (Swansong)*, staged in summer 2013 at the Festival d'Avignon.[23] On an empty stage, the soprano Kerstin Avemo stands alone, interpreting the Lieder of Schubert, accompanied by the pianist Alain Franco, sitting slightly lower. The audience are on 'standby' mode, when after some time the actress Valérie Dréville appears on stage, kneeling with her back to the audience. She repeats emphatically part of the lyrics and performs some stylized movements, fulfilling her duty as a dramatic artist.

Suddenly she interrupts the 'performance' when she realizes the presence of spectators. She turns and addresses them in a hushed and horrified voice: 'What's happening?', 'Is anyone here?', 'Who's there?', 'What are you doing here?' Later, in a crescendo of screams, she accuses the voyeuristic attitude of the audience by repeating the phrases: 'What are you looking at? You are looking at what? What are you looking at?', insulting and mocking the spectators. The actress-martyr reacts to the violence of the gaze with the violence of the words. All this in vain, for she will then succumb to our voracious gaze and to the pleasure of viewing, returning again to the humble safety of her role: 'Please forgive me, I am only an actress.'

Final thoughts

The pleasure of viewing in the theatre of Romeo Castellucci does not rely on a mundane view of nudity or violence, but stems from our ability to create as spectators our own object of viewing. The elements that compose the performances of Socìetas Raffaello Sanzio are not engaged in a dialectical relationship. Neither do they follow one another in a modular structure. On the contrary, they are interweaved, opposed and contradicted with each other in order to create an unexpected event, random and accidental. The concept of randomness, in the mind of the troupe, involves the element of beauty through the experiencing of a surprise (R. Castellucci 2001b: 306). Perhaps the best expression of the sensation of watching Castellucci's work comes from the words of Frie Leysen,[24] when addressed to the director himself:

> Watching your performances is undoubtedly what I call an experience. In your own words, 'only art, theatre and religion can revitalize the experience'. Yes, an exhilarating experience, this is what I feel towards your powerful theatre; an indescribable experience, which I accept as a sweet ignition that overwhelms me; an unheard-of experience, capturing the senses and touching me, sometimes it frightens me, sometimes it fascinates me, as my spirit senses its wise protocol. An experience that leaves me without the need of words ... See you soon, Romeo. Inside my head it's all messed up. Therefore, all is well. (2003: 27)

Throughout his work, what at first sight seems vague, arbitrary and confusing, slowly acquires the ability to open perspectives of reflection and apocalyptic interpretations. For that reason, the creative work of Romeo Castellucci is truly fertile and liberating, it is an intense visual experience imprinted on the senses and the brain of the audience.[25]

Notes

1. For Lemma «θέα», see Hofmann (1974: 126). This 'active' interpretation of the word is preferable to the merely 'passive' conception proposed by the more recent etymological dictionaries *GEW, DELG* and *EDG* as 'lieu ou se trouvent les spectateurs/place for spectators'.
2. The Socìetas Raffaello Sanzio was established in Cesena, Italy in 1981 by Romeo Castellucci, his sister Claudia and Chiara Guidi. The company's name refers to the term Socìeta, meaning 'guild', and Raffaello Sanzio is the well-known Renaissance Italian painter Raphael. Since 2006, the members of the company follow separate individual paths.
3. *Julius Caesar* (*Giulio Cesare*), directed by Romeo Castellucci, was first performed on 5 March 1997 at Teatro Fabbricone, Prato, Italy and toured European cities the following year.
4. The view of the female genitalia is also apparent in other creations of Castellucci's, such as the *C#1-Cesena* episode of the *Tragedia Endgonidia*, or the recent *Parsifal*. However, this motive is presented through a voyeuristic concept at the foreground in the episode *M.#10-Marseille* of the *Tragedia Endogonidia*. The voyeuristic mood of the spectators becomes stimulated in a crude manner, as they witness a porn scene: in the dark a blonde woman with a black face, dressed in white, spreads her legs and exposes her vagina. In order to emphasize the idea of viewing and voyeurism, Castellucci puts in front of this spectacle a male audience of the nineteenth century. The dark stage creates a sense of keyhole directly referring to a peep-show of the age; see also Ridout (2004), also published as Ridout (2007).
5. *I Miserabili*, directed by Romeo Castellucci, was first performed on 13 February 1987 at Teatro Petrella in Longiano, Italy.
6. Director's notes on *Giulio Cesare*, 11 June 1996. The 'Archivio' of Romeo Castellucci and the Socìetas Raffaello Sanzio, no. 53_01_13, Cesena, Italy.
7. Claudia Castellucci, 'Foreword' in the English version of the official programme of Socìetas Raffaello Sanzio's *Giulio Cesare*, 1997: 1.
8. For more details, see Papalexiou (2012: 77–8).
9. *Santa Sofia – Teatro Khmer*, directed by Romeo Castellucci, was first performed on 21 January 1986 at the Teatro Bonci in Cesena, Italy.
10. Claudia Manikón Castellucci, *Santa Sofia – Teatro Khmer, Dramma in due atti scritto*, Official poster (manifesto), 1986–87. The 'Archivio' of Romeo Castellucci and the Socìetas Raffaello Sanzio, no. 19_03_01, Cesena, Italy. Also published in C. Castellucci and R. Castellucci (1992: 9).
11. Ibid.
12. See also Romeo Castellucci interviewed by Eleni Papalexiou (Cesena, Italy, March 2009), in Papalexiou (2009: 105).

13. *Paradise* (*Paradiso*), the third part of the trilogy *The Divine Comedy* (*La Divina Commedia*), created by Romeo Castellucci, was initially presented as a site-specific installation on 11 July 2008, at the Catholic church Des Celestins, Avignon, France. The second version of *Paradiso* (the one described above), which followed, toured internationally for the following two years.
14. Francis Bacon, *Triptych May–June 1973*, Collection Saul Sternberg, New York.
15. *Purgatory* (*Purgatorio*), the second part of the trilogy *The Divine Comedy*, directed by Romeo Castellucci, opened on 9 July 2008 at Châteaublanc – Parc des Expositions, Avignon, France. The production toured internationally for the following two years.
16. *Genesi: From the Museum of Sleep*, directed by Romeo Castellucci, opened on 5 May 1999 at TTA Theatre, Westergas Fabriek, Amsterdam, The Netherlands. The production toured internationally in the following years.
17. *The Minister's Black Veil*, directed by Romeo Castellucci, opened on 15 March 2011 at the Théâtre National de Bretagne, Rennes, France.
18. *Hell* (*Inferno*), the first of the trilogy *The Divine Comedy*, directed by Romeo Castellucci, opened on 5 July 2008 at the Cour d'honneur du Palais des Papes, Avignon, France. The production toured internationally for the following two years.
19. The episode *R.#07-Roma* of *Tragedia Endogonidia* opened in Rome, Italy, on 21 November 2003 at the Teatro Vale.
20. The episode *BR.#04-Bruxelles* of *Tragedia Endogonidia* opened in Brussels, Belgium, on 4 May 2003 at La Rafinerie.
21. *On the Concept of the Face Regarding the Son of God* (*Sul concetto di volto nel Figlio di Dio*) opened at TheaterderWelt, Essen, Germany, on 15 July 2010. This production is still on international tour.
22. The episode *A.#02-Avignon* of *Tragedia Endogonidia* opened in Avignon, France, on 7 July 2002 at the Baraque Chabran.
23. *Schwanengesang* (D744) was produced on 25 July 2013 at the Opéra-Théâtre d'Avignon, Avignon, France.
24. Artistic director of KunstenFestivaldesArts of Brussels, which was a co-producer of many productions of Socìetas Raffaello Sanzio.
25. This research has been co-financed by the European Union (European Social Fund – ESF) and Greek national funds through the Operational Program 'Education and Lifelong Learning' of the National Strategic Reference Framework (NSRF) – Research Funding Program: Aristeia II – University of Athens – Archival Research and Cultural Heritage: *The Theatre Archive of the Socìetas Raffaello Sanzio*.

Bibliography

Aristotle. *Poetics*, 1448b.
Artaud, Antonin (1974) *Œuvres complètes*, XIII (Paris: Gallimard).
Artaud, Antonin (2004) 'Pour en finir avec le jugement de Dieu', in *Œuvres* (Paris: Gallimard).
Castellucci, Claudia (1992) '*I Miserabili*. Dall manifesto', in Claudia Castellucci and Romeo Castellucci, *Il teatro della Socìetas Raffaello Sanzio. Del teatro iconoplasta alla super-icona* (Milan: Ubulibri).

Castellucci, Claudia (2001) 'La sindrome di Platone nel teatro delle operazioni', in Romeo Castellucci, Chiara Guidi and Claudia Castellucci, *Epopea della polvere. Il teatro della Socìetas Raffaello Sanzio 1992–1999* (Milan: Ubulibri).

Castellucci, Claudia (2007) 'The picture, the place, the drama, us', in Claudia Castellucci, Romeo Castellucci, Chiara Guidi, Joe Kelleher and Nicholas Ridout, *The Theatre of Socìetas Raffaello Sanzio* (London and New York: Routledge).

Castellucci, Claudia and Romeo Castellucci (1992) 'Santa Sofia. Teatro Khmer Dal manifesto consegnato in teatro', in *Il teatro della Socìetas Raffaello Sanzio. Del teatro iconoplasta alla super-icona* (Milan: Ubulibri).

Castellucci, Romeo (2001a) 'Aliénation de la technique (ce qui mène au non-commun et ce qui mène à le mettre en commun)', in Claudia Castellucci and Romeo Castellucci, *Les pèlerins de la matière. Théorie et praxis du théâtre. Ecrits de la Socìetas Raffaello Sanzio* (Besançon: Les Solitaires Intempestifs).

Castellucci, Romeo (2001b) 'Attore: il nome non è esatto', in Romeo Castellucci, Chiara Guidi, Claudia Castellucci, *Epopea della polvere. Il teatro della Socìetas Raffaello Sanzio 1992–1999* (Milan: Ubulibri).

Castellucci, Romeo (2001c) 'Etica ed Estetica', in Romeo Castellucci, Chiara Guidi, Claudia Castellucci, *Epopea della polvere. Il teatro della Socìetas Raffaello Sanzio 1992–1999* (Milan: Ubulibri).

Castellucci, Romeo (2001d) 'L'iconoclastia della scena e il ritorno del corpo: la Potenza carnale del teatro', in Romeo Castellucci, Chiara Guidi and Claudia Castellucci, *Epopea della polvere. Il teatro della Socìetas Raffaello Sanzio 1992–1999* (Milan: Ubulibri).

Castellucci, Romeo (2008a) 'Système, fonctions et opérations pour une tragédie d'or', in Enrico Pitozzi and Annalisa Sacchi, *Itinera. Trajectoires de la forme. Tragedia Endogonidia* (Paris: Actes Sud).

Castellucci, Romeo (2008b) *Conversation pour le Festival d'Avignon 2008* (Avignon: P.O.L.).

Castellucci, Romeo (2011a) 'Il pellegrino della materia', in Romeo Castellucci, Chiara Guidi and Claudia Castellucci, *Epopea della polvere. Il teatro della Socìetas Raffaello Sanzio 1992–1999* (Milan: Ubulibri).

Castellucci, Romeo (2011b) Interviewed by Jean-Louis Perrier in the programme of the production *Sur le concept du visage du fils de dieu*, 65e Festival d'Avignon 2011.

Castellucci, Romeo (2013) 'La quinta parete / Le cinquième mur', in Nancy Delhalle (ed.), *Le théâtre et ses publics. La création partagée* (Besançon: Les Solitaires Intempestifs).

Debord, Guy (1995) *The Society of the Spectacle*, trans. Donald Nicholson-Smith (New York: Zone Books).

Debrinay-Rizos, Manuèle (2000) 'Romeo Castellucci', *La pensée de midi*, 2, Actes Sud, September.

Deleuze, Gilles (2002) *Francis Bacon. Logique de la sensation* (Paris: Editions du Seuil).

Delhalle, Nancy (ed.) (2013) *Le théâtre et ses publics. La création partagée* (Besançon: Les Solitaires Intempestifs).

Didi-Huberman, Georges (2002) *L'image survivante. Histoire de l'art et temps des fantômes selon Aby Warburg* (Paris: Les éditions de minuit).

Hofmann, Johann B. (1974) *Etymologisches Wörterbuch des Griechischen*, trans. Antonios D. Papadimitriou (Athens).

Levi, Primo (1965) *The Truce*, trans. Stuart Woolf (London: The Bodley Head).
Leysen, Frie (2003) 'Ho una gran confusione in testa. Quindi tutto bene!', in Socìetas Raffaello Sanzio and Romeo Castellucci, *Epitaph* (Milan: Ubulibri).
Nancy, Jean-Luc (2000) *Le regard du portrait* (Paris: Galilée).
Papalexiou, Eleni (2009) *Romeo Castellucci / Socìetas Raffaello Sanzio: When the Words Turn to Matter* (Athens: Plethron).
Papalexiou, Eleni (2011) 'Ecce Homo', *Theater der Zeit*, January (1), 67.
Papalexiou, Eleni (2012) 'The body as dramatic material in the theatre of Romeo Castellucci', in *Utopia and Critical Thinking in the Creative Process* (Besançon: Les Solitaires Intempestifs).
Papalexiou, Eleni (ed.) (forthcoming) *Rethinking la* Divina Commedia*: Proceedings of Romeo Castellucci's Meeting with the Greek Audience* (University of the Peloponnese-Dept. of Theatre Studies), 4 June 2009.
Plato, *Respublica* 3.394–6, 10.604–6.
Ridout, Nicholas (2004) 'Asking for it: 2. Make them go away', in Socìetas Raffaello Sanzio, *Tragedia Endogonidia di Romeo Castellucci: Idioma, Clima, Crono, VIII*, 5–6.
Ridout, Nicholas (2007) 'Beware what you wish for', in Claudia Castellucci, Romeo Castellucci, Chiara Guidi, Joe Kelleher and Nicholas Ridout, *The Theatre of Socìetas Raffaello Sanzio* (London and New York: Routledge), 178–80.
Sarrazac, Jean-Pierre (1999) *L'avenir du drame* (Paris: Circé/poche).
Socìetas Raffaello Sanzio (1999) *Genesi: From the Museum of Sleep*, Official Programme (Cesena), 25.

Part II
Voyeurism in Space

3
Intimacy, Immersion and the Desire to Touch: The Voyeur Within

David Shearing

> I discover a small, white cabin situated within a dark, misty forest. I approach the dilapidated structure and attempt to peer through the windows; I sense, for an unknown reason, a body. I attempt to open the door only to discover it is locked. I step back, disappointed that my attempts to find out what is inside have been thwarted. A second later, I hear the deep clunk of a key as it twists inside its chamber. A white-gloved hand appears through a small opening, beckoning me inside. Without hesitation I reach out: 'This is it, this is my moment,' I tell myself as I take hold of the hand and disappear into the darkened room.

In Punchdrunk's *The Drowned Man: A Hollywood Fable* (2013), the one-on-one experience recounted above is the immersive money shot – the ultimate reward for hours spent searching and seeking, until finally finding a body, a body to connect with, a body to touch me. This chapter examines voyeurism from a position of spatial centrality, in the form of theatre often referred to as 'immersive theatre'. Immersive theatre is a catch-all term: it depicts a range of practices concerned with experiential, embodied approaches to performance reception; such practices include promenade, site-specific, one-on-one, audio walks and installation. Immersive theatre privileges the promise of intimacy over distant spectatorship.

In this chapter, I explore the complex sensory and spatial functions I navigated when attending two different immersive experiences. Firstly, I examine the nature of aural intimacy in David Rosenberg's and Frauke Requardt's audio-visual production *Electric Hotel* (2010). Secondly, I explore the complex relationships between spectators, spectators and performers, spectators and space in Punchdrunk's *The Drowned Man: A Hollywood Fable* (2013), an epic, free to roam site-based performance loosely based on Georg Büchner's *Woyzeck*. In both these productions, I approach voyeurism from a scenographic perspective. I propose that the use of masks, headphones and the spatial organization of the works act as devices of concealment, creating spatial distances that situate voyeurism within an expanded immersive and intimate context – a field where touch and the promise of touch is an explicit dramaturgical tool.

Punchdrunk are arguably the UK's most recognized immersive theatre company. Their production *The Drowned Man*, in partnership with the National Theatre, has firmly positioned the company inside mainstream theatre culture. This Hollywood fable was set within a former Royal Mail sorting office tucked next to Paddington Station. The audience – wearing masks – were left free to roam the multiple floors of intricately designed sets. The performance was set within 'Temple Studios', a fictional film production company that provides the backdrop and voyeuristic frame in which two narratives unfold. Within the multiple spaces, two stories mirror each other; we follow one couple confined to the inside of Temple Studios, and the other follows a couple living on the outskirts of Hollywood. Encouraged to separate and go solo, participants pieced together the looped fragments of performance that were played out across the multiple floors of ultra-realist stage designs which included the film studios, motel rooms, a movie theatre, a market street, a trailer park and a more poetic landscape consisting of tonnes of rolling sand and dunes.

Single and collective performers, choreographed by Maxine Doyle, thrust, danced and fought their way around the building in sexualized motifs performed on cars, beds and dressing-room tables. The nature of voyeurism is explicit, both in the positioning of the spectator inside the world of theatrical action and within the cinematic frame of the production. Participants were encouraged to watch, open drawers, rummage through belongings, peek through windows, crawl through hidden tunnels, follow crowds and go it alone. These modes of engagement are doubled within the cinematic aesthetic of the work, which represents multiple angles and viewpoints, jump cuts and repeat shots of the stage action. The cinematic lens suggests the action is being filmed, and that the spectator is the filmmaker, responsible for getting the best shot, the best take on the action. Punchdrunk are not merely presenting performance, the spectator becomes an explicit vehicle for the performance dramaturgy – in a limited way, audience members direct the action.

Whilst Punchdrunk take an environmental approach that merges audience and performers within the same stage area, *Electric Hotel* uses aural augmentation to immerse its audience. With an increased application of pervasive mobile technologies into performance experiences, such as podcasts, binaural recordings and apps, the relationship between the seemingly distant observer and the theatrical event has become unstable. In intimate spatial configurations, the audience are thrust into bristling states of alertness as different sensory modalities are brought into theatrical play. The application of technology not only augments sensory experience, but also plays a crucial role in positioning spectatorship as a lived experience, where attention is drawn to the act perception.

Aural simulation, often neglected in the wider discourse of voyeurism, is seen here, in the example of *Electric Hotel*, to extend the possibility of and desire for touch through physiological bodily responses. *Electric Hotel* is an outdoor spectacle with the audience seated in front of a four-storey fly-by-night hotel looking in through the floor-to-ceiling windows. The audience caught glimpses of the 'do-not-disturb' behind closed-doors lives of the hotel guests and staff as they danced their way through private bedrooms, took late-night dips in the hotel pool and partied in the penthouse bar. Wearing headphones – that employ binaural recording – the audience eavesdrop into the internal private spaces of the hotel. Binaural recording captures the spatial qualities of sound through left and right channels. Sound material is recorded using microphones positioned inside the ear canals or a dummy head. The sound is then played back directly into the ears, recreating the volume, depth and spatial quality of the environment in which it was recorded. The resulting effect in the experience of *Electric Hotel* is the natural sound environment, the hustle of daily life, such as cars and sirens, is layered with recorded sounds of the city and merged with the musical and representational sound from the performance.

Through the isolation and manipulation of the audience's sense of hearing and sight, the two modalities are remerged to form a new spatial experience that creates an acoustic intimacy whilst simultaneously producing visual distance. The piece plays explicitly on themes of voyeurism as the audience watch skimpily clad characters engage in suspect and elicit behaviour; the delivering of a mysterious package and erotic dancing between different characters all aid to intrigue and entice the audience. In homage to Alfred Hitchcock's *Rear Window* (1954), the audience, like L.B. Jefferies in the film, attempt to piece together the fragments of performance material, constructing their own narratives – thus the nature of voyeurism is the subject of the theatrical spectacle, legitimizing voyeurism but ultimately, as we shall see, returning the gaze.

I consider voyeurism from a body-centred perspective. Rodosthenous has already redefined pleasure in voyeurism by extracting its sexual connotations and suggesting that voyeurism is 'an intense curiosity which generates a compulsive desire to observe people (un)aware in natural states or performed primal acts and leads to a heightening of pleasure for the viewer' (p. 6, above). Whilst the forbidden and the taboo are explicitly referenced in my chosen case studies, my focus is on the physiological responses of the spectating body in acts of watching supposedly 'unaware' performers. I replace the sexual pleasure for a more nuanced erotics: a desire for touch.

Touch and aural intimacy

According to Maurice Merleau-Ponty, 'the world is not an object such that I have in my possession the law of its making; it is the natural setting of, and field for, all my thoughts and all my explicit perceptions' (Merleau-Ponty 2002: xi–xii). From a phenomenological perspective, the body and the world are mutually dependant. Perception, in Merleau-Ponty's account, is the essential interconnectedness of sensory and motor response for a being in and of the world. However, the interconnectedness of the body's various parts (visual, tactical, motor aspects) are not simply co-ordinated, as Merleau-Ponty asserts:

> [i]f I am sitting at my table and I want to reach the telephone, the movement of my hand towards it, the straightening of the upper part of the body, the tautening of the leg muscles are enveloped in each other. (Merleau-Ponty 2002: 172)

Sensorial motor action is enacted through the whole body. To reduce voyeurism – or the act of looking – to a single sensory mode of engagement, such as sight, neglects the synthesis of bodily engagement. To see more clearly, I stretch my neck, to hear more accurately, I rotate my torso, or tilt my head. In reaching, the whole body is mobilized. In our experience of the world and in performance, perception is a multi-sensory synthesis; in *Electric Hotel* the usual co-operation of the senses is challenged.

Electric Hotel was a touring production; I shall draw upon the Sadler's Wells staging of the event, which took place in a disused plot of land behind King's Cross Station in London, 2010. In this incarnation, at the start of the production, city sounds such as sirens and traffic were underscored by the sound of an orchestra tuning up. In this opening moment, the dual sound fields interpenetrated each other, creating a blurring between actual and fictional sounds. The orchestra tuning up becomes a theatrical play on that awkward transition between theatrical representation and noise; a signal perhaps for the audience to tune in to their own perceptual engagement.

Noise is the background against which all theatre sound is created, a position Ross Brown (2010) firmly asserts. The body, according to Brown, is by default always immersed in sound, and therefore the design of sound starts from a position of omnidirectional distraction. Brown argues that our daily sonic environments are a 'mashed up soundscape of possibility' in which the contamination of sound is a part of our everyday landscape (2010: 1–3). This 'urban drone', as Jean-François Augoyard and Henry Torgue term it, creates 'a permanent framework over which individual sonic activities are superimposed' (Augoyard and Torgue 2005: 65). In essence, we are always immersed in sound. Immersion in an aural sense is a 'dominance of sonic micromilieu that takes precedence over a distant or secondary perceptive field' (2005: 64). The city becomes the permanent background against which *Electric Hotel* is scored, causing the audience to tune in through the multiple sonic fields. A sense of immersion in *Electric Hotel* is gained as the spectator attempts to grasp their shifting perception between the background noise of the city and the theatrically foregrounded sound of the hotel space – immersing the audience in an active perceptual juggling. This juggling takes place through semi-porous headphones, which ultimately merge the sonic fields. The headphones do not completely isolate the recorded sound; sonic material still penetrates the plastic shell, much the same way as listening with in-ear headphones whilst walking down the street. The experience is not fully isolating; the headphones do not create a barrier, but allow for sonic material of the everyday to creep into the musical score.

Our daily sound environments are complex compositions of ecological sounds (such as wind and rain) that are layered by human activity (such as traffic, sirens and the bustle of crowds). The voyeur is primarily concerned with human activity; pervasive music players and in-ear headphones allow for an aestheticization of human activity whilst providing the appearance of distance and separation with the world. In most cases, we do not simply listen to headphones, we listen through headphones, while our bodily action continues our immersion in the world. The technology becomes what Merleau-Ponty might call a 'bodily auxiliary, an extension of the bodily synthesis' (Merleau-Ponty 2002: 176). Although the spectator in *Electric Hotel* is seated in an end-on formation, watching the action through the window frame, the body of the spectator is active though a perceptual sonic juggling between foreground and background; between the intimate and the distant.

The perceptual shifting of sound in *Electric Hotel* develops as the piece unfolds. At one moment, as spectators, we watch from the outside whilst hearing through the headphones, as if up-close, a pair of red stilettos marching across the hotel hallway. The sexuality and iconography of this moment is striking; it is the intimacy and spatial operation of sound that I propose offers the potential for, and activates, the desire for touch. In his seminal essay *The Eyes of the Skin: Architecture and the Senses* (2005), Juhani Pallasmaa examines the nature of the senses in the experience of architecture. Pallasmaa's perspective unites the senses through the skin, where he proposes that '[a]ll the senses, including vision, can be regarded as extensions of the sense of touch – as specialisations of the skin. They define the interface of the body and the exteriority of the world' (2005: 42). For Pallasmaa, vision is a form of touch; each sensory organ is a fleshy membrane of sensing tissue. Although Pallasmaa regards vision as a distance sense, he suggests that

> [v]ision reveals what the touch already knows. We could think of the sense of touch as the unconscious of vision. Our eyes stroke distant surfaces, contours and edges, and the unconscious tactile sensation determines the agreeableness or unpleasantness of experience. The distant and the near are experienced with the same intensity, and they merge into one coherent experience. (Pallasmaa 2005: 42)

Vision is not an isolated distant process; vision is co-opted with other sense modalities to create intimate skin impressions. Whilst this is appealing, Pallasmaa is not totally convincing, as he does not outline the ways in which the 'distant and near' can be experienced with the 'same intensity'. In a performance context, Yvon Bonenfant (2011) explores Pallasmaa's non-ocularcentric perspective to form his own architecture of touch between sonic voice and haptic visuality. Bonenfant's practice is centred upon extended vocal technique in which the voice can be felt as a 'vocal body' extending into space. What makes Bonenfant's argument compelling is that the voice is seen as an agent for sensory simulation via vibration of the skin. Bonenfant draws on Steven Connor's concept of a vocalic space and the vocalic body. He suggests that as the receiver responds to vocal vibration and vocal gesture, a form of haptic feeling 'lead[s] us to a reaching, an extension, a feeling outward' (2011: 52). Vocal sound fields, according to Bonenfant, represent other bodies, as the voice is always connected to a body. The argument is that the spectator, in reaching towards the sound, comes to touch it. Bonenfant suggests that

> [w]e come out towards these as we sense touch – attention, blood and juices flow towards tissues that are mobilized into action, even if that action is as subtle as pricking up our ears or turning our cheek towards sensation. (Bonenfant 2011: 52)

To hear sound is to feel vibration; the whole body is mobilized as it reaches towards it. This concept of 'reaching' is especially compelling for articulating the phenomena of vocal vibration between live physical bodies (that is, from performer to audience); however, in *Electric Hotel* the technological interference with the sound vibrations – the amplification, processed sounds and separation of audience and performer via a Perspex screen – problematizes this concept. The vocal body no longer extends into space. Yet my own experience was of a deep physical relationship with the performers – one where my body was brought into bristling states of sensorial arousal.

The pre-recorded sound in *Electric Hotel* is detached from its source, processed (with echo, reverberation and other digital adjustments), and then reattached by approximate layering to visual material. The technology offers a new perceptual mode of engagement, hinged between the unstable visual and sonic material. The perceptual linkage between sound and source is what Denis Smalley calls 'source bonding'. Source bonding, according to Smalley, is 'the natural tendency to relate sounds to supposed sources and causes, and to relate sounds to each other because they appear to have shared or associated origins' (Smalley 1994: 37). It is natural to seek out sound and source; we perceptually hook sound and visual objects together through shared and associated attributes. However, the two need not be precise. Approximate but comprehensive timbres are all that are needed to create a source–cause linkage. Although window blinds covering the rooms are used to focus the audience's attention, so too does sound via source bonding; sound as much as light and stage mechanics manipulate the audience focus. By creating a linkage between sounds and visual source, the spectator's vision is drawn around the four-storey building towards objects and characters. Within the process of source bonding there is a window of tolerance in which the theatrical manipulation of timbre can be used for creative effect; this opens up a space of perceptual ambiguity. To return to the example of the red stiletto, mentioned above, the use of amplified sound focuses the audience's attention on a specific object and thus imbues that object with a theatrical power. No longer does the stiletto merely traverse the floor, it struts with long piercing punctuation, revealing through its resonance a spatial depth forged as it clunks upon the otherwise soft theatrical floor. The symbolic red gains its theatrical power bound with a sonic resonance – the sound of a red stiletto is not feeble, it is powerful and erotic. The processing, manipulation and reorchestration of sonic and visual material via source bonding raises sensory alertness; the body becomes aroused in a space of perceptual ambiguity between visual source and sonic representation.

In a space where the audience and performers do not share the same direct sound field, source bonding and the digital manipulation of sonic material is one possible way to bridge the spatial gulf between audience and performer. In another moment, I recall how sound caused my skin to mobilize and affect my whole body. The amplification of the sound of a maid salivating as she rolled chewing gum around her mouth – delivered directly into my ears – caused the hairs on my arms to rise in a bristling state of arousal – a shiver ran down my spine. The sound of the maid's salivating brought the distant visual stimuli into an almost uncomfortably close proximity, exemplifying the intimacy that sound can facilitate. Pallasmaa acknowledges the power of sound to create intimate acoustic spaces:

> [s]light isolates, whereas sound incorporates; vision is directional, whereas sound is omni-directional. The sense of sight implies exteriority, but sound creates an experience of interiority. I regard an object, but sound approaches me; the eye reaches but the ear receives. (Pallasmaa 2005: 49)

When the maid rolled her gum around her mouth, the image of a body was carved directly into the mind through an acoustic intimacy. Vision, when combined with sound in this way, becomes part of the experience of interiority. The sound of the salivating mouth draws on what Bonenfant might call a 'feelingness' (2011: 52) of another body – in this case the specific body of the maid. Pallasmaa's assertion that sound has the ability to create internal intimate spaces is useful to consider how we carve internal spatial impressions. Internal impressions are part imaginary and part physiological response.

On discussing listening in darkness, Pallasmaa notes that

> [a]nyone who has become entranced by the sound of dripping water in the darkness of a ruin can attest to the extraordinary capacity of

the ear to carve a volume into the void of darkness. The space traced by the ear in the darkness becomes a cavity sculpted directly in the interior of the mind. (Pallasmaa 2005: 50)

Imaginative listening creates an aural intimacy. The mono recording in this example positions the sound experience inside the head, between the ears. The positioning of sound inside the head felt violating. The sound of the chewing mouth invaded my personal intimate space; it was close and bordered on repulsive.

In spatial terms, intimacy is usually associated with proxemic relations between bodies in space, and is useful in the analysis of the experience of *Electric Hotel*. Edward T. Hall's (1966) clarification of spatial distance between humans provides a framework in which to consider the sensory impact of the spatial relations between audience and performer. By considering distance not as fixed perspective but as a series of 'expanding and contracting fields' (Hall 1966: 109), spatial proxemics reveal information about many different kinds of human behaviour and personality. Hall identifies four distance zones; Scott Palmer (2011) has usefully outlined these for the analysis of space in performance (see Table 3.1). I have further visualized this in Figure 3.1.

In an end-on performance the audience are usually at a spatial proxemic of 'public space'. At this distance, the skill of the performers needs to communicate across the performance area, as Hall notes that '[m]ost actors know that at thirty or more feet the subtle shades of meaning conveyed by the normal voice are lost as are the details of facial expression and movement. Not only the voice but everything must be exaggerated or amplified' (Hall 1966: 120). Whilst this may be a simplification of performer training, some truth may be found in the natural desire to shift bodily presentation in order to communicate more fully, and where the performer's whole body becomes a vehicle of communication.

In *Electric Hotel* the intimacy of sound as it penetrates the central cavity between the ears might be considered an extension of the 'intimate space'. Hall notes that '[t]he detail that can be seen at this distance is extraordinary' (Hall 1966: 111). The spectromorphology at this distance reveals microscopic detail as to the texture of the material that would otherwise go unnoticed. The heightening of the chewing-gum popping takes on a much greater significance; the salivating mouth 'touches' the spectating body in a cross-sensory fertilization between the wet mouth and the intimate inner-ear canal.

The distant visual stimuli and intimate sound stimuli in *Electric Hotel* merge through the spectator's body. This creates a new space of

Table 3.1 Spacing behaviour (after Hall 1966)

Bodily distances	Imperial measurement	Metric equivalent	
Public space	10 feet and beyond	over 3 metres	Domain of impersonal and relatively anonymous public interaction such as in a shopping precinct or public park.
Social-consultative space	4–10 feet	120cm–3m	Typical of routine social interactions and includes interactions with acquaintances and strangers and of more formal social occasions.
Personal-casual space	1.5–4 feet	45–120cm	Area of interaction with good personal friends and people whom you know well. This category tends to have the greatest variation between cultures.
Intimate space	0–18 inches	Below 45cm	The closest 'bubble' of space beginning at the body. This is a space reserved for the closest of friends and family. Interactions may include hugging, whispers, close conversation, kissing and touch.

Source: Palmer 2011: 83.

sensory embodiment: see Figure 3.2. The orchestration of the senses in *Electric Hotel* creates a unified space in which the pleasure of watching is activated by an intimate internal impression of sound. In this physiological response of hearing and viewing the maid chewing gum, the voyeuristic gaze is returned. The audience cross a threshold in which the thrill of closeness becomes an actualized internal intimacy. The perceptual ambiguity between vision and hearing is lost in favour of a predominantly aural one – revealing sound's power to touch us. The salivating mouth of the performer, heard at microscopic level, disrupts the balance of power, shifting it from spectator to performer, towards performer to spectator.

Through this brief examination of the interplay between vision and hearing, it is clear that voyeurism through aural augmentation can bring about a closeness between audience and performer via a reaching of the body, brought forth and disrupted by the technology. In 'reaching' we

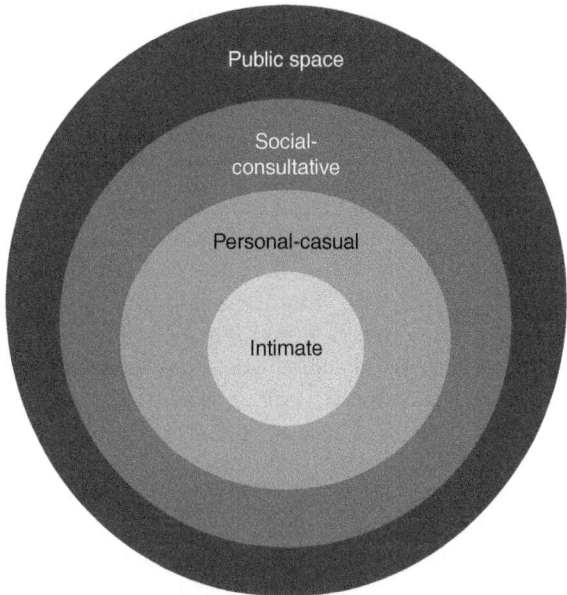

Figure 3.1 Concentric bubbles of spatial distance

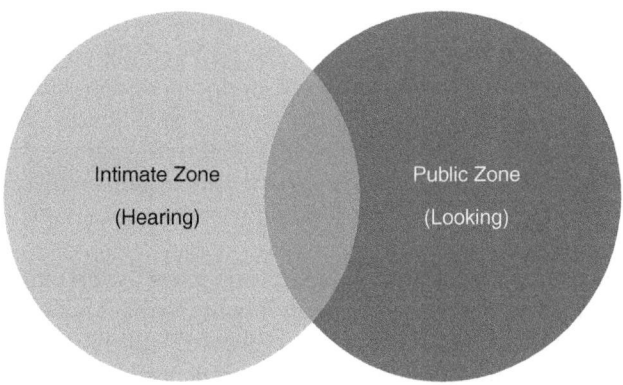

Figure 3.2 The unification of sensory engagement via spatial proxemics

open ourselves up, a space of vulnerability forms as we give over our intimate sense of hearing. Reaching, Bonenfant proclaims, 'also requires an erotics, an anticipation, a hope. It requires us to want and express and explore more' (Bonenfant 2011: 56); voyeurism is a body reaching. Augmenting perceptual experience can be revealing and erotic, as desire is part actualized. As the body opens up we become vulnerable – equally, repulsion lingers dangerously close.

Touch in immersive space

The spatial relationships offered in Punchdrunk's epic labyrinthine performances further thrust the spectator into acts of voyeurism. In *The Drowned Man*, the mask – which the audience wear throughout the performance – is a complex and ultimately important scenographic tool in the construction of spatial distance. Far from immersing the audience, the mask creates the theatrical distance of end-on proscenium theatre. It creates a spatial distance where the desire for intimacy and touch expands into a spectatorial gulf between the audience's body and the stage action. It conceals the spectators from the gaze of other audience members, but it also brings about what Heidegger would term the 'deficient' mode of our usual concern with the world (cited in Leder 1990: 19). This deficient mode of engagement can be seen against our usual absent mode of engagement with the world. Drew Leder articulates how 'actions are motivated and organized by outer-directed concern' (1990: 19); he argues that in action the body recedes and thus absence becomes the norm. As the spectator moves through the space of a Punchdrunk performance, the mask continuously returns the spectator to an awareness of their body. The perspiration in the rising heat and the general discomfort of the mask can be seen to bring about a deficient mode of engagement from the absent norm. In wearing the mask, far from being liberated, the audience are aware of their 'limited role' (Nield 2008: 534) as a spectator. Sophie Nield questions the nature of the mask in Punchdrunk's work; she proposes that it does not simply provide a cloak of anonymity, but appears to stop the performance ingesting itself:

> behind our masks, the actors STILL cannot see us spectating. Could the hood, the mask, the enforced anonymity, perhaps not be merely to give the audience the illusion of freedom? Does it not also continue to protect the theatre from having to see us seeing it, to watch itself be watched, by covering our faces and creating us all as an individual black hole, with a personal and portable visor-effect: still invisible, still what Derrida calls 'the other side of the eye.' (Nield 2008: 534)

In wearing the mask the fourth wall remains intact, only now displaying explicit rules as to how to behave, rather than the implicit rules of usual theatre attendance. As Nield suggests, the spectators are obscured from seeing themselves seeing, saving the performance from ingesting itself. Thus, the audience become silent witnesses to acts of murder, sex and debauchery.

Because the spectators occupy the same social/personal casual space as the actors, the one desire that looms over the whole Punchdrunk experience is the craving, possibility and anticipation of touch. The voyeurism evoked by *The Drowned Man* is not simply an acceptance to passively watch as bodies thrust against the hoods of cars, strip naked in caravans and fight in market streets – it is compounded by the desire for individual contact. Adam Alston explores the neoliberal and entrepreneurial premise of Punchdrunk's work; he suggests that immersive theatre is often built upon 'hedonistic and narcissistic desire: hedonistic, because the experiences are often pleasurable, with pleasure often sought as an end in itself, as a site of self-indulgence or even eroticism; narcissistic, because the experience is all about you, the participant' (Alston 2013: 130). The desire for intimacy is fetishized within Punchdrunk's work; it feels as though hours could pass without seeing a performer. The performing body therefore becomes a rare commodity that is quite literally hunted down by large numbers of the audience.

Whilst the performance invites participants to touch objects, performing bodies remain firmly out of bounds; unless, of course, you are one of the privileged few to experience a one-on-one encounter. Peppered throughout the performance are several intimate experiences, where solo performers invite individual audience members into a private space to hear a ritualized telling of a short story. The possibility that, at any moment, you might be whisked off into your own private room, away from the crowd, and offered your own intimate – albeit repeatable – performance glosses the one-on-one encounter with a 'sense of privilege' (Gordon 2013). Colette Gordon examines the desire for touch in Punchdrunk's one-on-ones, suggesting that they are 'designed to feed the audience's desire for touch and recognition, the *desire* being fed regardless of whether you are the one on the inside or the hundreds on the outside' (Gordon 2013). In Punchdrunk's work, you are always left wanting more, and willing to pay for the pleasure. Many audience members come back again and again – two, three, four, five times – in order to seek out a deeper connection with the performance. Premium tickets are sold on the premise that you receive your own entrance to the studio with additional performance material and hospitality. Sensory immersion – the desire for touch – is created within a space that rewards what Alston calls 'entrepreneurial participation' (Alston 2013: 133). The entrepreneurial individual is rewarded with hidden tunnels, or undiscovered rooms, as they push their way to seek out the best shot and perhaps find themselves a one-on-one encounter.

> I find myself sat in a swinging seat on a wooden porch, overlooking a set of rundown motel rooms. I sit for perhaps fifteen minutes as the crowds come and go. For a brief period, I am totally alone; content to bask in the hazy warm night air. From a distance, I see a masked female figure enter one of the motel rooms. I shift on my seat to catch a better look through the window. I am curious; she begins to rummage through the bedside tables. Perched on the side of the bed she flicks through a small book. She removes a piece of paper; she rolls it up and places it in her pocket. I imagine her story as it simultaneously unfolds in front me. In the thickness of the air, tension is brewing. As she stands, a couple enter the room behind her. Startled, she places the book back on the bedside table and leaves. For a brief moment, I meditate on in this brewing atmosphere. When I feel the urge to leave, I stand up and walk away. Looking back toward the wooden house where I was sat, I see a figure through the window; I'm being watched, I shiver as a tingling sensation shoots through my body.

As the audience enter the performance they are instructed by the voice of the fictional director of 'Temple Studios': 'Do not take photos, remain silent and keep your mask on at all times.' Despite the seemingly open environment, we are always under the watchful eye of someone else – of ushers and other spectators. Far from being emancipatory, spectators are bound to strict rules on how to behave – this might explain the numerous rebellious accounts of audience members stealing items from the set. Breaking the implied etiquette can see you removed from the premises.

In my own one-on-one encounter, described at the opening of this chapter, I recounted my desire to seek out an intimate moment with a performer. Having not received a one-on-one encounter during my first experience of the performance I was determined to seek one out the second time. As detailed, my encounter started as I approached the white cabin in the forest. When I entered the cabin, the door was locked behind me; other spectators, outside, continuously attempted to open it – this was my moment. A 'Pierrot' clown greeted me, removed my mask, and sat me gently down on a bed. The bed was covered with soft furnishing and blankets. The clown held my hand and whispered a short story in my ear. Through the make-up and the costume, I was unable to identify the clown's gender, but it felt warm and safe. After the story was finished, I was taken through a back door into a dark concrete space that led down like a car-park ramp into cold black darkness – a stark contrast to the vivid detailed world from which I had just been removed. Hand in hand, we followed a thin piece of red thread laid out on the floor. The thread ran up the ceiling and hung broken in the thick darkness. As I followed the thread to its broken conclusion above my head, suddenly the performance space had inverted and I became the spectacle – a chilling sensation ran through my body. The darkness stared back against me. For a split second, I was blinded by a flash of light revealing an image of a dead white horse on the floor. Before I regained any sense of orientation, I was thrust back into the arena.

The one-on-one experience disrupts notions of voyeurism, as the gap between performer and spectator is collapsed, indicative of one of the multiple spectatorial relationships within Punchdrunk's work. The experience of attending a performance by Punchdrunk does not operate on any one set of relationships. The watcher, at any moment, can become the watched – with or without awareness. The space, in my case the darkness and the thread as it hung above my head, turned the gaze towards me. What is common with all these relationships is that they are built upon notions of concealment and directionality. I have listed these directional relationships in Figure 3.3.

The Drowned Man is built upon the premise of watching both aware and unaware bodies in a personal-social space. It is not a mutual or reciprocal exchange; spectatorship, like that of *Electric Hotel*, is directional. The distance created by this non-reciprocation only highlights the desire for closeness. The intimacy of the scenographic material and bodies foregrounds that desire. Throughout my experiences, I can identify with these different modes of directional spectatorship that continuously

SPECTATOR > ACTOR

SPECTATOR > SPECTATOR (MASKED)

SPECTATOR > SPACE

SPACE > SPECTATOR

USHERS > SPECTATOR

ONE-ON-ONE: ACTOR > SPECTATOR

Figure 3.3 Directional spectatorships

changed throughout the production. Layered within these modes of spectatorship is the notion and premise of voyeurism.

For some, the immersive space exploits the individual, fuelling their personal desires for closeness and deeper engagement. The brief encounters only increase the desire for more. Any notion of uniqueness in these moments of bodily closeness is merely an illusion, as Alston contests: '[t]he non-reproducible element comes largely from the consumer narcissistically investing their own personality and desire' (2013: 131). This is reproducible exploitation, where spatial closeness and a heightened sensory awareness gesture towards the impression of uniqueness – ultimately Punchdrunk know who is really being watched, and who is paying for the pleasure.

Conclusion

Explicit in the experiences offered by *Electric Hotel* and *The Drowned Man* is the promise and desire of touch. In attending *Electric Hotel* the body is brought into bristling states of sensorial alertness. The body becomes a site of sensory-spatial merging in a rewiring between the public distant sense of sight and an intimate spatial sense of hearing. The skin's reaction to the intimacy of sound activates a touch-like sensation; the body of another is felt at an intimate proximity. However, the concealment of the stage action through the use of window blinds and the fixed seated position stimulates the audience's desire further, as two sensory modalities are brought tantalizingly close. This is the desire for closeness; the desire of touch through a body reaching.

In Punchdrunk's *The Drowned Man*, I argue that it is not the bodies on display that compel the audience in their desire for touch. The mask acts as a device of concealment that ultimately creates a spectatorial gulf between audience body and stage action. The gulf is filled with *the desire to become closer*. In both experiences, this is not an immersion built upon a shared exchange, but on the directionality of watching: one that is structurally voyeuristic.

The intimate experiences offered in both performances, the one-on-ones, the salivating mouth of the maid chewing gum brought uncomfortably close, shattered the *desire* for intimacy. The performance space of Punchdrunk's *The Drowned Man* commodifies the performing body; the spectator is always kept at a distance that compels the desire for touch. However, the desire for touch is lost when it is – in the end – revealed that *you* are the subject being watched. The spectator's self-desire is framed within a space that encourages the possibility of closeness.

The voyeur is, by nature, entrepreneurial. The immersive space of Punchdrunk's 'Temple Studios' plays on the spectator's innate voyeuristic tendencies; it compounds their desire for closeness, but ultimately it does not, in fact, grant it.

Bibliography

Alston, Adam (2013) 'Audience participation and neoliberal value: risk, agency and responsibility in immersive theatre', *Performance Research*, 18:2, 128–38.

Augoyard, Jean-François and Henry Torgue (2005) *Sonic Experience: A Guide to Everyday Sounds* (Montréal and London: McGill-Queen's University Press).

Bonenfant, Yvon (2011) 'Architecting sensation: voice, light and touch', *Choreographic Practice*, Intellect Ltd, 2, 43–67.

Brown, Ross (2010) *Sound: A Reader in Theatre Practice* (Basingstoke: Palgrave Macmillan).

Gordon, Colette (2013) 'Touching the spectator: intimacy, immersion, and the theater of the velvet rope', *The Journal of Shakespeare and Appropriation*, www.borrowers.uga.edu/472/show (accessed 24 January 2014).

Hall, Edward T. (1966) *The Hidden Dimension: Man's Use of Space in Public and Private* (Garden City, NY: Doubleday).

Leder, Drew (1990) *The Absent Body* (University of Chicago Press).

Merleau-Ponty, Maurice (2002) *Phenomenology of Perception* (London: Routledge).

Nield, Sophie (2008) 'The rise of the character named spectator', *Contemporary Theatre Review*, 18:4, 531–44.

Pallasmaa, Juhani (2005) *The Eyes of the Skin: Architecture and the Senses* (Chichester: John Wiley).

Palmer, S. (2011) 'Space', in J. Pitches and S. Popat (eds), *Performance Perspectives* (Basingstoke: Palgrave Macmillan), 52–87.

Smalley, Denis (1994) 'Defining timbre – refining timbre', *Contemporary Music Review*, 10:2, 35–48.

4
In Between the Visible and the Hidden: Modalities of Seeing in Site-Specific Performance

William McEvoy

This chapter explores the relationship between the visual and the textual by proposing some ways for thinking about how site-specific performance can be conceptualized and theorized. It argues that site-specific performance turns us simultaneously into voyeurs, writers and critics, searching, inscribing and staging meaning through types of theatre that bring the verbal and the physical (objects, spaces) into dialogue with one another. My main contribution to this book's theme of voyeurism is to suggest that the visible and the linguistic operate in dialectical tension with one another in site-specific work. The act of seeing in such contexts is never coincident with itself, but is displaced and restaged through the process of writing and critical restaging that accompany it. By looking at a site-specific production and some critical scenes of writing, I hope to construct a sense of the voyeuristic spectator-critic of site-specific theatre, one whose subjectivity is evoked, invoked and provoked by modes of performance that erode the barriers between self and work, between immanent and projected meanings, between found and fabricated objects and settings. The site-specific spectator looks for meaning, but such acts of looking are also acts of introspection, reversing the spectatorial gaze so that it also becomes a self-analytical one. Site-specific theatre, as much as anything else, stages and exposes the desires that structure our voyeuristic search for meaning in art and performance.

This chapter begins with my critical recollections of a site-specific production I saw in 2011, Hydrocracker's *The New World Order*, and then continues with three disparate sets of theoretical reflections from the writings of Max Frisch, Guy Scarpetta and Tadeusz Kantor, to approach site-specific performance from different angles. Its principal objective is to propose a disjunctive set of theoretical ideas that emerge from, rather than frame, the site-specific theatre event. It will examine how site-specificity blurs boundaries between performance and writing, the real and the staged, the found and the fabricated. And most importantly: the visual and the verbal. The voyeuristic gaze of site-specific performance will be conceptualized as contingent upon text, theatricality and self-reflection. In site-specific work, voyeurism is reconfigured as a circulation of text, object and self in a processual writing and critical investigation of the theatre event. In such events, the dialectics of the visible and the hidden, the voyeuristic spectator and the unstable object of perception, reveal the complexity one experiences in site-specific work, where voyeurism can no longer be conceived of as object-oriented, but has to be seen as part of a much wider phenomenological and affective experience derived from the participatory nature of this type of performance.

Voyeurism, visibility and the hidden object of site-specific performance in *The New World Order*

The conventional approach to reconstructing an experience of seeing the production *The New World Order*, based on five of Pinter's plays, would take me to the theatre archives (we shall return to archives shortly) to record the fact that the production I saw was the revival of a show that first took place in Brighton Old Town Hall in May 2007, and then again at the Brighton Festival at the same venue in 2011. The reviews help you recollect the bare outlines of the performance, the journey 'from the oak-panelled council chamber, where the silky new minister of culture [...] is being questioned [...] down into the bowels of the building where the dirty work is carried out' (Gardner 2011). Reviews will tend to name the performance's genre, 'site-specific', list some or all of the plays performed – *One for the Road*, *The New World Order*, *Precisely*, *Mountain Language* and *Press Conference* – and narrate some of the key scenes, indicating whether they were 'powerful' or not, or try to offer some analysis of their objective, as my own review for *The Stage* did, saying the production showed 'Pinter's grasp of how political repression operates through brainwashing, fear and psychological violence' (McEvoy 2011). In a video report made about the production, Andrew Dickson for *The Guardian* interviewed director Ellie Jones and actor Richard Hahlo. Hahlo provides the important historical information that the underground venue used to be Brighton's police station until 1967, while Jones explains how the piece related to its site: 'the rooms gave us ideas for which plays we would do, and then which scenes from those plays in which rooms', describing it as an 'organic process very much based on the building' (Jones in Dickson 2011).

While reviews tend to focus on the text and space, and in the video cited above Hahlo talks about the sense of closeness and intimacy one can feel in site-specific performance, the site itself also leaves a most powerful impression and forms part of the phenomenological or visual memory of the performance. Ellie Jones speaks of the way this closeness makes the invisible visible, perhaps in the Brechtian sense of defamiliarizing it, or by a process of theatricalizing and then detheatricalizing the object in performance, the space or the event. More precisely, one could say that site-specificity releases the object into a dynamic relationship to the aesthetic. In Jones' words, the events of the play 'are happening and we don't really look at them and if they were actually happening to us and we could actually see them up close and personal, I think our audience would be galvanized to do something about them' (Jones in Dickson 2011).

In discussing site-specific performances, Pearson and Shanks offer this well-known definition from *Theatre/Archaeology*:

> They rely, for their conception and their interpretation, upon the complex coexistence, superimposition and interpenetration of a number of narratives and architectures, historical and contemporary, of two basic orders: that which is of the site, its fixtures and fittings, and that which is brought to the site, the performance and its scenography. (Pearson and Shanks 2001: 23)

This definition separates site and performance as a prelude to a complete deconstruction, a merging or 'interpenetration' of the two parts of the binary opposition, via the two disciplinary practices of theatre and archaeology. But arguably 'that which is brought to the site' most obviously comes from the audience member(s): their phenomenological presence as bodies in spaces, their perceptual, haptic, aural responses, their memories, desires and subjectivities. As David Shearing suggests in his essay in this volume, the 'synthesis of bodily engagement' and the unpredictable 'proxemic relations between bodies in space' (pp. 74 and 79, above) mean that the spectator is the key determining variable in site-specific performance.

What remains after the event of the Pinter performance, aside from these fragmentary verbal documentations in reviews and via video reporting, are the trace-memories of objects of performance, as I noted in my original review: 'Ministry of Culture diktats line the walls. Old Council files double as files on political prisoners. The lower rooms are dilapidated, functional, intimidating' (McEvoy 2011). These found objects, part of the fictional universe of the plays, and objects in the real, document people's lives as shaped and contained by bureaucracy, and in doing so they have an uncanny double existence. They are like the open dictionary from Deborah Warner's site-specific *Tower Project* in 1998, the word glimpsed having potentially revelatory significance (see McEvoy 2006). They remind you of the documents and the found objects that Camilo José Vergara saw when cataloguing abandoned buildings in the US in his book *American Ruins*, objects whose status as non-aesthetic is troubled by their transmission as writing in Vergara's own text (see McEvoy 2006). The dual ontology of the object, both significant and random, aestheticized and resistant to co-option into the aesthetic, prompts a self-reflexive curiosity, a probing voyeurism in the site-specific spectator, which Shearing, quoting Bonenfant, says 'requires us to want and express and explore more' (p. 81, above).

The site-specific voyeur wants to unveil the contents of these text-objects, to exhaust their meaning, to read them with double vision as both objects-in-themselves and metonymies of the performance, minor mises-en-abime that will unlock the hidden, secret side of the performance.

Secret watching, failed recording, hidden objects

This chapter will continue by suggesting the ways in which site-specific theatre moves from the logic of the voyeuristic to a type of seeing which is bound up with writing and self-reflexivity. The voyeuristic urge of the theatre spectator, the desire to unveil or expose meaning, is diffracted and commuted in site-specific work, where the visual is a function of the verbal and vice versa. Site-specificity relies on reconstruction, on the dialectics between the hidden and the visible, the readable and the unreadable, and this indeterminacy creates rich figurations of the new epistemologies of reception that shape site-specific work.

I will be juxtaposing three textual-theatrical events to reflect critically on the self-reflexive voyeurism of site-specific work, the allure of the indeterminate or dual ontology object, and the problematic recordability of fleeting impressions. One is based on a moment of secret watching, one on failed photographing, and one on veiled objects and their inscription as or in texts. The first involves the merging of the real and the performed, charting the impact this has on our understanding of the viewer's subjectivity in the theatrical process. The second places emphasis on the ephemeral, the unrepeatable and the unrecordable, suggesting the applicability of these qualities to site-specific work. The third example explores how this type of performance relies on the hidden or the secret for its meaning.

The overall aim is to think about how the conventionally voyeuristic gaze of theatre, seeking to reveal or expose its subject, gives way to a more generalized and plural form of reception which is based on the emergence of critico-creative writing and the staging of the self. Site-specific work mixes the visual, the verbal, the perceived and the remembered in a generalized reinscription of the event. I use these three readings to think about the self-reflexivity of the viewer in performance, the role of the uncanny in site-specific work, the relationship between perceiving and writing, and the tropes of reconstruction and deduction.

I begin with what could be called a site-specific event in an actual theatre: an incident that combines the secret, offstage watching of the voyeur with a transition to aesthetic analysis and self-reflection about one's viewing position. This event makes the theatre a discursive space, reconstructed through theory and as a result of writing (and its unconscious processes). In the extract from Max Frisch's diary analysed below, Frisch shows himself to be the ideal critic for a site-specific performance.

In an entry in his 1957 *Tagebuch* (Frisch 1962),[1] Frisch describes a visit to the theatre which left a deep impression on him. Planning to attend a rehearsal, he arrives too early and decides to enter a private box. From his vantage point, he catches sight of two people on stage, a man in overalls and an actress with her coat and hat on, going about their daily business. Some words are spoken, and later the actress eats an apple. The event is 'devoid of magic', 'the speech which sounds from the stage is utterly conventional, anything but literary' (8).

Yet the incident preoccupies the writer and leads him to question his perceptions. Frisch's record of the scene follows the shift of his thought process from intuition to analysis. A note of understatement suits the insignificance of the event and captures his scepticism about the ability of language to convey its fragile beauty. The transition to theoretical reflection is also a moment of uncertainty about putting words to his emotions: 'There is something in this small event which seems significant to me' (8).

This minor scene paradoxically strikes Frisch as no less than an exposure of ontology, '[t]hese two people, just as they crossed the stage, had a being, a presence, a destiny, which naturally I know nothing of, nevertheless it was here, even if only secretly, it had a presence which filled all this large space' (8). At the same time, it is nothing out of the ordinary, 'repeated a thousandfold on the street outside' (8). It calls to mind not the scripted scenes one might find in theatre performance, but the unscripted space of the street. Frisch's thinking is structured by opposites which no longer seem stable. He reacts to the incident by trying to discern what factors contributed to the force of its impact on him; in short, he assumes the role of the critic.

Turning to aesthetic theory for help, he begins with a focus on framing. One way of characterizing the aesthetic is by 'its self-sufficiency, its capacity to trap us within itself, to keep us from moving beyond it to further knowledge or to practical efforts' (Rudnytsky 1993: 40). The frame apparently offers this clear division. But why should Frisch refer to the frame, a device used in pictorial art, when he is assessing the effect of being in a *theatre*? The misapplication is symptomatic of the difficulty of theorizing the incident's meaning, of 'framing' theatre, as event and concept, without omissions or gaps.

Equally curious is Frisch's discussion of the *effect* of framing, which begins with an apparent, perhaps unconscious, *negation* of the work of art (just as the fascination for this powerful incident may be prompted by an unconscious negation of theatre). What happens, he asks, when you put a frame around an *ordinary piece of plaster* on a wall? The framed plaster is no different to the unframed wall around it, yet at the same time it is transformed. A picture frame gives lasting significance, showing 'not the flower that fades, but the likeness of all flowers, or as has already been said: the symbol' (9). What is inside the frame becomes representative, allowing one to 'see this individual who represents the millions and who alone is real' (9).

The frame offers Frisch a special form of viewing, allowing him to see what he 'would not otherwise see' (9). It permits the double move from looking to *seeing*, with its attendant philosophical metaphors of knowledge and understanding, and from blindness to insight. In 'this small event', with its minor details and simple exchanges, Frisch encounters the plural being of the other, 'even', as he crucially adds, 'if only secretly' (8).

A negation of art and the aesthetic pervades Frisch's text as soon as we hear that the words were 'anything but literary'. For Frisch, the literary is the sign of a desire to create the exemplary and beautiful, and the dangerous effect that would cancel out the beauty of what he has seen. The 'literary' is therefore the *space of a desire* for the beautiful, necessarily negated in order for that desire to find its object. As the event's structuring absence, the literary is rigorously excluded by the 'conventional' nature of the exchange, only to return as a powerful *effect* apprehended from the perspective of negation.

We quickly feel the subliminal undertow of personal memory and subjectivity in Frisch's art theory. The piece of framed wall is 'in a room in which we may have lived for a number of years: now, however, for the first time, we notice how the wall is really plastered' (8). Autobiography casts its shadow over Frisch's aesthetics and the first person plural cannot disguise the trace of the 'I' and the scene of a room once lived in.

Frisch appeals to reason, since 'reason tells us that the plaster which I have framed can be no different from that on the rest of the wall' (8). Yet the borders of reason are not reliable: the framed wall *'compels* us to look', 'becomes evident, it is there, it *speaks*' (8; my italics). Pictures removed from their frames 'are suddenly no longer secure [...] one has the feeling that they are *falling apart*, and one feels *disillusioned* in the fact' (8; my italics). The removal of the frame presages mental disintegration, insecurity and disenchantment. The frame gives the ordinary plaster some of the qualities of the work of art, while its removal from a painting makes the work of art volatile. Frisch's heuristic mind experiment shows the aesthetic to be intermittent, a construction of the mind, a form of memory imprint. The frame contaminates the ordinary plaster with the structures of memory and cognition which have been built through previous exposure to art, and, in the process, exposes the critical self as the unconscious, desiring producer of art's effects.

'Even if only secretly'

However, Frisch's account of his experience involves an 'other scene' and hinges upon his secret position as voyeur of the real, and theorist of its spectral theatricality. His response to the end of the episode is close to a form of mourning, for which the text's poetics try to compensate: 'then everything is past, inexplicably, as if a human being had died, inexplicable that he ever existed, that he ever stood in front of us for us to see, that he spoke, conventionally and without consequence, but nevertheless stimulatingly' (8). Words tumble forwards and hold back, hesitant or headstrong, as minor and major endings (the end of an everyday scene, the aftermath of death) coincide. In reaction to a sense of mortality, Frisch's words mimic the irregular syntax of consciousness.

We learn at the start of the account that the theatre box was 'dark as a confessional' (7), and indeed Frisch's text can be read as a form of confession, in spite of its aesthetic/epistemological tropes. Its 'other scene', I suggest, revolves around the (missing) figure of Frisch himself, shrouded in darkness and privacy, at once onlooker and voyeuristic observer, writer and theorist. Like the voyeur, he occupies a space of latent criminality and potential guilt, *overhearing* a moment of 'not-quite' theatre which he has accidentally discovered.[2] It was not meant for his ears or, indeed, for anyone's. Simultaneously eavesdropper and voyeur, intruder and trespasser, witness and scribe, the writer is hidden, unseen, his presence is obscene.

He is a dangerous figure who brings the distortions of an aesthetic consciousness into the arena of the everyday. Frisch the writer becomes the episode's hidden determinant, its structural centre and the threat of its dispersal. His private, confessional box is the displaced scene of writing. The reader, given a model of writerly fascination, is fascinated in turn by Frisch's own (missing) self-presentation, and becomes implicated in a textual detective process.

The psychoanalyst and critic André Green thinks of theatre as the art of the misheard and misunderstood. The foregoing version of events fits Green's suggestion in 'The psycho-analytic reading of tragedy' that theatre is the embodiment of the scene of the unconscious (Green 1997: 136). Frisch's reconstruction of the episode stems from a misreading of his position as voyeuristic intruder in the theatre space, the figure who will turn his viewing experience into writing, thereby recording and erasing it (converting it into writing will threaten its status as *memory*).

In theatre, according to Green, the text re-emerges even as we try to do without it: 'Even the destruction of the text still leaves a text. Even its abolition in a theater given over to action will refer us back to the notional text implied by the action' (1997: 140). Bound up with his rejection of the literary, I suggest that Frisch's account recognizes that perception and its textual revision are simultaneous, that writing (or, more precisely, the unconscious pleasure and narcissistic desire to write) unavoidably contaminates his viewing experience. The focus on his *theatre* location is in fact an unconscious displacement of his primary concern about the contagious and contaminating act of *writing*.

In this text, which searches to give structure through theory and criticism to the sudden force of an unanticipated emotion, Frisch is mourning his own and human mortality, and, equally, the lost idea of purity (perceptual, aesthetic) and the consequent permeability of the frame (already catachrestic when applied to theatre theory). Frisch's mourning is a recognition of intertextuality, a realization that even his momentary epiphany about ontology is tragically impure. There is no such thing as pure viewing in theatre, and his act of voyeurism from a place of darkness becomes a phantasmatic site of theorizing, self-analysis and metaphorical association. Roland Barthes' distinction in *The Pleasure of the Text* between figuration and representation is useful here, since

Frisch's act of voyeurism manifests the emergence of the spectator from a place of epistemological darkness. As Barthes says, '[f]iguration is the way in which the erotic body appears (to whatever degree and in whatever form that may be) in the profile of the text' (Barthes 1975: 55–6). Here, Frisch's own text is an erotics of reading, interpretation, a kind of critico-creative self-figuration that captures the way in which the voyeuristic gaze of conventional theatre is reversed onto the writerly reconstruction of the watching self.

Theatre, site and writing: Frisch's critico-creative text

In Frisch's text, we witness the intersection of the self, the act of writing and the process of viewing. The (writerly) self is both an agent and an elusive figure in the reconstruction of the minor incident, the author of critical reflections and the subject of repression, searching for elucidation (through theory or reason), but in fact located in a position of epistemological darkness. At first glance, the focus of Frisch's writing is the stage space, shown not to have intrinsic meaning, but in relation to the plural spaces which the incident evokes. However, the stage space turns out not to be the real site of interest at all. The reader's fascination with Frisch's encounter occupies a third space, neither physical, nor imaginary, but the hybrid space of a negative poetics, of writing becoming unwritten, disguising its tracks.

In the extract, the relation of the stage action to the underlying concepts of theatre and performance is mediated through an act of (critical) writing generated by a voyeuristic gaze that has been turned back onto the watcher and subjected to critical and textual translation. Writing is the voyeuristic event's other scene, figuratively marginalized and hidden.

Frisch's hybrid role as witness, critic, writer and confessor, and the text this produces, are exemplified in wider critical responses to site-specific theatre and performance. Site-specificity leads to a reinscription of the scene of writing into other spaces, sending writing, to borrow the cinematic phrase, 'on location'. Site-specific performances change the act of criticism, as Max Frisch demonstrates, from a meta-textual framing of performance to a creative (and often unconscious) re-inscription of it.

Furthermore, site-specific theatre and performance implicate us, in several senses of the word,[3] in the act of criticism, giving the critic a greater sense of creative agency. Site-specificity posits critics and spectators as creators who experience the sense of exposure, the tendency to confession, and the impulse to narcissism associated with the genre of autobiography. They turn us into autobiographical critics, producing writing whose other scene is the staging of the secret self, a powerful, disfiguring force in our attempts, like Frisch's, to categorize experience according to aesthetic theory or epistemological frameworks.

It has been suggested that site-specific theatre and performance are prompted by a *fit* between the site and performance (see for example Wilkie 2002). I would adapt this to argue that they are often distinguished by a lack of fit, the lack of fitting response, on the part of the critic or spectator. Critical responses to site-specific performance are frequently marked by indecency, the troubling inability to find the right vocabulary or the proper idiom to avoid betraying, or even, in some cases, negating the performance.

Elin Diamond claims that theatre may be understood 'as a symptomatic cultural site that ruthlessly maps out normative spectatorial positions by occluding its own means of production' (Diamond 1997: iii). Site-specific theatre and performance are, on the contrary, crucially concerned with exposing their own means of production by turning spectators into critics of their own critical impulses (alerting us to the latent critic/theorist, the guilty producer of writing, the hidden Frisch, in all of us). In addition, the sites used in these performance modes are both the inaccessible supplement of/to language (especially sites of decay which expose their excess of materiality) and the endless generators and mobilizers of signs in the creative-critical act.

As with Hydrocracker's production *The New World Order*, we are no longer sure where to look in site-specific performance, nor whether the existing theatre text or the wider, plural signifying mechanisms released by the site should take priority. It is this indeterminacy that makes the voyeuristic gaze of conventional theatre a self-reflexive one in site-specific work. As objects oscillate between the real and the fictional, as filing cabinets contain both the parking fines collected by Brighton Town Hall and the records of dissidents in Pinter's fictional totalitarian state, the act of interpretation itself is staged and put on trial.

Failed recording: Scarpetta and Kantor, theatre-effects and the critic

Frisch in the above episode is a hidden voyeur, a secret critic, a figure trying to account for the non-aestheticized performance theoretically, but whose writing inevitably distorts its object. I want to examine another aspect of site-specific work, its ephemerality and the difficulty of recording it, by looking at a set of reflections by Guy Scarpetta about Tadeusz Kantor. Kantor's critical work, questioning the status of the art object, rejecting the frame of aesthetics, foregrounding the real, the functional and inartistic, offers resonant ways of thinking about the dynamics of site-specific theatre. Once again, I am interested in the relationship between visibility and invisibility as tropes in the process of viewing theatre and as ways of staging the engagement of complex subjectivities and temporalities in writing about performance, especially site-specific performance that destabilizes clear categories of real and performed, objective and subjective, present and remembered.

In 2000, Scarpetta published a collection of essays and interviews about the Polish director Tadeusz Kantor. Scarpetta's texts are haunted by the figure of Kantor, the failure of memory, and the effects of theatre and theatricality. While they do not depict site-specific performances, they have all the hallmarks of site-specific performance criticism. I use Scarpetta's texts to demonstrate what I perceive to be the effects of site-specific performances, but also to underline those performances' powerful negation of the distinction between the real and the performed, which is played out in the scene of failed visual recording and (critical) writing.

Guy Scarpetta's *Kantor au présent* (2000) is subtitled 'a long conversation'.[4] The collection is as much a staging of the critical self as it is the encounter with the other. In the book, the author relates his own biographical encounters, or missed encounters, first with Kantor's work, and then with the man himself.

Through Scarpetta's meetings with Kantor in texts, the theatre and in person, the negative, in terms of decay, the failure to remember and the compulsion to work through emotions which have no clear focus, dominates. He begins with a confession:

> I confess that at the moment I am not able to pinpoint clearly the impressions I felt during the first of his shows I was exposed to. Everything that has taken its place since [...] has definitively overloaded and blurred that initial feeling. (Scarpetta 2000: 20)

Scarpetta's text is haunted by a sense of decline, taking evident pleasure in lingering on the aspects of decay and waste so central to Kantor's imagination. The performance he tries to recollect has lost its definition and cannot be reconstructed, apart from in blurred form, more like an emotion than an event to be analysed. The absence of a distinct memory clears the way for a charged critical writing, exposing the writer as a subject-in-process, remembering, forgetting, reinscribing a theatre experience as more powerful because it has faded from memory. Crucially, it is the blurring of the visible, of the clear memory of the visual, that permits the emergence of a critical writing of the event.

The negative takes a number of forms in Scarpetta's texts. When Scarpetta reflects on the Polish city of Krakow in the light of his relationship with Kantor, he says of it: '[I] was going into his universe, Krakow, that proud and desolate city – with its gothic, baroque splendours, its churches, its ancient university, and something, at the same time, obscurely devastated' (2000: 76). Entering the city represents a threshold moment, a crossing-over into the world of Kantor's imagination, and Krakow incarnates not merely an aesthetic, but a built actuality of decay fundamental to an understanding of Kantor's work. As Scarpetta visits Krakow for the first time, Kantor's theatre and theory shape a response to the city, providing a map for finding one's way around not only its streets, but also its meanings. Yet the city also withholds its meanings, and the 'something' which remains left over and obscure is what stays unthought, the part of Scarpetta's experience of Krakow which waits to be summoned up later not as a memory, but as an emotion. Such cities weave themselves into the memory-text of the self as moments of hesitation, as Georges Perec suggests in relation to the cities of Edinburgh, Sarajevo and Belgrade:

> We often retain the memory of an indefinable charm from the cities that we have scarcely encountered: the memory of indecisiveness, of hesitant footsteps, of not knowing where to look and of feeling emotion at the slightest thing. (Perec 1974: 88)

Connected to this pervasive sense of decay, Scarpetta characterizes Kantor's theatre work as 'what one could call a scenic writing of *generalized corruption*' (2000: 80). Corruption is not merely a trope in Kantor's work, according to Scarpetta, but a tentative ontology. It is a way of engaging with the disintegration or decay of the logic of the trope as it tries to construct meaning. Any form of 'scenic writing' would also be subject to the effect of generalized corruption which it endeavoured to stage. Memory falls prey to this corruption: but what is the role of writing, of Scarpetta's own critical writing, in this generalized corruption?

His critical writing about the *negation* of memory reconstructs the work of memory as bound up with its own erasure, enacted in and through the writing process.

In his collection, Scarpetta reports Kantor's own mercurial negations of the work of art. At one point, Kantor tells Scarpetta about an intimate part of his life: '[I] have at home a lot of objects that come from my plays: they're not merely props, but could also be considered works of art' (2000: 32). Kantor's words test the boundary between private self/space and art/aesthetic public space. The objects in question cross the border between home and performance, circulating between domestic space and public performance space. Those objects are in counterpoint with themselves, gesturing towards the other spaces in which they might equally feel *at home*.

Finally, firmly entrenched in Kantor's world, Scarpetta recounts a journey with him to 'the edge of the forest' (2000: 108). The journey is the prelude to a strange meeting with one of Kantor's neighbours. The neighbour's house, full of 'precious old items of furniture on the point of collapsing' (2000: 109), indeed the whole atmosphere of decay, throws Scarpetta into a state of doubt:

> I totter a little, all of a sudden I am not at all sure where I am. *In a Kantor play, perhaps.* Or in one of his paintings. As if reality had suddenly merged with his universe, invading it, magnifying it. (2000: 110; my italics)

The sudden disorientation, the instability of the writer's senses and of the borders of things, lead him to a point at which the aesthetic (at least memories of it) and the real interpenetrate. No one incident triggers the sense of vertigo which prompts him to imagine he might be '[i]n a Kantor play, perhaps'. Instead, it is attributable to a gradual process or initiation, accompanied by the entry into the tangled space of the wood and the sense that appearances cannot be trusted.

Crucially and uncannily, the photographic evidence, the potential proof that all the experiences (and emotions) have not merely been an effect of the imagination, fails to materialize, further confirming the writer in his bewilderment:

> What is more, all the photos that we took that day failed. A problem with the film ... all you can see are vague, fluid, fleeting silhouettes – as if everything had to remain hidden, suppressed, disguised, before or beyond all figuration. (2000: 110)

In a vertiginous moment, the negative returns at the level of the signifier, as the photographic 'negative' is itself negated. The voyeuristic gaze seeking to fix the visible fails, permitting writing to become the necessary act of reconstruction through memory and deduction.

The failure of the evidence to attest to what has been witnessed, the lack of a permanent record, are explained both by a simple accident (film not working) and a complex desire to remain in a fluid space of doubt and scepticism. In this case, the reliability of the photograph as the apparatus which fixes a moment in time is replaced by the alternative, diachronic economy of memory and reconstruction. The experience is haunted by its own unrecordability, an intensity of emotion leaving only vestigial traces in the mind.

Scarpetta's encounters with Kantor embody many of the characteristics of site-specific performances in general and a production like *The New World Order* in particular. They show the critic haunted by the *memory* of theatre and performance which translates itself into critical writing that compensates for the loss of clarity of the visual. Theatre pervades his text as an effect, troubling the distinction between the real, which he hoped the photographs would replicate, and the performed or theatricalized. Negatives haunt the text, challenging the boundaries of the self. The failure of the images represents a projection of critical paranoia and the pleasure of replacing them with a creative writing of the negative. Scarpetta's writing reconstructs the scene of his disorientation by focusing on decaying objects, accumulating them as evidence, but is haunted by another scene, a ghostly trace of the aesthetic which makes the tangible incorporeal, turning the evidence of the senses into a ghostly world of signs.

As with Hydrocracker's work, meaning is hidden in site-specific performances, distanced from the penetration of the voyeuristic gaze, in files, in spaces to be explored. The events of the performance are not presented to us for consumption but have to be discovered as the audience navigates the multiple rooms of the venue. We are unclear what has been especially fabricated for performance and what was found at the site and incorporated by our aestheticizing desire and impulse. And crucially, that back and forth between text and venue, between Pinter's writing and the material eloquence of the venue and its objects, creates an overlapping set of memories, interpretations and experiences, since the undirected gaze and the different ways of navigating a site-specific performance mean that its significance has to be reconstructed after the event, and will be a composite of multiple different perspectives and viewing positions. The pressure of the one-directional voyeuristic gaze of conventional theatre, seeking to expose meaning and reveal the object, has changed to a multiple, circulatory mode of reception that emphasizes writing, memory and other sensory perceptions as much as the visual.

Reconstructing the hidden

The final set of perspectives on site-specific work will explore the visibility/invisibility binary by looking at the idea that the meaning of site-specific work is often hidden. I turn to Kantor's own art criticism and examine his idea of the 'emballage', a wrapping of the art object which leads us to engage with meaning and epistemology from the viewpoint of negation and absence. The emballage rejects the voyeuristic gaze, or rather, deprives it of its object of desire: more specifically, one might say it disrupts and plays around with the voyeuristic.

Kantor's critical reflections on the emballage help us see the meaning of site-specific performance as secret or deferred, hidden from the gaze and having to be reconstructed by bypassing the visual: through memory, deduction or inference. The emballage embodies the hidden poetics of the negative and discarded, the unresolved dialectic of secrecy and exposure.

In the 1964 'Emballage Manifesto' (Kobialka 1993: 77–81), Kantor analyses the emballage's status as a denigrated supplement to the primary object. This text is the poetic transgression of a prose genre (the manifesto) in which theory intersects with a poetics, forcing the metalanguage of criticism to fold in on itself. In the text, signifiers pile up in a sustained attempt to construct the meaning of an emballage, yet the text is haunted by echoes and repetitions, words displaced from sites of fixed meaning as they form residues of optical and aural memory for the reader.

Kantor's language in the 'Emballage Manifesto' is both a scientific analysis and a performance of the limits of codification. The word 'emballage' recurs in the text, alone, repeated, elongated or capitalized, undergoing visual mutations and shifts in meaning. Attempts to *classify* what an emballage is lead to 'misunderstanding and contradictions' (2000: 79). The emballage does not have an essence. One cannot say what it *is*, but only what it *does*: it folds, ties up and seals, stores, isolates and hides, evoking hope, temptation and the unknown.

At the end of the text, the concept of the emballage seems to be coming unwrapped as language disintegrates into a flux of adjectives and infinitives, until a triple repetition of 'emballage' folds the meaning back up and returns its plural secrets to it:

> Emballage –
> when we want to send
> something important,
> something significant,
> and something private.
> Emballage –
> when we want to shelter
> and protect,
> to preserve,
> to escape the passage of time.
> Emballage –
> when we want to
> hide something
> deeply.
> EMBALLAGE –
> must be isolated,
> protected from trespassing,
> ignorance,
> and vulgarity.
> Emballage.
> Emballage.
> Emballage. (2000: 81)

The emballage moulds itself to the object's contours. It highlights limits while temporarily negating the object's provision of vision-based knowledge. Instead, our interaction with the object comes from emotions (like curiosity), desires and expectations. By emphasizing the emballage itself, Kantor's theory and art question the idea that the meaning of the object is confined to our visual perception of it. In the brevity of its functional role in hiding the object (its *suitability*), its inexorable drift towards rejection and waste, its future displacement (being cast aside) and abasement (being ripped up, thrown away, reduced to the merely superfluous in relation to what it wrapped), Kantor finds in the emballage a resonant poetics of the negative. The triple, end-stopped repetition of the word 'emballage' at the end of the manifesto represents the limits of theoretical analysis and the return of the object. The word is opened on to its own negation, producing an imagination hole for the object to occupy.

Kantor uses the emballage to question the priority of inside over outside and our perception of the object's borders. It reinvests what has been designated as negation and waste with the desire and human emotions so easily forgotten and cast aside with the unwanted wrapping. By evaluating the emballage's duality as metaphysical essence and throwaway adjunct, Kantor launches a poetic retrieval of the secondary. Such a revaluation of the negative and its emotional associations, especially in terms of how to capture them in language, are central components of site-specific theatre and performance.

The emballage offers us an exciting model of engagement with site-specific performance. It hides the object, just as site-specific performance often hides its meanings, rather than exposing the work to the logic of the voyeuristic gaze or the visual as with many other forms of theatre. We are led to reconstruct meaning using the other senses or other modes of knowledge rather than visual evidence: we infer, deduce, imagine and invent in this engagement with site-specific work. Because the object is hidden with an emballage, it exists in a state of multiple possibilities: we cannot be sure whether our knowledge of it is accurate or fanciful, revealing of our own subjective obsessions and memories, or validated by the shape and form of the emballage itself.

As with shows like *The New World Order*, site-specific theatre, in blurring the boundaries between the real and the performed, releases a categorical instability into the way we construct meaning and interpret performance. It is a mode of theatre no longer dominated by the visual, but offering a more plural, phenomenological engagement of the senses and of memory; we move through the work, from room to room, between texts and multi-signifying objects, guessing at meanings, doubting our former epistemological certainties: a multi-sensory voyeurism.

Conclusion

Hydrocracker's *The New World Order*, bringing together five Pinter texts, took his work into a site whose found objects, history (as a police station) and current role (as Brighton Town Hall) reinforced the plays' exploration of faceless state power and bureaucracy. The site echoed and amplified the plays' themes: the desire to put people under surveillance and to control their actions, both invisibly, through internalized fear of state power, and visibly, in the form of human rights abuses and torture. Yet, what remains of this site-specific performance, for this spectator at least, were the secret moments of looking, the desire to read the hidden files and objects, to think through their dual ontology, their translocation from the real town hall to the theatrical fictional, performed spaces of prison cells in Turkey or nameless dystopian states. Such encounters with objects in the performance, generated by the spectator's voyeuristic search for meaning, predicated on the ocular-centric drive to unveil the secret, or on the spectator achieving an unrecordable, singular moment in the performance, are a fundamental part of the invisible and visible dialectic of site-specific performance. The unrecordable moment of reading or hesitation about the aesthetic, generated by the found or fabricated object, invisible to other spectators, hard to verbalize or capture theoretically, fragile and ephemeral and thus potentially destroyed by the heavy framework of critical analysis: these are the facets of site-specific theatre this essay has sought to highlight.

Looking at three encounters with site-specific theatre from oblique angles has allowed us to model some of the processes the spectator of site-specific performance engages in. In Frisch's mini philosophical essay on performance aesthetics, we are presented with a playwright reflecting on the way in which theatre contaminates the real. Emerging from that detailed analysis is a staging of the voyeuristic self, the centrifugal force around whom converge theory, critical thinking, the pleasures of viewing and of being unseen. Frisch asks us to reflect on how the act of looking and verbalizing might distort the event he observes, incorporating the theorizing self into the construction of the meaning of what he sees: he is implicated, as all site-specific work implicates the viewer.

Looking at Scarpetta's thoughts, we see the writer as memoried and embodied subject, his recollections full of holes, gaps and digressions, refusing to adhere to one aesthetic category, but instead drawing on experiences of Kantor's performance work, his negotiation of the city, his meetings with the director, and sudden uncanny moments like the failure of a camera film to record the events he witnesses. This writing aims to capture the fluidity of impressions and the ephemerality of events in the absence of a clear visual record; indeed, this failure of the camera-gaze to preserve its subject is what prompts writing, both critical and creative, to emerge. Kantor's theatre is part of a wider set of multi-layered narratives that emerge from the reflective subject: the intimate, the remembered, the definable and the indefinable all overlap in this fluid and unstable critical flux. Scarpetta's work shows us the effect of theatre overlapping and merging with the real in the uncanny way it does in site-specific performance, and the categorical instability that results.

Finally, with Kantor's 'emballage manifesto', the visible and the invisible undo one another as structural opposites: the object is hidden and meaning has to be deduced, fantasized, projected or created.

The voyeuristic gaze has been specularized and emerges as the trace of a phenomenological memory derived from modes of seeing, being and viewing in the world. As with the emballage, in site-specific performance there is an outline, in the form of a space, or a building, or an architecture, but we are not sure how to interpret it, or the objects within it. Was the object found or fabricated? Are we reading too much into it, and does that say more about us than we are willing to expose? Site-specific work, like the wrapped object, presents us with the bare outline of the thing, the room, the space, the object, and opens it up to multiple histories, narratives and poetic connotations: it releases our desires, our obsessions and our paranoias, and mobilizes signs because they are no longer restricted by the empirical logic of the visual.

By approaching site-specific performance via these three encounters, dealing in turn with a moment of the untheatrical within the theatre, with the staging of the self that is attuned to site-specific effects, and with a text that performs its own embrace of the negative, this chapter makes the argument that site-specific performance opens criticism up to new modes of verbalizing the experience of theatre that do not simply rely on the visual gaze. Instead, it implicates the act of writing into the performance event, making it a structural necessity that emerges as a result of the questioning of the primacy of the voyeuristic and the visual. Likewise, it blurs the subjective–objective binary, allowing self and other, self and external world, to intersect and overlap more fluidly. Finally, it removes the dominance of the visual and creates a critical space receptive to memories, digressions, drawing on what belongs to the event and what precedes the event, refusing to delimit what is relevant to the construction of the meaning of performance, but prompting instead a stratigraphic writing (see Pearson and Shanks 2001), multi-layered, multi-temporal and critical of all fixity.

Notes

1. All quotations from Frisch are taken from this article, with page references given in parentheses.
2. In their book *Theatre/Archaeology* (2001), Pearson and Shanks link site-specific performance and the crime in terms of how both are reconstructed after the event: 'Aftermath – think of the scene of crime as a paradigm for our documentary efforts' (Pearson and Shanks 2001: 59).
3. Alongside more neutral definitions of 'implicate', for example 'to intertwine' and 'to involve', the *OED* (2b) points to the use of the term to denote involvement in a crime. The links between criticism and criminality are explored below. Most often used transitively when referring to crime, 'to implicate someone', or in the passive, 'to be implicated', I conceive of site-specific theatre

and performance criticism in relation to the verb's reflexive use, underlining the agency of 'implicating oneself' in the scene of the performance/crime.
4. All translations from the French are mine.

Bibliography

Barthes, Roland (1975) *The Pleasure of the Text*, trans. Richard Miller (New York: Hill and Wang).
Damian, Diana (2011) 'The New World Order – review', *British Theatre Guide*, Barbican BITE, Shoreditch Town Hall, London.
Diamond, Elin (1997) *Unmaking Mimesis: Essays on Feminism and Theater* (London and New York: Routledge).
Dickson, Andrew (2011) 'Pinter in a police cell: Hydrocracker at Brighton Festival – video', 12 May, www.theguardian.com/stage/video/2011/may/12/pinter-theatre-brighton-festival-hydrocracker (accessed 8 February 2014).
Frisch, Max (1962) 'On the nature of theatre', trans. Carl Richard Mueller, *TDR*, 6:3, 3–13.
Gardner, Lyn (2011) 'The New World Order – review', *Guardian*, 16 May.
Green, André (1997) 'The psycho-analytic reading of tragedy', trans. Alan Sheridan, in Timothy Murray, *Mimesis, Masochism and Mime: The Politics of Theatricality in Contemporary French Thought* (Ann Arbor: University of Michigan Press), 136–62.
Kobialka, Michal (1993) *A Journey Through Other Spaces: Essays and Manifestos 1944–1990. Tadeusz Kantor* (Berkeley and London: University of California Press).
Machon, Josephine (2013) *Immersive Theatres: Intimacy and Immediacy in Contemporary Performance* (Basingstoke: Palgrave Macmillan).
McEvoy, William (2006) 'Writing, texts and site-specific performance in the recent work of Deborah Warner', *Textual Practice*, 20:6, 591–614.
McEvoy, William (2011) 'Brighton Festival: The New World Order', *The Stage*, 19 May.
Pearson, Mike and Michael Shanks (2001) *Theatre/Archaeology* (London: Routledge).
Perec, Georges (1974) *Espèces d'espaces* (Paris: Editions Galilée).
Rudnytsky, Peter (ed.) (1993) *Transitional Objects and Potential Spaces: Literary Uses of D.W. Winnicott* (New York and Chichester: Columbia University Press).
Scarpetta, Guy (2000) *Kantor au présent. Une longue conversation. Essai* (Arles: Actes du Sud).
Wilkie, Fiona (2002) 'Mapping the terrain: a survey of site-specific performance in Britain', *New Theatre Quarterly*, 18:2, 140–60.

Part III
Voyeurism and Acts of Watching

5
The Pleasure of Looking Behind Curtains: Naked Bodies from Titian to Fabre and LeRoy

Luk Van den Dries

What do we see when we look at naked bodies on a theatrical stage? Are we still looking at the representation of the person, or possibly – ultimately – the person himself, who is no longer concealed by a costume? Has a naked actor become more himself – a biographical person – now that he appears to us in the nude? Do the nude actor on stage and the dressed spectator watching him per definition constitute a voyeuristic set-up? Why does the audience always fall tensely silent when an actor disrobes himself? Why do we not encourage him or her like we do at other times, in other settings? Why are we interested at all in nudity in the theatre when it has become so evident, so commonplace? This contribution relates to these and other questions; to the relation between the glance and the (nude) body: to looking at naked bodies on stage.

In this chapter, I want to zoom in on two examples of the use of nudity on the contemporary stage. These two examples are taken from a much broader spectrum because today nudity is used more than ever on the stage, in some cases gratuitously, in others as an effect: established traditional companies as well as the most radical neo-avant-garde companies and everything in between have already used nude scenes as an evident component of the contemporary theatrical language. The two examples which I have selected show two ends of the spectrum: on the one hand Jan Fabre (born in 1958, Belgium), a visual artist and theatre maker who is known for his rather controversial performances, and Xavier LeRoy (born in 1963, France) on the other hand, who switched from biochemistry to a career as a dancer and a choreographer. In this chapter I have explicitly chosen to limit myself to contemporary theatre and I do not pretend to make any statements about other historic periods: the glance and the body are eminently susceptible to cultural and historic transformations. Like Richard Leppert I believe that 'every image embodies historically, socially, and culturally specific ways of seeing' (2007: 236). I wish to examine the two conditions of the voyeuristic glance, which I defined above in more detail using these two examples: how is the complicit glance of the spectator directed in a performance? How is the violent revelation of the hidden reality of the body effectively staged in the theatre? To do so I will start from a classical painting by Titian in which the 'act of looking' is the central motor and focus of attention.

From painting to stage: the look as violence, curtains and silencing the gaze

The notion of 'voyeurism' in the book's title instantly offers an interesting framework to start from. This term immediately places the act of looking in a given perspective. Voyeurism seems to contradict the theatrical situation in which we are invited to look at actors, performing naked as part of their aesthetic choices. At the same time we feel sometimes to be positioned in the role of a voyeur looking at scenes that exhibit an intimacy, seemingly not meant for our eyes. It is precisely this mixed notion of voyeurism, that uneasy position of the spectator, that is central to my contribution.

The core of this 'mixed', 'double' voyeuristic act that I want to discuss here can also be found in some classical paintings in which the 'act of looking' at undressed bodies is implicitly part of the painting. An apt example is Titian's classic painting of the myth of Actaeon.[1] In Ovid's tradition, which draws from several Hellenistic sources, Actaeon was a heroic hunter, who was always accompanied by a pack of perfectly trained dogs. One day, as he was walking through the forest, he suddenly came upon Diana, the goddess of the hunt, who was bathing. Intrigued by the spectacle, he continued to look, and the vengeful goddess meted out a horrific punishment. Diana transformed Actaeon into a deer, and his pack of dogs immediately set upon him, hunting him down till his death. His 34 loyal dogs – Ovid names them all – devoured our hero, and he disappeared into their innards, where he was swallowed and digested.

In Titian's painting of this scene the exchange of glances is especially striking. Actaeon appears behind the drape which aims to conceal the bathing goddess and her servants and peeks at Diana who, in vain, attempts to cover her nude body with a towel, casting a murderous look at the intruder from under her raised arm. At her feet Titian has added a lap dog which, wishing to defend its mistress, has risen as if to attack

Actaeon. One of Actaeon's hunting dogs is by his side and raises its head to look at its master, held back by the leash. Diana's servants in a way reflect the dramaturgy of the various glances: one woman hides behind a towel, we can only see the back of her body, while another woman spies Actaeon from behind a small pillar, casting admiring looks. It is a sublime scene of concealment and revelation, an interaction of skin and fabric, of beauty and violence, a complicated network of horizontal and vertical lines. Actaeon's glance, which started it all, is cast to and fro between the various characters, and the onlooker is invited to follow this interaction of glances through the various perspectives of the characters until it finally ends with the painting's central character, who looks away from the scene and into the distance to an opening in the Renaissance-style landscape.

The motoric instant which Titian captures in this scene is the moment of 'being caught in the act'. Diana is surprised during an intimate moment where no onlookers are tolerated, an intimate act that you only share with people you trust. Naturally you look at one another, but not with a penetrating glance. The glances that are cast are complicit; they are a mark of enjoyment. Until someone else walks in on the act and everything is changed and pleasure is transformed into violence. The Arcadian setting in which Diana takes her bath changes dramatically and forcibly into a perversion of itself through the penetrating gaze of the hunter. But at the same time Actaeon is also caught in the act, from behind the rather hapless curtain. The glance he casts on this innocent scene is transformed into penance and a gruesome punishment: he is changed into an appetizing prey before the eyes of his most loyal servants. The glance cast by the voyeur on the virgin goddess becomes the sight of the hunt in which the hero must eventually perish. He dies as a result of his own hunting prowess and his perfectly trained dogs. The positions of the hunter and the hunted are reversed. The hunter becomes the prey. The prey becomes the hunter.

In this famous painting Titian almost seems to suggest that the core of the voyeuristic set-up lies in the clumsy curtain, which separates the hunter from his prey, the voyeur from his object of desire. It is a red piece of fabric, which is vaguely reminiscent of a stage curtain, and which I, for the sake of the argument, want to connect with the concept of the half-curtain which Bertolt Brecht introduced in the mid-1900s.[2] Although it still refers to the traditional stage curtain, especially because of its colour and the way in which it is draped, it is nothing more than that: a reference, a memory of what once used to be a theatrical code in the traditional bourgeois spectacle. In Brecht's concept of theatre the half-curtain is not a veil which conceals or seals off something. In fact it is more of an 'eye-opener'. It is a curtain which invites you to look in, which is put up so you can look through or past it. The half-curtain explicitly toys with the spectator's glance. It seems to say: 'Look, I have nothing to hide, just look, this is theatre. We are playing for you, we know you are looking; what's more, we want you to look.' The Brechtian half-curtain surprises the spectator in his own viewing behaviour. In his bundled essays written between 1918 and 1956 and first published as *Schriften zum Theater. Über eine nicht-aristotelische Dramatik* (1957), Brecht calls on the theatre to use the half-curtain in a way to show and to hide at the same time: 'zeigt ihm zuviel nicht / Aber zeigt etwas! Und lasst ihn gewahren / Dass ihr nicht zaubert, sondern / Arbeitet, Freunde' (Brecht 1957: 260). At the same time it also wants to surprise reality and reveal its hidden truth. Brechtian theatre wishes to better penetrate that which reality attempts to conceal so fiercely through the means of theatre, stripped of any illusion. The red piece of fabric in Titian's painting affords Actaeon a view of the naked Diana, much like Brecht's half-curtain affords the spectator a view of what 'they' wish to hide from us: the veiled reality.

At the same time, and that is the second prerequisite for the voyeuristic set-up which we can deduce from Titian's painting, this involves a hefty dose of violence. The scene of the voyeur is the scene of being caught in the act. Actaeon sees something that he was not allowed to see, something which he has not been invited to see: he surprises Diana, he intrudes upon an intimacy which is not his, and this gives rise to a voyeuristic desire. The desire to be part of something that was not designed for a scene, a form of violent desire which appropriates something that did not belong to you in the first place. When Actaeon is surprised this unleashes an even greater desire, which transforms lust into some sort of blind violence and which ultimately causes a bloodbath. In that sense the voyeuristic act is strongly linked to the intoxication of the prohibition about which Georges Bataille also writes:

> L'interdit donne à ce qu'il frappe un sens qu'en elle-même l'action interdite n'avait pas. L'interdit engage à la transgression, sans laquelle l'action n'aurait pas eu la lueur mauvaise qui séduit ... C'est la transgression de l'interdit qui envoûte ... (Bataille 1987: 607)[3]

The heady state in which Actaeon finds himself when he stumbles on the intimate scene of a bathing Diana rather unexpectedly is the intoxication associated with the transgression of a prohibition. The various versions of the myth diverge on the interpretation of the locus of the act of looking – did Actaeon really fall upon her involuntarily or was he curious, maybe even in love? In any event his glance was prohibited and he transgressed the prohibition of the goddess of the hunt. Consequently she exacted her revenge by sprinkling water over him, which resulted in the well-known metamorphosis. This is not the place to digress on the nature of this specific prohibition.[4] In his version Ovid only mentions the colour of Diana's face when she is surprised and the words she addresses to the man who came upon her: 'Now you are free to tell that you have seen me all unrobed – if you can tell' (Ovid 1960: 137). It is clear that she feels shame and that this is clearly a case of what today in legal terms is known as a 'violation of her privacy'.

A vexed glance: unveiling and the complicity of looking

Actaeon's glance changes the nature of Diana's bath into an erotic scene. The naked bodies of the women take on an erotic colour in his eyes and become nude.[5] This is certainly the case in Titian's painting, which is dominated by human nudity: seven women are revealed to the spectator in various states of undress. They all adopt different positions (half-sitting, reclining, crouching, standing) and great emphasis has been placed on their voluptuous female figures – even Actaeon himself, the hunter, appears to be wearing clothing that reveals his body rather than conceal it. Titian affords the spectator a full view of the partly voluptuous, partly muscular bodies and then directs his or her glance to the many curves and folds of skin.

At first glance this seems to be an almost Arcadian scene, replete with explicitly shown beauty, except that the gruesome tipping point is already announced by a number of details: the deer's antlers which are displayed, as the trophy of the goddess of the hunt, the laughing lion's mask, which Titian has added as an ornament to the base of the fountain, the dragon's head from which the water trickles,[6] and naturally, and last but not least: the serp-spitting eyes of the goddess herself. Actaeon's erotic glance, in other words, is reflected in the violent eyes of the woman who looks back at him, of the woman who catches the intruder in the act, of the woman who will exact revenge for his transgression of the prohibition. Once again the link with Bataille, who considered eroticism and death to be inseparably related, becomes clear: 'Eroticism is the assenting to life up to the point of death' (1957: 17).

What I have defined as the two conditions for a voyeuristic set-up in Titian's composition are also conditions which are reflected on the stage in contemporary theatre. One might say that the use of the naked body on the contemporary stage is always filled with the condition of Bertolt Brecht's half-curtain: it is aware of the spectator's glance, it toys with his viewing behaviour and continuously questions the nature and the consequence of this act of looking. At the same time a 'violent' component is also involved, which ignores the act of merely taking pleasure in this conscious interaction of glances, which one might define as a 'vexed glance'. It is the moment when one is caught in the act, the unveiling, the revelation if you like of what was hidden. It ties in with Georges Didi-Huberman's analysis of Venus' nudity: 'Toute la question de la nudité semble suspendue à cette dialectique. Structure ou blessure? Forme ou informe? Convenance ou conflit?' (1999: 41).

These are two conditions which seemingly behave like each other's counterparts: the complicity of looking versus the 'dévoilé' or unveiling of what was hidden. But it is precisely the intertwining of these basic conditions for the appearance of nudity in contemporary theatre that differs from nudity in the 1960s. In his analysis of the use of naked performers in the theatre of the sixties, Toepfer formulated this as follows: 'Nudity signified a release or "freedom" of the body from "oppressive" constraints imposed on it by texts, language, communication codes which "clothe" the disclosure of an "authentic" level of being or reality' (1996: 78). The nudity here grants it a different complexity and layeredness than the 'release' or 'freedom' of the nude scenes in *Paradise Now*, *Dionysus in 69* or *Oh! Calcutta!*, to name but three iconic examples of a historical use of nudity in the theatre in the past.[7]

Jan Fabre's transformations: tangible corporeality, obscenity and the body's explosive plasticity

Jan Fabre has been using naked bodies from the start of his career in theatre. In *Theater met een K is een kater* (*Theatre with a K is a Tomcat*, 1980) he used the motto of performance art, real time/real action for the first time in a number of harsh scenes in which naked actors push each other to the limits of exhaustion and pain. During a guest performance of this production in Milwaukee he was sued for obscenity. In the breakthrough production which he created afterwards, entitled *Het is theater zoals te verwachten en te voorzien was* (*This is Theatre like it Was to be Expected and Foreseen*, 1982), he once again made frequent use of naked bodies, which carry out a number of daily rituals, often repeated in a loop, for longer periods of time (the performance lasts eight hours): dressing or undressing or lathering themselves with sun cream. The actors do not make the slightest effort to conceal themselves in the phantom of another body, another person or another character. They enter the stage and go about their business.

The presence of the tangible corporeality takes precedence in this production. The ordinary banal body is displayed to the spectators. This especially applies to the penultimate scene: the actors are sitting on a row of chairs which have been lined up near the end of the stage. When their names are called by a (dressed) actor who stands to the extreme left of the stage, the actors rise one by one, their profession is called out, while they stand up and fall over, once again in an endless loop. They are naked during this scene, but even more than naked: they resist being looked at as a 'nude',[8] they resist any artistic frame; they show their passports as it were, they show who they are. These ordinary bodies repeat that they are simply that: ordinary bodies. Naturally this ties in with the strategy of the radical dismantling of the fiction which is at the centre of this production.

This *a fortiori* also applies to the third part of this trilogy, *De macht der theaterlijke dwaasheden* (*The Power of Theatrical Madness*, 1984). Fabre brings Hans Andersen's fairy tale 'The emperor's new clothes' to life as a crucial metaphor of the illusion. At the centre of this production is an emperor, armed with a sceptre and crown, who drapes his invisible clothes around his naked body and in so doing hopes to impress his subjects. The naked emperor struts to and fro before our eyes for most of the performance. Fabre reveals the nature of the stage in a way which simultaneously and inherently contains an evocation and a destruction with the demonstration of this sublime lie, of the ultimate masquerade.

In *Parrots & Guinea Pigs* Fabre uses nudity in a completely different way in his theatrical universe. This production examines the relationship between man and animals. Here the theme is associated with the primary scene of shame which kicks in when Adam and Eve transgress God's prohibition[9] and in that sense it also ties in with Titian's painting, which I discussed above. In one of the scenes of the production the dancers are 'surprised' in their nudity and they immediately cover their parts – as already mentioned, a primary image of Christian civilization, the sense of shame after the Fall. It is interesting that Fabre mirrors this scene with another one in which naked actors wearing animal masks perform some sort of wild, Dionysian fuck dance. In contrast with the female actors, however, the male actors seem completely unaware of their nakedness. They feel no sense of shame, the impulse of shame has to be rammed into them with beatings and reprimands. These animals are civilized in a violent way, they are tamed, a civilization process which involves several strategies of repression and punishment.[10]

As I already explained, nudity is an important ingredient in Fabre's work. It is an evident tool to produce Fabrian corporeal images. And Fabre is, of course, well aware of the always double nature of nudity in art, also mentioned in the contribution of Daniël Ploeger in this volume: there is not a clear boundary between the sexualized naked body and the nude representation in an art frame: 'naked subjects also afford sexualized readings by members of a "conventional" high-art audience, which *do* acknowledge the work's artistic frame' (p. 152, below). In so doing, Fabre also revisits an iconographic tradition, which he quotes and which he incorporates into his own visual language. In traditional painting and sculpture the (nude) model plays a very important role,[11] and he often literally refers to this great tradition in which the naked body is portrayed on canvas, in bronze or marble.

But the theme of the metamorphosis[12] is more fundamental in his examination of the human body. Fabre is fascinated by hybrid creations between man and animals, bodies which are in a state of transformation and which, consequently, extract themselves from any form of fixation. Fabre goes in search of the body's explosive elasticity, the elasticity between the body, an object, an animal. This fascinating plasticity is most pronounced in the naked body. As a spectator you can read the alphabet of the muscles, the joints, the vertebrae and the bones and you can see how different 'forms of being' are demonstrated again and again.

The violent revelation of the hidden reality of the body is situated precisely at this point of the body's unknowability. The voyeurism and eroticism on Fabre's stage associates itself with the contingency of the transformation. The spectator witnesses a revelation which transcends the act of disrobing or denuding oneself: the glance is exposed to another state of the body, the body slips into a more animal form, abandoning any sense of shame. It is here that the controversial nature of Fabre's physical work is revealed. This becomes apparent in a scene from *The Crying Body* (2004), in which Fabre introduces the weeping body on the stage. This performance is an ode to the humid body. The three primary streams in this watery body are perspiration, tears and piss. They form channels between our most intimate skin folds and the world beyond our body. They constitute the body's secretions: sweat, tears and piss are poured out, expelled, expressed. But secretions are also secrets, such as the secret code of the odour of sweat or the invisible boundaries with which a urine trail demarcates the boundaries of a

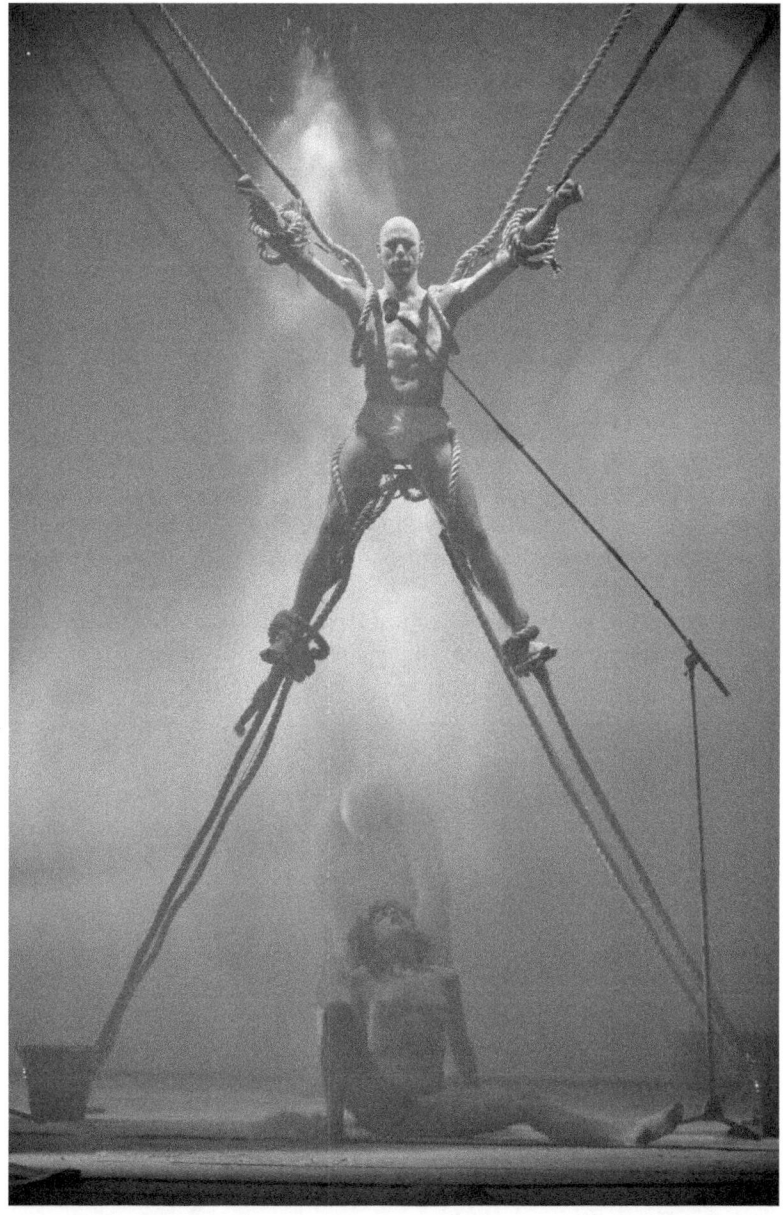

Figure 5.1 *Promethean Landscape II* by Jan Fabre (Photo: Wonge Bergmann)

territory. The body's instincts are triumphant in these secretions: urine as a warm shower, sweat which tingles, tears which weaken. These jets of urine, the pearling perspiration, the bath full of tears inform us that the inside of this body is humid. A body full of repositories of snot and slime. Without these sacred corporeal oils in the various nooks and crannies of our body, it would become stiff and even rigid.

When Fabre puts three women on stage who graciously lift their legs and produce a strong jet of urine, the result is an explicitly voyeuristic dispositive: this is a highly intimate activity which you are invited to witness as a spectator and which is almost misleading. Fabre is showing much more than is visible in this scene. He is highlighting the body's hidden aspect, its nature which is founded on water; he is showing the body's secretions. This may come as a shock to some spectators but more fundamentally Fabre seems to catch a corporeal quality in the act: he puts this juicy body on the stage as an anachronism of our time, which is under threat from draught, the denial of nature, and excessive reason and control. We are becoming increasingly alienated from our humid nature. He rehabilitates the body of grace, which can participate directly in the mystery of the cycle of life and death. The production celebrates the liquid body, which continuously transforms itself and thus withdraws from the petrifying glance.

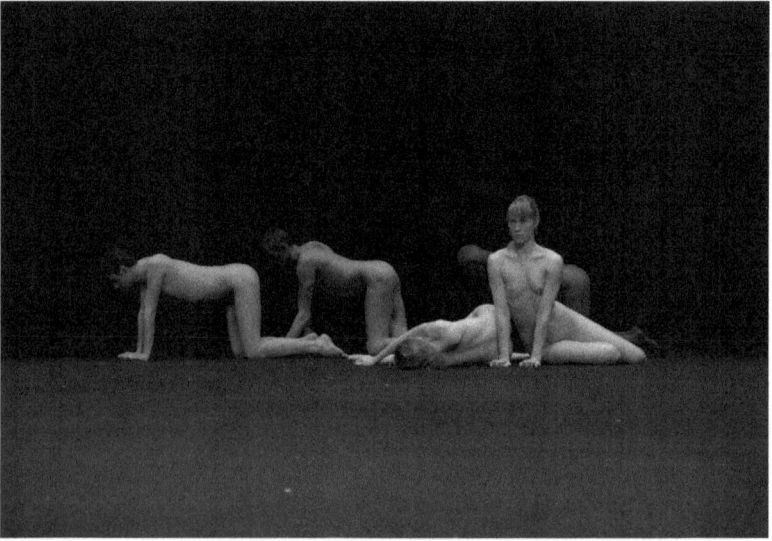

Figure 5.2 *Low Pieces* by Xavier LeRoy (Photo: Xavier LeRoy)

The same can be said about Fabre's most recent production, *Promethean Landscape II* (2011). Fabre considers Prometheus, who brought the gift of fire to our world, as a figurehead of proud autonomy. He eschews the Olympic laws, goes against the flow, and his acts are founded on his own convictions. As the accessory of fire he also has all the tools at hand to transform matter. Both artist and alchemist, he becomes like a lighthouse for humanity. He is contemptuous of death as he demonstrates man's skills. But in this production Fabre shows how mankind has traded the Promethean fire and its emancipatory potential for a society with a deeply rooted aversion to and an absolute prohibition of anything unrestrained and fiery. This evolved society with its rules and laws has banished fire and in so doing has also restrained the imagination: fires are continuously extinguished in this production with buckets of sand, or heavy CO_2-based fire extinguishers.

But at the same time new fires are lit: because the individuals continue to search feverishly for moments of passion, something which sets their body, their soul alight. Naked bodies rub up against each other until sparks fly. Men and women turn themselves into pyres of desire. A rod is transformed into a torch at a glance, a vagina becomes a fuse of sulphur and phosphor: the pubic area is an ideal striking surface for

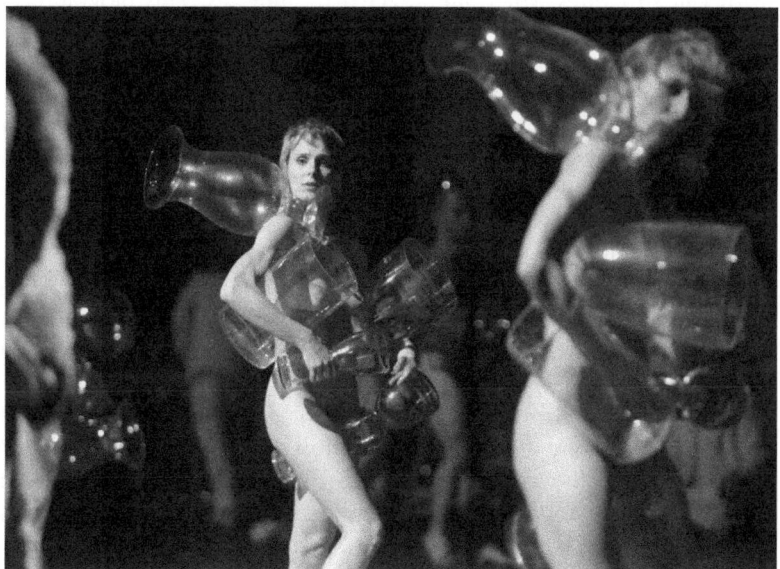

Figure 5.3 *History of Tears* (Photo: Wonge Bergmann)

anything combustible. In this way Fabre transforms the pubic area, in which all the Christian shame of Diana and Eve is contained, into a passionate call for the assent to eroticism until the point of death, much like Bataille, and make us, the voyeuristic spectator, aware of dimensions of a sexual fire that is at the same time extremely attractive as it is dangerous.

Xavier LeRoy: activating the act of looking, vociferous nudity and the curtains of the glance

I would like to place Xavier LeRoy, who is one of the pioneers of so-called conceptual dance, together with Jerôme Bel, at the other end of the voyeuristic spectrum, which I sketched in what preceded. He, too, is fascinated by the body's 'flexibility', by the fact that it can always be remade, by its transformative power. But he uses this theme quite differently, starting from a completely different relation with the spectator's glance.

In the performance *Lecture-Performance* (1998),[13] Xavier LeRoy also introduces his own biography in the piece. In the 'lecture' part of the performance he discusses his past as a researcher in the biochemical industry and shows images relating to his research: multicoloured slides with cell structures which are affected by illnesses. This biographical take is then interrupted and intersected with another tale, namely that of his introduction to the world of dance and how it gave rise to another relation with the/his body. He had already demonstrated that other route to the body in the Performance part of this piece in which he adopted a series of positions sitting nude under a table and against a wall. He exhibits himself to the audience in a completely unspectacular way. We see him naked on his back, in a folded 'candle'-like position. His legs, which are folded over, his arms and shoulders create various transformations or corporeal landscapes without wishing to narrate a story *per se*. These are transforming corporeal images, much like in Fabre's productions, but the entire setting of this production is aimed at repressing the visual language of this body.

In her analysis of this performance, Gabriele Brandstetter emphasized the anecdotal nature of the body: 'Er nimmt die Stelle des "anek-doton" ein – als das nicht Veröffentlichte, nicht zu Veröffentlichende' (1999: 34). The anecdotal aspect of this body is some sort of 'residue', says Brandstetter, which you cannot immediately grasp. She associates this with a typical feature of the performances in the nineties, which followed a different narrative structure, which do their best to not tell a story at all, or rather a different type of story, 'die kleine pointierte Geschichte, die die Lücke zwischen Faktum und Fiktion zugleich füllt und wieder öffnet' (1999: 38). It is precisely this feature of corporeal history which Xavier LeRoy narrates with this production which can be associated with the clumsy drape in Titian's painting: 'filling the void between fact and fiction', as Brandstetter put it so nicely, is nothing else than tooling around with the awareness of the spectator who is watching the performance. The continuous variation between lecture and performance, between biography and fiction, between the naked body and the colourful slides of degraded cell structures, creates a viewing framework which was not designed with a violent revelation in mind as is the case in Fabre's productions. Instead it focuses on the playful construct of the body and the happy conclusion that there is nothing to reveal!

In subsequent performances Xavier LeRoy will focus on this viewing framework even more in order to avoid the development that spectators start to search for a meaning or deduce a metaphor from the fragments of his corporeal narrative. 'At the same time the reception of my work seems to emphasise the idea of a body in parts and created an image or a metaphor for a schizophrenic body which was not my purpose. That pushed me to think about how to escape the production of metaphor and to look for ways to open up the possibilities of perception' (LeRoy 2003).

I will now take a great leap through this body of work to discuss a production, *Low Pieces*, which premiered in Vienna in 2010 and which once again centres on nude bodies. In Avignon, where I saw the performance, six women and five men, whose ages vary from the early twenties to the late sixties, receive the audience as they enter the theatre. They stand on the stage, quite relaxed, dressed in streetwear. Now and then they smile at someone they know, which immediately fosters a sense of complicity. We see the actors, the actors see us. We look, they receive our glance and look back at us. Then Xavier LeRoy takes to the stage and explains the structure of the performance: first there will be a 15-minute discussion with the audience, after which the lights will be completely switched off, and then switched on again after some time. He also promises that the discussion will be reprised at some point during the performance.

The audience is taken seriously in this performance, or, more precisely, the audience is given an active role without resorting to a form of interactive theatre. The act of looking itself is activated in this production; the spectator catches his own viewing behaviour in the act. LeRoy is not interested in the staging of this act of looking. Instead he wants spectators to become aware of what happens during the act of looking. In other words, he is questioning the basic contract of theatre: what happens during the act of looking at a theatrical performance? How democratic is this form of communication? What are the audience's expectations? What happens when you rip up this contract? Can we approach looking in any other way? In the 15 minutes of discussion with which this performance opens, the French audience shows its most avid side, but at the same veers towards a very traditional take when it comes to determining its position. The audience asks the actors questions and thus starts from the idea that they know the answers to these questions, in other words that there is a difference between the knowledge of those who watch and those who perform.

As a consequence, the questions almost all relate to the basic contract of theatre: 'Is this a dialogue or a discussion?', 'Why is this discussion with the audience necessary?', 'How was this discussion incorporated in the rehearsal process?', 'Does the discussion replace the programme?' The actors carefully formulate their point of view in their answers, but their aim is not to be right at any cost. And then suddenly darkness falls. Five naked actors, sitting or reclining, with headphones, make small, almost spastic, robotic movements, again and again. For quite a long time. The effect is exhausting. Until the light is switched off again for quite some time and a new scene is formed, now with bodies lying about on the stage and a forest of arms and legs, stretched out, swinging to and fro in the air, like a landscape of limbs moving in the wind.

Once again the light is dimmed for yet another new scene in which actors enter the stage slowly, like tigers, sniffing at each other and lying down in different formations. The last scene, finally, consists of an image of bodies which barely breathe, like solidified matter. The naked bodies on the stage are actually quite ordinary. *Low Pieces* maintains a form of low energy, without emphasis, exhaustion or theatricalization. The actors carry out actions which, in principle, are quite open. The production highlights a landscape of skin, of young and old, male and female. The skin moves in time, fades out and transforms, and may be seen as a highly formal exercise which is almost abstract in nature. Or maybe the skin also forms constructs between human, automated and animal representations.

But the moments of darkness, in which the spectator can no longer see, in which his glance is blocked off, are just as important as the corporeal imagery which unfolds on the stage. While the audience responds in a contained manner, in silence even when confronted with the actors' nudity, it is vociferous during the long blacked-out moments of the performance, as if their *pudor* is unleashed and they are free to voice their dissent and impatience. The audience recovers its voice in this anonymity, in an almost ob-scene way. This culminates in the last

15 minutes of the performance during which the actors once again engage in a dialogue with the audience, but in complete darkness now. 'How much are you paid for this?', 'Why do you never stand up?' But also testimonials of spectators who are moved by the performance and who explain how the alternation of light and dark leaves impressions on their retina and subconsciously moves them.

In this way the spectator's glance is provided with a platform. Each spectator with their own sensitivities, own references and considerations. The pleasure or the displeasure associated with the act of looking at these naked bodies is put into words. And in so doing this performance succeeds in turning the act of looking into a theme: it shows that looking always takes place within a framework, in the frame of a contract with many expectations and unwritten rules. It calls upon the spectator to move past this point, to look starting from his own body, to let one's glance become corporeal. At the same time the performance also always makes you aware of the construct within which this occurs. In other words, it toys with the curtain of your glance: it continuously opens and closes that curtain. Reveals and conceals. And draws the spectator's attention to his or her own perceptive behaviour.

Conclusion

These two examples of Fabre and LeRoy highlight a wide range of possibilities for dealing with nudity on stage today. They demonstrate two extremes of viewing behaviour and physical staging that we recognized also in the painting of Titian: on the one hand the complicity of the spectator is staged within an encounter with a scene of nudity in which the gaze of the spectator is reflected in many mirror effects on his position as a spectator. That is exactly the effect of LeRoy's *Low Pieces*, who is challenging the comfort zone of the spectator by explicitly questioning his passive position as a voyeur and by inviting him during the show to speak about his own position whilst looking at naked bodies on stage. Fabre, on the other hand, connects with the more violent aspect of Titian's painting by focusing on the violent forces released with the disclosure of an intimacy which was not meant to be seen. In his nude scenes, Fabre reveals hidden powers of the body and violent layers of sexuality that, for the spectator, can be at the same time attractive and unpleasant to look at.

As I mentioned above, these two examples of looking at naked bodies on stage only represent two points in a drawn-out continuum. It is exactly the space between these two points which affords the theatrical world a lot of time and the opportunity to experiment. Precisely because nudity continues to be a sensitive theme – also in the sense of exhausted, too much, too naked, not naked enough, impossible – this continues to be an interesting area for development. And precisely because, as spectators, we keep on being attracted to watch scenes of revelation, to be the witness of a hidden dimension: to look behind the curtain. But this pleasure is always mixed as Anne Übersfeld pointed out in her chapter 'The pleasure of the spectator': 'comme tout plasir, il sent le soufre: voyeurisme, c'est un villain mot, catharsis, c'est plus distingué, mais il est clair que se passe au théâtre quelque chose qui à la fois satisfait et ne satisfait pas le spectateur, qui unit pour lui le plaisir et la frustration' (1981: 338).

Notes

1. Titian, *Diana and Actaeon*, 1556–59.
2. See De Ponte (2006: 163).
3. 'Prohibition gives to what it proscribes a meaning that in itself the prohibited action never had. A prohibited act invites transgression, without which the act would not have the wicked glow which is so seductive ... In the transgression of the prohibition a spell is cast ...' (my translation).
4. Giorgio Agamben makes a convincing attempt to understand this prohibition from a theological perspective in his essay *Nudities*, written on the occasion of a performance by Vanessa Beecroft. After the Fall of Man the naked body is no longer visible, says Agamben, as the Fall has forever cast a veil on our eyes when we look at the naked body (Agamben 2011: 91–144).
5. See the difference between naked and nude in John Berger's famous quote 'To be naked is to be oneself. To be nude is to be seen naked by others and yet not recognised for oneself' (Berger 1997: 54).
6. Both ornaments have been painted under the buttocks of one of the nymphs, which is quite a telling detail!
7. *Dionysus in 69* of The Performance Group premiered in 1968, the same year in which Living Theater's *Paradise Now* opened. Kenneth Tynan's amazingly successful musical *Oh! Calcutta!* was performed for the first time in 1969.
8. See again Berger (1997).
9. This primary scene is also referenced in the opening scene of another production, *As Long as the World Needs a Warrior's Soul* (2000), in which a naked man and a naked woman are forced to admit that they did 'it' in a shrill confession scene.
10. Foucault's analysis of power and punishment constitutes an important source of inspiration in Fabre's work; see Hrvatin (1994: 77–101) and Van den Dries (2006: 21–2).
11. Some of his productions even use the relationship between the artist and the model as a theme, including *Vervalsing zoals ze is, onvervalst* (1992), *Lichaampje, Lichaampje aan de wand* (1997), *Elle était et elle est, même* (2004) and *Etant donnés* (2004).

12. See the analysis by Hertmans (2003) on this theme in Fabre's work.
13. I am referring to the description by Brandstetter (1999: 31–3). The performance part of this performance was reprised as *Self-Unfinished*.

Bibliography

Agamben, Giorgio (2011) *Naaktheden* (Amsterdam: Sjibbolet). Originally published in 2009 as *Nudità* (Rome: Nottetempo).
Bataille, G. (1957) *L'érotisme* (Paris: Editions de minuit).
Bataille, G. (1987) *Oeuvres complètes, tome X, Les larmes d'Eros* (Paris: Gallimard).
Berger, John (1997) *Ways of Seeing* (London: British Broadcasting Corporation and Penguin Books).
Brandstetter, Gabriele (1999) 'Geschichte(n) Erzählen im Performance/theater der neunziger Jahre', in E. Fischer-Lichte, D. Kolesch and C. Weiler (eds), *Transformationen der Neunziger Jahre* (Berlin: Theater der Zeit).
Brecht, Bertolt (1957) *Schriften zum Theater* (Frankfurt-am-Main: Suhrkamp).
De Ponte, Susanne (2006) *Caspar Neher – Bertolt Brecht. Eine Bühne für das epische Theater* (Berlin: Henschel Verlag).
Didi-Huberman, Georges (1999) *Ouvrir Vénus. Nudité, rêve, cruauté* (Paris: Gallimard).
Hertmans, Stefan (2003) *L'ange de la métamorphose – sur Jan Fabre* (Paris: L'Arche).
Hrvatin, Emil (1994) *Jan Fabre. La discipline du chaos, le chaos de la discipline* (Seine-Saint-Denis: Armand Collin).
Leppert, Richard (2007) *The Nude: The Cultural Rhetoric of the Body in Western Modernity* (Boulder, CO: Westview Press).
LeRoy, Xavier (2003) Interview by Dorothea von Hantelmann – Xavier Le Roy, 9 November 2002 / version 30 January 2003. www.insituproductions.net/_fr/frameset.html.
Ovid (1960) *Metamorphoses*, trans. Frank Justus Miller (London: Heinemann and Cambridge, MA: Harvard University Press).
Toepfer, Karl E. (1996) 'Nudity and textuality in postmodern performance', *Performing Arts Journal*, 54, 76–91.
Übersfeld, Anne (1981) *L'école du spectateur* (Paris: Editions Sociales).
Van den Dries, Luk (2006) *Corpus Jan Fabre: Observations of a Creative Process* (Gent: Imschoot).

6
Baring All on Stage: Active Encounters with Voyeurism, Performance Aesthetics and 'Absorbed Acts of Seeing'

Fiona Bannon

W.B. Yeats writes in 1952 that '[a]rt bids us touch and taste and hear and see the world, and shrinks from [...] all that is of the brain only, from all that is not a fountain jetting from the entire hopes, memories and sensations of the body' (1961: 292). That we are, as he suggests, so continuously and radically in relation with the world, and with others, underlines the importance of the experiences we grasp as we go along. Our capacity for affecting and being affected moves us beyond the taming of the spirit and towards a fuller capacity of the intensity of our lives. There is a long and detailed history of practitioners, directors and designers inventively teasing how they might explore theatrical space. In doing so, they succeeded in recasting the gaze of the performer, audience and voyeur. What becomes evident through the entire venture is that it is the affect of spatial tensions felt amidst bodily proximity that contributes significantly to how we each experience performance. Where this is achieved, it switches attention away from contemplating idealist agendas, and towards the very material nature of shared physical existence; in a moment of co-presence, we are hooked on experiences that are both intense and unpredictable.

From the chosen vantage point of the voyeur, there is more to the event than casting a gaze across a spectacle and feigning engagement from the safety of a darkened seat. Instead, there are choices to be made, discriminating adventures to be seized. A journey that, at first, may appear to have no clear destination, can flourish in an array of manifestations, often in excess of our imaginings. For philosopher and psychotherapist Gendlin, it is the mutuality felt in such experiences that holds significance. He argues that,

What one feels at any moment is always interactional, it is living in an infinite universe and in situations, a context of other people, of words, and signs, of physical surroundings, of events past, present and future. (Gendlin 1973: 324)

In these terms, it is the relationships experienced in performance in terms of presence between performer, work and audience that are significant: to be 'touched' but with no physical contact. The performer articulates potential experiences as part of a dialogue with work and audience, each conjuring ways that individually and together get under the skin of the emerging ideas. In terms of the variations in reception, the continuum from ecstasy to dis-ease can be felt as the affect of the experience in context of decisions made during the encounter which are always in flux. It is never a singular relationship. Through the guts and glory of such felt experience comes an unravelling of performance as a physical response that echoes as a 'blaze of consciousness' (Armitage 2011). Arguably, in such instances, live performance generates 'bodily thinking' which is sparked by the spectacle, where literally whole embodied selves are expressed (Schenck 1986). As voyeurs, we effectively shift the demeanour of Rancière's *Emancipated Spectator* (2009) beyond an ease of cognitive episodes to an active and individual intimacy that peels back layers of sensuous perception to reasoning with the senses (Bleeker 2008).

In the themes that run through this chapter, I consider the fervent desire of some audiences who revel in 'stolen pleasures' when watching selves made bare and the moralizing habits of those who are ill at ease when confronted by the visceral presence of human flesh. From the spectre of the voyeur, I will discuss the audience as active participants who make discriminating choices about their experience and sense of embodiment. Through the social context and interaction of being immersed in the realm of a performance, a glance can serve as a key: to make meaning and to take pleasure. I will explore material ideas from a number of experimental performance artists whose works prioritize movement as a way to communicate ideas. In the examples chosen, I suggest a privileging of affective relations as something 'co-determined' between performers who are often unclothed, and audiences often invited to view the work from varied vantage points.

The works span a 50-year time period in terms of the theatre and Western culture coming to terms with naked bodies in performance. My personal experience, being part of the audience for the majority of the works, also contributes to the discussion. With the artists hailing from France (Olivier Dubois, Xavier LeRoy), Germany (Felix Ruckert), Canada (Dave St-Pierre), Australia (Clare Dyson) and North America (Anna Halprin), they form an eclectic mix of Western physical performance. Whilst their individual motivations and methods vary, I find in their work a recurring desire to question the presence of bodies in relation with power in works that are decidedly social and shared encounters. They have each created work received as subversive, disgusting, even prurient. Though it is not always clear what may trigger such reactions from audiences, the situation is made more difficult to understand when one considers the social and political questions that the artists aim to investigate in making the works.

What will become evident in unravelling something of the practice of these artists is the attention given to proximity in terms of felt spatial tension between audience and performer and the distinct role this can play in the manner of reception. For sociologist Georg Simmel, 'The union and interaction of individuals is based upon glances [...] What occurs in this direct mutual reciprocity is the entire field of human relationships' (Simmel in Waskul and Vannini 2006: 4). In adopting such a perspective towards a glance, we can see a nuanced form of awareness, a connection that, for me, resides between aesthetic experiences and relational ethics. Through the guise of the voyeur, we can gaze upon others and, in the process, observe and discriminate with regard to power, possession, vulnerability and desire in what is, effectively, a meeting of our own 'being', in relation with others and with our world.

Baring all for the stage: flesh and sensibilities challenged

For art historian Kenneth Clark there were clear distinctions between the words 'naked' and 'nude'. He suggested that these fed the attitude to involvement with our sensory experience of an artwork. He argued that the word 'naked' implied an embarrassment due to being without, or deprived of, clothes, whereas 'nude' carried 'no uncomfortable overtone' (Clark 1956: 3). This was not the case for Duchamp who, in 1912, attempted to exhibit *Nude Descending the Stairs*, only to be denied by Metzinger and Gleizer because the nude was said to have the vitality of being in motion. For Clark, the nude presents what he saw as a balanced, prosperous and confident body, which cuts a swathe through any case for revealing the fullness of human experience. Although in the world of Fine Art nude portraits may continue to hold a sanctified, though somewhat inactive, status, in the fleshy world of performance we often encounter something different. A moving, active body that is sweaty and pulsating presents a sensuous threat in an otherwise sanitized etiquette. Later in the chapter, *Parades and Changes* (1965), a work by Anna Halprin, is discussed for the echoes that resonate some ten years after Clark was writing in terms of her difficulty challenging the acquired systems of belief in the conceptions of nudity and stillness. A difficulty that was to result in her being threatened with arrest and the work banned from performance.

In Toepfer's (1996) consideration of the conceptual troubles in coming to terms with nudity in theatre, he concerns himself with 'truth'. In a discussion that addresses varied modes of textual correspondence, he argues that there are difficulties in working with nudity because of its association with truth or reality, which in turn sits uneasily with the artificiality of theatre. To compel the audience 'to see the body in a new way' (1996: 78) and to make what is thought to be the most 'private' public can evoke fears by association. It is rare in theatre to be alerted to your own physical realm whilst in the audience. The visceral presence of a nude body can change what we think to be familiar. In this sense, nude performance operates at a level beneath the veil of clothes, casting a mirror onto bodily realities, particularities and the functioning of real people. When stripped of the manners of clothing and revealed as animal, a reality of sweating, urinating, farting, masturbating, scarring with limbs of weight, form and proportion present a reality beyond theatre. The scenario can shock, cradling a fragile range of emotional turbulence that reflects our own human bodily knowledge back at us. As voyeurs, we may be more teased by a partial reveal, by the fragmentary secret show from a chosen vantage point. For, arguably, the more naked the body, the less voyeuristic we become and potentially the more confounded by our own identity.

Hiding with the lights up: responses to flesh

It is worth considering the change in social relations that exist between a performer, a work and an audience. The co-presence of actor and audience remains an identifying feature of the reciprocity of performance and is often made more acute where a performance invades the personal space of audience members. The results of such endeavours can be of heightened anxiety, disengagement or even flight. Where traditional roles are breached, the perceived safety boundary is suspended, often with unexpected consequences. At a safe, respectful distance the performer remains an actor, with protocols upheld and roles fulfilled.

For many, this scenario provides security, a sense of order in the implicit contract between host and client. Where a performance is less predictable, even intent on presenting a state of disruption, audience members can flounder in trying to grasp their new, non-negotiated role. The tables are turned, in a spatial relationship that merges performer, work and audience. It can generate increased vulnerability in trying to stabilize the unpredictable context in which they are now complicit. With the privacy of darkness and the security of a fixed seat gone, they are left in a place of not-knowing.

Such episodes can generate affective responses long after the encounter, felt by both performer and audience. This power to transform draws on both aesthetic sensibility and relational ethics. Aligning ethics in this way with responsible and responsive engagement with others involves being explicitly in-relation with people through an enhanced attentiveness. From this dialogic perspective, we can forge links with aesthetics, addressing interactions between sensory experiences, environments and interpretations. In this context, both involve appreciation for the connections between sensual and reasoned knowledge and coalesce as sensuous accounts of experience with the potential to transform our implicit understandings.

Absorbed acts of seeing: multi-sensory reactions

In terms of transgressions, MacKendrick argues that what might be considered transgressive, for a host of reasons, may in the first instance not be thought of as rule breaking. She suggests that a popular sense of transgression might arise from a situation that,

> [r]ather than indicating a hostile and intentionally destructive reaction against its object (or the law the boundaries of which it crosses) [...] may arise as a fluid and highly desirous response to that (or those), object(s) (or laws). (MacKendrick 2004: 140)

MacKendrick goes on to argue that, in and by the very act of transgressing, the object, law or sensibility in question may be significantly and irrevocably changed. What can be found in the experience is a way to realize ideas and responses differently, to acknowledge that our ways of perceiving, of feeling our reactions are not fixed or final but instead are in constant motion. Sometimes an unnerving or unexpected intimacy in a performance can catch you off-guard. In combining ideas that resonate with previous experiences, audience members can find themselves with unresolved responses, almost a reluctant voyeur of circumstance. Such unguarded intimacy can trigger memories or associations that individuals are not ready to address which can emerge in the immediacy of a moment and intensify futures.

In the writings of John Dewey (1934) there are connections between such ongoing flows of life that unite the idea of thought as being both affective and perceptual. He emphasizes how we are each inextricably entwined with bodies as our common meeting place with others. It is through our embodied selves that we feel our way into experiences as 'bodiliness': breathing, seeing, hearing, smelling and feeling. Whilst thinking this way offers something familiar and tangible, many people self-censor, thereby prohibiting such experience in compliance with cultural norms. As a voyeur we are never of only one opinion, for the richness found in a 'moment' of experience might be 'fleeting but decisive sensations (of delight, surrender, disgust, surprise, horror, or outrage) [...] somehow revelatory of the totality of possibilities' (Lefebvre 1991: 429). It is through such 'totality of possibilities' that we move between an inside feeling of individual experience, the complex realm of negotiation in what is a reciprocal engagement with others. In this realm of perceptual and emotional turbulence, we are, as Bachelard argues 'in a community of dangers' (1994: 176). This reveals the core of the struggle: to learn to value the affect of experiences where intimate inter-corporeal interactions are brought to our attention through our own corporeal specificity. Voyeuristic experiences are entwined with understandings of the self/body that are always unstable and always culturally variable.

Placing 'affect' under a lens leads to concern for the passage of experience, or the movement of thoughts, from one body to another. Through what is effectively continuous negotiation, the potential for interference, nuisance or disturbance lingers. We can, at one and the same time, feel engaged and estranged, drawn towards and repelled in a tease of visceral sensation. We might find ourselves unable to engage with the material content of a performance for reasons we cannot articulate. Something about the work generates an intensity that puts us ill at ease with our surroundings and with ourselves. Equally, we may be captured by the unimagined possibility of a performance, finding ourselves intensely surprised and drawn to new fascinations which were previously only imagined.

Certainly the vitality evident in the works of Eiko & Koma exemplifies the tentative nature of relations to varied states of body, time and intimacy. In *Residue and Nakedness* (2012), designed as a video installation, they share the indelible imprint of time on the body. The work on the screen isolates the naked bodies whilst revealing close-up and intimate physical performance which exists in another time and space. As spectators, we are drawn in, but soon come to realize that our choices are restricted. With your view obscured you peer, select and become captured by your attention being directed, by the camera, towards small detailed movements. Such motion reveals ideas with no recourse to language, erupting to express feelings as a social and affective force (Lepecki 2010). Underscoring this active encounter with the body comes a self-questioning concerned with distinctive responses found when watching nude performer/s.

Parades and Changes and *Low Pieces*: trust

When Anna Halprin choreographed *Parades and Changes* in Stockholm in 1965 it brought her notoriety, later followed in New York (1967) by threatened arrest for indecent exposure. Halprin describes how she aimed to challenge conceptions of nudity, stillness and what she calls the 'ceremony of trust' (2010) between performers and audience trying to 'by-pass acquired belief systems and move directly to our physical bodies which hold all our life experiences' (Halprin 2000). In a reconstruction of the dance during *Move: Choreographing You* (2010), the work opened with each performer standing close to the front of the stage slowly removing individual articles of clothing as if part of a routine daily activity. The clothes were reminiscent of unisex office suits and were methodically removed and draped about their feet. Once removed, the performers paused and stood, then started to redress. There was never a change to their focus; never a glance to the audience or to their fellow performers. They kept a measured pace, maintained their distance and progress through their task, watched by hushed and expectant spectators.

The sense of voyeurism in watching such a mundane task was fuelled by the hypnotic sensation of feeling myself slow down to watch bodies working through daily tasks, as if unseen. The detail of the activity revealed the individuality and vulnerability of the performers. From archival images, it appears that the original work was presented in-the-round, a less formal setting with the audience closer to the performers. In this setting, the audience would have glimpsed other audience members, been close to the performers, aware of more detail of physical presence. The programme note for a retrospective staged in 2000 notes, 'the piece was created in reverence of the human form, as an extension of Halprin's work in the natural environment' (Worth and

Poynor 2004: 78). The slowed and sustained dynamic of the gradual reveal subdued the audience as they watched a hushed, private disrobing. In 2010, the feeling was of a complicit play for power, between an audience seated in rows and the dutiful performers stripping in demure compliance. Maybe it was the auditorium that fostered this sense of control. We were seated higher than the performers, who came as far to the edge of the stage as they could to attract our attention.

Other sections of the work offer different dynamic range where the company tear long scrolls of brown paper, which they fold, roll and rip in the air as they progress together across the space. Bathed in rich golden light, the nude bodies become entwined in an ever-changing design of a river of mellow brown paper. A torrent of energy emerges as they churn the paper, working in a calm, ongoing collaboration. The connections are of rhythmic relationships in time and space, with nudity contributing shape and range in an environment of curves and rolling lines. Watching is mesmeric, hypnotic and sensual, with the space between performers and audience diminishing with every step.

In earlier reviews the work was exposed as 'indecent exposure', yet for others, a liberation of restraint. For writer and critic Arthur Bloomfield, who saw a number of early projects guided by Halprin in San Francisco, her use of nudity was never about rebellion, but more fully about the affirmation of the body as part of a broader ecology: 'In the highest sense, she feels a performance involving bare facts can make for an honest situation re-enforcing the idea of a communion between audience and performers' (Bloomfield 1967). For Halprin, the work was a way to formally frame a series of tasks where the manner of observation became key to what was in the first instance a functional exchange. Worthy of note is a chance letter written to Halprin by a farmer, Sven Kyberg, after the performance in Sweden where much of the intention of the work was revealed. He wrote:

> The dance impressed me very deeply [...] At first I was very sceptical, because a lot of modern art seems to me to be much too egocentric and without humanity or humility. But in the taking off of clothes and the rolling out of paper [...] I saw the naked human animal slowly and unafraid and shy and clean, just like one of my own newborn cattle or lambs, approaching, going near and near, something unknown [...] I felt cleansed and washed and shaken. (Kyberg 1965)

In *Low Pieces*, choreographed by Xavier LeRoy, the contract between work, performer and audience again aims at questioning physical resonance in dialogue with the social milieu of the event. Luk Van den Dries in Chapter 5 speaks of ways that the spectator glance might be directed in a performance. He reviews his experience of being part of an audience, suggesting that '[t]he act of looking itself is activated [...] the spectator catches his own viewing behaviour in the act' (p. 123, above). My experience was to be made alert to an absorbed act of seeing, something markedly different from an idea of looking or surveying. I do not doubt the veracity of the arguments about the theatrical contract, or the expectations of audiences, but what remains fascinating is the ways that we each come to apprehend experience. How do we allow or find ourselves affected by experience and, in a range of our life encounters, prepare and/or repair ourselves to encounter more? Do we learn when to invest in the potential for being 'moved'?

As the lights began to rise on *Low Pieces* they revealed a landscape of nude bodies performing episodes that I associated with an animate ecology. The scene included oscillating sea anemones, formed of legs and arms; the curve of eroded rocks, formed from spines, buttocks and thighs, and dozing, inquisitive lions made through a motion study of bodily dynamics. Each episode, all performed naked, echoed the thoughts shared and repeated in the chapter that our physical body is the meeting place of worlds.

On being aware: *Human Sex, Ring* and *The Voyeur*

In the work of Berleant (1986) characterization of aesthetic experience as unitary perception includes the full range of sensory and somatic responses. This position helps to form a valuable cornerstone from which to appreciate aesthetic experience as both intellectual and emotional. From this perspective involvement with experience can be characterized as 'ranging from multi-sensory synaesthesia to somatic action' (Berleant 1986: 101).

In terms of the present discussion, these notions also offer a means to appreciate that lived experiences have directness and cohesion, that are immediate, and 'of the moment'. I remember my own exhilaration watching Louise Lecavalier, the diminutive, muscular-framed, barechested, peroxide blonde dancer of LaLaLa Human Steps performing in *Human Sex* (1986). Maybe Thompson captures it well, remembering how, when watching, 'You lean forward, on edge. The hair on your neck stands up. Fuck gravity, and escape the laws of nature: for a moment, her leap is yours' (Thompson 2002: 229). For me, it is a leap shaped as a mutual aesthetic experience, a trait that I see evident in the work of an increasing number of practitioners, creating performances that determinably engage with bodily intensity and sensation.

The seductive nature of works where artists challenge audiences by engaging them 'up-close' further disrupts the long-standing etiquette of respectful distance. *Ring* by Ruckert (1999) is such a work, formed by an intimacy of close relationships that progressively develop between audience and performer. Ruckert's intention was for the work to explore the ways that individuals might interact through energized invisible and actual contact with each other. Audience members were invited in the caress of a whisper directly into their ear to dance with their performer/guide. The process was one of melting what Ruckert calls 'choreographic know-how with the intelligence of the genuine personal body language' (Burt n.d.). In his more recent work and now based at Schwelle 7, Berlin, he continues to explore interaction and participation, no longer working with divisions between audience and performer but in explorations of sexual politics and politics of sex within club/art environments, where the whole community are, at once, performers and audience. With a similar drive to explore the potentiality of roles existing at the edge of performance resides *The Voyeur* (2010), a performance created by choreographer Clare Dyson. The content of the work evolved through an intentional investigation of audience relationships with intimacy, choice, and what Dyson identifies as the performative act of revealing. In order to investigate the changing role/experience/power of audiences, the work focused on behavioural traits, where it was directly up to audience members to decide what they experience, and how they experience performance. They were free to roam and embrace a series of encounters with their own watching habits, without being seen, but in close proximity with the two performers. The work is staged in a large wooden box placed on a stage, which the performers inhabit throughout the work and from which there is no obvious way out. Some may see the box acting as a protective barrier, a lens, a sanctuary or even a cage to look into, at the performers, or across to other audience members. The walls of the box are punctured with peepholes of various sizes, sited at different levels. Some peepholes are big enough to share the view, others no larger than an eye. Peepholes that are sited higher than head height can be accessed by climbing steps, and some have headphones and/or binoculars for audience use. It is easy to see that the work is as much about audience as the performers. There are advantages and disadvantages to the choices made; there may be opportunities missed and chanced.

When purchasing a ticket, the audience were unaware that there would be no seat for them in the auditorium. When they entered the auditorium they were invited to the stage and their tasks were introduced. They each chose how they watched and what they watched. If they chose to spend time watching one performer whilst perched on a seat looking through one peephole or to wander around the box glimpsing fleeting views as they passed by, the experience was distinct. It is what each audience member makes of it. Choosing to attend to other intimate details is available through the headphones and/or binoculars. Listening to personal stories or watching a person carefully wash their hair becomes reciprocal moments. Decisions have consequences; there are things you can't quite see or hear from the place you choose to site yourself as an audience. There are things you think you shouldn't see but can't resist watching. The outcome for many appears to have been asking questions of themselves in terms of their own vulnerability, what it means to watch other people and be watched yourself, and what it means to make decisions about your right to decide.

Un peu de tendresse bordel de merde and *Tragédie*: impressions on the skin of the voyeur

So, imagine sitting safely in the middle of Row J: you see a naked man clambering over the chairs and heading straight at you. Not only is your safe vantage point under threat of invasion but when the performer arrives they want to sit on your knee, climb over your head with little regard for even a handshake. Your personal space shrinks and a new intensity rises in your gut, in your breathing, in your sweat. There may be respite in the realization that you are not alone in suddenly feeling yourself to be an unwitting performer, but those people seated in the rows beside you are temporary acquaintances, you haven't even been introduced. This is what happened for many of the audience attending a recent staging of a performance by Dave St-Pierre at Sadler's Wells, London (2011). So when outraged from the very beginning of a performance, do you decide to stay or to leave? Deciding to stay, you engage and witness the work as it continues to unfold; deciding to leave, you fix your experience forever in the 'what if' realm of apprehension. Are audiences confronted with indecent exposure or self liberation?

Dave St-Pierre, a choreographer based in Montreal, speaks through his work of the vulnerabilities of the body and of our human relationships, using the impetus of his own deteriorating health condition. At the time of writing he has been suffering from advanced cystic fibrosis, a life force behind much of the emotional turmoil fuelling his work. In his most recent work, a film entitled *Over My Dead Body* (2013), director

Brigitte Poupart makes public St-Pierre's private turmoil with life and death as he awaits a lung transplant. Often referred to as a new-generation *enfant terrible* and provocateur, he says his aim is to test boundaries between our vulnerability, consumption and intimacy. In *Un peu de tendresse bordel de merde* (A Little Tenderness for Crying Out Loud, 2007) we see these desires laid bare. The work is the second part of a triptych entitled *Sociologie et autres utopies contemporaines* (Sociology and Other Contemporary Utopias), in which he not only presents the company alternatingly dressed and undressed, but early in the work encourages the male members of the cast to leave the stage and invade the auditorium. The first instalment of the triptych, entitled *La pornographie des âmes* (Bare Naked Souls, 2004), met with critical acclaim for what some felt to be an extraordinary potency.

Back in the middle of Row J, the lights stay up on audience members who only moments ago felt themselves to be at a safe distance; now they find themselves befriended by performers in search of attention, affection or indeed any lively response. In this early section of the work, the male members (only the men) of the company, all naked except for their blonde wigs, climb over the heads of the audience, clambering along rows of seats, targeting some audience members to linger with and sit on their knees. They drape themselves across and around the often visibly startled audience members with legs, arms, wigs, buttocks and genitals flailing in all directions.

As you might expect, there was a range of responses; some people walked out, some jokingly played along, whilst others tried to fade away, to be invisible and endure in the hope that the performers would stop and return to the safe distance of the stage where normal relations can be re-established. For the season at Sadler's Wells, the box office acknowledged that whilst there had been 'walk-outs', tickets for seats at the front of the auditorium sold first, which suggested that the production was popular. Sanjoy Roy, in a review entitled 'Pleasures of the flesh: how a nerve-shredding new dance production from Dave St-Pierre has divided the critics' (2011), captures the array of positive and negative responses, saying of the performance that, 'It was certainly impossible to remain unaffected', that 'the boundary-breaking felt physical'. For Thain and Preston (2013), the responses to St-Pierre's choreography highlight the intensity of affective engagement by amplifying our present tense. They say of his work that it, 'marks the potential of the anticipatory as indeterminancy' (2013: 33), that amidst the unfolding of the work we attend to and are affected by a deepening relational bound. For the critic from *Toronto Life*, it is a sense of underlying sincerity that 'gives his productions integrity: they demonstrate both the ugliness and the beauty of our basic instincts'.

In reference to his own experience in making work, St-Pierre writes that he was able to encounter human beings, that in the process he 'experienced their splendour, their foolhardiness, their lack of discipline [...] I flirted with their beauty, their artistic whim, their ideals, their energies, their zeal' (St-Pierre 2011). He speaks of an interest in seeing monsters on stage, capturing something of an energy unbounded when working with raw, complex extremes of emotion. The performances seem to draw audiences to the limits of their social and visceral sense, nudging them to question their own moral stance in relation to the ideas of the work and maybe to be shocked to be asked to deal with them, now. For some, the combination of outrage at the public display of the body prevents their engagement with the driving themes of the work. For others, a silent community with a shared sense of relief in being part of a crowd was only disturbed when individuals broke the bond by choosing to leave. It is interesting to consider the fragility of crowds where ultimately we each experience alone but through a multiplicity of temporary snatched relationships that are eventually eclipsed.

What is evident in a range of exit interviews with audience members is a developing sense of respect for persons. That being in such unexpected relation to other people became something they felt to be quite irreducible. The work seems to have encouraged them to reflect on social interaction underpinned by something of an 'accountability' to (an) other person/s through ethical relations. In sharing his response, Sanjoy Roy (2011) recounted how the opening of the work with the invasion of the audience by naked, attention-seeking men affectively shredded his nerves, peeling back the social skin between audience and performer: 'And from then on, I was sensitised: the scenes of brutality, need and innocence felt as tender as a wound' (Roy 2011).

Another choreographer who uses the naked body extensively in his work is Olivier Dubois. He describes *Tragédie*, a work he created in 2012, as an exploration of the gulf between being human and embracing our full humanity. What was most captivating when watching the work was observing the individuality of 18 naked men and women performing for over 90 minutes in plain sight. This was most marked in the footfall of the whole company during the first 30 minutes of the work as they create a pounding rhythm striding down and up stage in repetitive, though nuanced, choreography, before disappearing momentarily through an upstage scrim. What unfolded was an ongoing game with proximity where we were alternatingly in close and ever distant relations, tantalized by focused perspective.

From my position in the auditorium with the need to peer into a dimly lit stage, I was drawn by the array of idiosyncrasies being gradually revealed as I chose who and what to scrutinize. The thrill of the driving force of biomechanics was reminiscent of Muybridge's human motion studies. The quality of being in-relation with the performers changed as they disappeared into the distance only to return in ever increasing size and detail as they approached the threshold of the stage. For 30 minutes I remained unseen, presented with a fleeting spectacle where my gaze could settle on one performer only for them to disappear at the very moment that a new opportunity burst forward. I had time to understand the form, to predict my choices of who to wait for, only to be thwarted by a shift in location. Performer and audience came to know the game we played. The bombarding physical presence gave way to allegiances forged by individuals who worked in temporary groupings in jerking moments of unison, rhythm and spatial design. There were connections between them that jolted my individual relationships. With no physical contact between performers throughout the 90 minutes of performance, the play with proximity was heightened. Even though at times they ran violently across the stage with arms and legs flailing in the air, there were other moments of stillness that cancelled out the increasing frenzy. Their presence was made more tangible by not moving. Each protagonist was to live, have sex and to die in close proximity with others but always alone.

The spatial tension, and play with proximity, left a lasting impact, as much for the performers on the stage as for those seated in the auditorium. It was an exhilarating introduction to the work of a choreographer who when talking of his work emphasizes that he belongs to no family, seeing himself as a transgressive choreographic hybrid. He is not held by the past, instead he is intent on devouring experience in order to make his own statements and future. At the curtain call, we were all jolted back into our seats, giving a respectful distance to performers who this time appeared clothed. It was disturbing to feel I knew nothing of these dressed people; my relationship was with naked people now vanished behind dresses, trousers, shirts and smiles.

Forging affective relations: voyeurism being with bodies

The range of discussion here revolves around acknowledging that our embodiment generates life experiences, driving us beyond an habitual self to be affected by our unexpected and unruly responses. The mind's eye is an idea found in the body that in turn nudges me to appreciate what Howes (2005: 7) refers to as a 'sensuous interrelationship' between body, mind and environment and to championing this as aesthetic sensibility that we find being in relations with others.

In considering the ways that bodily sensation informs knowledge generation through the affective reception of performance, attention can be drawn to the ways that we relate from the inside-out. Such experiences, it can be argued, exist beyond language, even before language, residing in our individual expressive potentialities. What is evident is that we continuously negotiate realms of experience that include perceptions and affective experiences. In such a tender embrace of 'violent relatedness' (Nancy 2000), what we might find is a sense of respect for persons as something irreducible in our subjectivity. What we might secure is the need of tenderness towards ourselves and towards others that St-Pierre reminds us of in his attempts to tenderize our senses in *Un peu de tendresse bordel de merde* and Dubois in *Tragédie* and that Clare Dyson speaks of in *The Voyeur*, where the outcome for many audience members was to ask questions of themselves in terms of their own vulnerability: of being watched. For, it is through such relationality that an adaptive practice of ethics of voyeurism in performance resides. Through our chosen observations emerge an appreciation of an arena where the corporeal and inter-corporeal are inescapable, where seeing, thinking and feeling are about concurrency and interdependency. The questions and responses of the artists discussed evolve through the social practice of the performances themselves, where theorizing understandings of the body mingles with a sense of what it is to be present and to be sentient.

It remains the case that performances that prioritize 'the body' receive unsettled reception in terms of the meaningful role they have to play in questioning experience, our relationship to self and to others. Where the body is bare, the cultural materiality of vulnerability, impact, power and gender remains as affectively at play as it did in 1960, 1912 and before. Whilst the idea of being bare, undressed, nude, naked may carry different socio-cultural ideas in the popular imagination at different times where works are denounced as insensitive, immoral or boorish, the result can be that the works are stripped of other meaning through complicit moral indignation. A more progressive debate asks of the risks we take when adopting such prurient manners, that through fear we further disassociate ourselves from our bodies. In the realities of the body, voyeuristic engagement offers the potential to understand more about self/body as something unstable and culturally variable. Learning the affect of experiences that are sourced through your own corporeal specificity, effectively means learning to cope with the responsibility of being in relation with others, and that is the basis of our socialization.

Though the guise of the voyeur may be interpreted through multiple perspectives, it does allow us to gaze upon others whilst discriminating our own sense of power, possession, vulnerability and desire. In shifting away from a one-dimensional dismissal of nudity in performance and merging relationships of power, affect and 'bodied' interaction, there is a route to grant ourselves permission, to notice, to glimpse and to be excited. As voyeurs of the performers who bare all, we become absorbed in moments of reflective pleasure, glimpsed as we explore the civilizing and social processes of art, in a context of being in the world.

Bibliography

Ahmed, Sara (2000) *Strange Encounters: Embodied Others in Post-coloniality* (London: Routledge).
Armitage, K. (2011) Interview Transcript, 4 January.
Bachelard, Gaston (1994) *The Poetics of Space* (Boston: Beacon Press).
Berleant, Arnold (1986) 'Experience and theory in aesthetics', in M.H. Mitias (ed.), *Possibility of Aesthetic Experience* (Dordrecht: Martinus Nijhoff), 91–106.
Bleeker, Maaike (2008) *Visuality in the Theatre: The Locus of Looking* (Basingstoke: Palgrave Macmillan).
Bloomfield, Arthur (1967) 'When nudity is defensible in dancing', *San Francisco Sunday Examiner and Chronicle*, 15 October.
Burt, Ramsay (n.d.) *Felix Ruckert's Intimate Theatre of Seduction*. www.felixruckert.de/_Seduction.html (accessed 20 June 2013).
Clark, Kenneth (1956) *The Nude: A Study of Ideal Form* (New York: Pantheon Books).
Dewey, John (1934) *Art as Experience* (New York: Minton).
Eiko & Koma (2012) *Residue and Nakedness*. http://eikoandkoma.org/works (accessed 14 November 2013).
Gendlin, Eugene T. (1973) 'Experiential psychotherapy', in R.J. Corsini (ed.), *Current Psychotherapies* (Itasca, IL: Peacock), 317–52.
Halprin, A. (2000) Programme notes for Anna Halprin's Eightieth-Year Retrospective, Cowell Theater, Fort Mason, San Francisco, June.
Halprin, A. (2010) *Move: Choreographing You: Art and Dance since the 1960s* (London: Hayward Gallery). http://move.southbankcentre.co.uk/microsite/.
Howes, David (ed.) (2005) *Empire of the Senses: The Sensory Culture Reader* (Oxford: Berg).
Kyberg, Sven (1965) Letter to Anna Halprin (via Swedish TV station), 16 December; in Anna Halprin Archives.
Lefebvre, Henri (1991) *The Production of Space*, trans. Donald Nicholson-Smith (Oxford: Blackwell).
Lepecki, Andre (2010) 'Zones of resonance: mutual formations in dance and the visual arts since the 1960', in S. Rosenthal (ed.), *Move: Choreographing You: Art and Dance since the 1960s* (London: Hayward Publishing).

Le Roy, Xavier (2010) *Low Pieces*. UK Premiere, 28 November, Queen Elizabeth Hall, SouthBank Centre, London.

MacKendrick, Karen (2004) 'Embodying transgression', in A. Lepecki (ed.), *Of the Presence of the Body: Essays on Dance and Performance Theory* (Middleton, CT: Wesleyan University Press).

Nancy, Jean-Luc (2000) *Being Singular Plural* (Stanford University Press).

Poupart, Brigtte (2013) '*Over My Dead Body*', *Dave St Pierre Documentary*. http://tendu.tv/catalogue/dave-st-pierre-over-my-dead-body/ (accessed 17 October 2013).

Rancière, J. (2009) *The Emancipated Spectator* (London: Verso).

Ross, Janice (2009) *Anna Halprin: Experience as Dance* (Berkeley: University of California Press).

Roy, Sanjoy (2011) 'Pleasures of the flesh: how a nerve-shredding new dance production from Dave St-Pierre has divided the critics', *New Statesman*, 6 June.

Ruckert, Felix (1999) Ring, www.felixruckert.de/_Ring.html (accessed 20 June 2013).

St-Pierre, Dave (2011) *Un peu de tendresse bodel de merde!* Dave St-Pierre Company Programme Notes. Sadler's Wells, London.

Schenck, David (1986) 'The texture of embodiment: foundation for medical ethics', *Human Studies*, 9, 43–54.

Thain, A. and V. Preston (2013) 'Tendering the flesh: the ABCs of Dave St-Pierre's contemporary utopias', *The Drama Review*, 57:4, 28–51.

Thompson, M.J. (2002) 'Le refus corporeal: a manifesto after Paul-Emile Borduas and Louise Lecavalier', *Women and Performance: A Journal of Feminist Theory*, 12:2, 217–33.

Toepfer, Karl E. (1996) 'Nudity and textuality in postmodern performance', *Performing Arts Journal* 54, 18:3, 76–91.

Waskul, D. and P. Vannini (eds) (2006) *Body/Embodiment: Symbolic Interaction and the Sociology of the Body* (Aldershot: Ashgate).

Worth, Libby and Helen Poynor (2004) *Anna Halprin* (London: Routledge).

Yeats, W.B. (1961) *Essays and Introductions* (New York: Macmillan).

Part IV
Voyeurism and Exhibiting the Body

7
Thinking Critical/Looking Sexy: A Naked Male Body in Performance

Daniël Ploeger

Naked bodies in Western performance and installation art are frequently taken for granted by artists, or treated as a primarily aesthetic feature, whilst the broader cultural significations of unclothed bodies are often ignored in the conceptualization of work. Such treatment of naked bodies as isolated from popular cultural – often sexualized – readings of nakedness may to an extent have been effective in the past due to the framing of the work as 'high art'. However, this approach has become problematic in recent times: the boundaries between popular culture and 'high-art' audiences have become increasingly blurred. This process has arguably been accelerated by the broad accessibility and intermingling of contents from different contexts on web platforms; work previously designated to the 'high-art' frame of the gallery is now accessed equally by a range of audiences with different – at times voyeuristic – interests and reading practices. I suggest that this shift should be taken into account in the conceptualization of performance artwork.

In this chapter, I will propose a conceptual approach to nakedness in performance art that engages with the different ways bodies may be read by audiences, drawing from research in psychology on the framed perception of naked bodies, and perspectives from performance and cultural studies on the collapse of the distinction between 'high' and 'low' art, and perceptual frameworks of nakedness, respectively. In the first part of the chapter, I will examine nakedness in installation and performance work by Spencer Tunick, Marina Abramović and in one of my own works. These analyses will form the basis for three propositions on the conceptualization of naked bodies in performance art. In the second part, I will discuss the practical implementation of this approach in my performance installation *ELECTRODE* (2011).

Naked bodies and the art frame

In the summer of 2007, American photographer Spencer Tunick made an installation in the centre of Amsterdam that encompassed 2000 naked people. Tunick's photographic work concerns different spatial arrangements of large groups of unclothed people in public spaces. In Amsterdam, he positioned naked volunteers on canal bridges and in the Europarking garage, an architectural landmark designed by architects Zanstra, Gmelig Meyling & De Clercq Zubli in the late 1960s. In the photos, the naked bodies are arranged as an articulation or extension of the architectural structures of the environment they are presented in. Commenting on the motivations behind this practice, Tunick emphasizes that he is interested in using naked bodies 'in an almost abstract form' and that his work 'has nothing to do with sex or eroticism' (Tunick in Dutch Amsterdam 2007). This approach to naked bodies as material to realize aesthetic objectives, regardless of their potential cultural signification, is also apparent in his statement that he uses his website to 'collect [...] men and women with different skin colors', whom he is planning to use in the creation of 'a more painting-like photo [...] For example by drawing a line of black bodies through a group of only white bodies' (2007).

In his approach and rhetoric, Tunick seems to make an effort to place his work into what psychologist Beth Eck (2001) describes as the 'art frame' in her study of people's perception of representations of naked bodies. Drawing from outcomes of focus group experiments in which participants were asked to describe images of naked people, Eck suggests that the interpretation of representations of naked bodies is to a considerable extent dependent on the context they are situated in. She initially identifies three contextual frames: art, information and pornography. If a representation of a naked body is perceived as (part of) an artwork, it is more likely to be experienced as an aesthetic phenomenon, rather than a sexual (pornographic) spectacle. Likewise, the informational frame of medical drawings prevents depictions of naked bodies in this context from being experienced as sexually explicit and 'indecent'.

Eck's findings correspond with art theorist Kenneth Clark's (1956) suggestion that the presentation of naked bodies in a high-art context renders these bodies into 'nudes'. His writing suggests that 'nude' is to be understood as equivalent to a certain form of clothing, which one might choose to wear. Thus, 'being nude' is different from 'being naked'; only when naked, a person is truly exposed and in a state where sexual activity would be conceivable. Considering this, do Tunick's attempts to render his naked models into 'nudes' effectively exempt his work from sexualized readings?

Comments by participants in his works seem to confirm Tunick's point of view and emphasize that their experience of participating in his work was more about spirituality, aesthetics or tolerance of bodily diversity, rather than sexuality (Robinson 2010; McNulty 2010; Phillips 2010). However, when we look at responses from observers of Internet documentation of Tunick's work, it becomes clear that Eck's categories and Clark's theory do not always apply in such clear-cut manner. The following comments from a thread, accompanying video documentation of Tunick's work *Mardi Gras: The Base* around the Sydney Opera House in 2010, show that many observers do not share Tunick's conviction that the naked bodies in his work have 'nothing to do with sex or eroticism':

> i always wondered if there was a place where u can just say hi to a women [sic] introduce yourself and shove it in. this setting would be perfect for that. (abelucious in insideoutXS 2011)
>
> the brunette on the left holy fuck her tits are huge and her ass is fine. (lordwirt338244 in insideoutXS 2011)
>
> I could never do this, I would have a erection around those two hot girls in the front. How can these guys not have a boner? [...] These guys might need Viagra. (MisterRepoMan in insideoutXS 2011)

This discrepancy between the artists' and participants' conceptualization of nakedness as 'nudity' in the work, and its sexualized perception by members of a broader audience, particularly in the context of publicly accessible net-based resources, is not confined to Tunick's practice. A similar pattern can frequently be observed in performance artwork. A good example of this is provided by Marina Abramović's conceptualization of her work *Nude with Skeleton* (2002–5) and some of the public's responses to this work. In the performance, Abramović is lying on the floor with a replica skeleton on top of her. In an audio interview accompanying the retrospective exhibition of her work in the Museum of Modern Art in New York in 2010, she explains the concept of the work as follows:

> The work is really about facing your own mortality. It's about fear of pain, and fear of dying, something that in our life we fear the most. And again, in my own work, I always like to confront with [sic] the fears, so being close to the skeleton, washing it, caring it [sic], breathing through, and looking at, confronting it, it's the way to deal with that fear. (Abramović in MoMA Multimedia n.d.)

However, quite contrary to Abramović's own account of the work, many respondents to footage of the performance on YouTube read Abramović's naked body from a sexual perspective. One respondent succinctly states: 'this is the worst porn I've ever seen' (10jjoff in benkratschmer 2007), whilst another person claims that 'if this is art then [...] I'm Rembrandt, Picasso, Da Vinci, and Michelangelo all rolled into one! She sure looks nice naked, though. I hope she makes some more "art"' (imallpissedoff in benkratschmer 2007). A more explicit reading of Abramović's nakedness as a sexual transgression is offered by a third, who suggests that '[i]f you have normal sexual relationships with somebody you just would not pay attention to Marina's deviations a.k.a "modern art"!' (kalek100 in benkratschmer 2007). The latter two comments also touch on another tendency in the reactions to both this video and the documentation of Tunick's work: the majority of the commentators do not seem to acknowledge the work as art at all. If we recall Beth Eck's suggestion that the way naked bodies are read is affected by the context in which they are perceived, we might then attribute the prominence of sexualized readings of these works to their failure to be perceived in the context of the 'art frame'.

What could be the reasons for the ineffective containment of these works by this frame? A rather straightforward explanation would be that the sexualized responses come from people who are simply not part of the intended audience of the work. However, in this case the question arises, to what extent can such a clear-cut distinction between a category of 'high-art' (or 'high-performance') audience and a mainstream culture of the 'uninitiated' still be made? Does a 'high-art audience', which perceives nakedness in art completely detached from its apparent mainstream sexualization, really exist?

To engage with this question, it is of interest to consider Philip Auslander's (1989) writing on the relationship between the notions of high art and popular culture. Auslander has argued that, by the late 1980s, performance art could no longer be regarded as a niche art form situated outside mass culture, which it had predominantly been throughout the 1960s and 1970s. Drawing from cultural theorist Craig Owens (1984), he suggested that post-1970s performance art 'problematizes, but does not reject' (Auslander 1989: 132) the representational forms of popular culture. Much of the performance work of American artist Paul McCarthy, for example, draws heavily from popular culture and advertising imagery. In *Caribbean Pirates* (2005), he assimilates the puppet style of a Disneyland attraction and uses this setting to present an orgy of consumerist transgressions involving ketchup and chocolate sauce.

A development from the other side has taken place as well though: since the 1980s, performance art has gradually been getting more attention in popular media and is much discussed outside its traditional niche audience of contemporary art enthusiasts. The success of Laurie Anderson's work on the mainstream music market, initiated by her hit single 'O Superman' in 1981, shows how the blending of popular culture idioms and 'high-art' performance contributed to this development. However, the media coverage of Lady Gaga's visit to Abramović's *The Artist is Present* (Avalos 2010) and her enthusiasm about the artist's work, as well as the references to *Room with an Ocean View* (2002) in an episode of *Sex and the City*, show also that performance art forms that do *not* actively engage with popular cultural idioms enjoy increased interest outside the exclusive circles of 'high-art' audiences. Wondering about the mass-media compatibility of transgressive performance art like Austrian artist Hermann Nitsch's *Orgies Mysteries Theatres* (1962–), which involve ritual crucifixions of performers and animal slaughter, Auslander suggests that even when performance art does not fit in with mass-entertainment idioms 'it can still be recuperated as oddity or freak show' (1989: 122). This is apparent in the association of Abramović with Lady Gaga, who cultivates an image of self-proclaimed freak herself and famously declared to her fans that 'it's OK to be a freak' (Vena 2009). Abramović's work might not be suitable for mass consumption as such, but by presenting it in conjunction with the 'freak brand' Lady Gaga, it is conveniently framed as an oddity, suitable for mass-media representation.

Returning to Eck's research on the contextual perception of nakedness, this blurring of the boundaries between 'high art' and popular culture, as well as the increasing representation of different forms of performance art in mainstream media, can be read in the context a fourth category, which Eck added to her initial three frames: the 'commodified frame'. She describes how the interpretation of naked bodies becomes increasingly ambiguous, in terms of the perception of their adherence to one of the three previously mentioned frames, if the context of representation is less bounded. This is often the case in representations of naked and partially naked bodies in commodity culture; whereas the depiction of a pregnant woman in a medical textbook is generally clearly perceived as informational, a similar image on the cover of a popular magazine is likely to raise debates on whether the representation is either informational, artistic or pornographic.[1]

In this context, cultural theorist Rob Cover argues that the increased sexualization of nakedness in contemporary culture is a result of what he calls the '"postmodern" destabilization of contexts' (2003: 55).

Focusing on the presentation and representation of nakedness in everyday situations, Cover points out that practices and sites that were formerly identified as non-sexual tend to increasingly afford a sexualized reading as a result of the collapse of clear contextual demarcations. Same-sex showers, for example, were much easier to perceive as strictly non-sexual when homosexuality was not commonly acknowledged. With the public acknowledgement of homosexuality, the gaze in the public shower room has become sexualized; openly looking at other naked bodies in this context is likely to be experienced as sexual intimidation.[2] Similarly, in the context of the availability of child pornography on the Internet, photographs taken by parents of their naked children have in recent years frequently been read as pornographic material, resulting in a number of legal prosecutions of parents who had photographed innocent scenarios of their kids enjoying a bath.

I suggest that Cover's argument should also be considered in the analysis of contemporary performance-art practices involving naked bodies. The sexualized readings of Tunick's and Abramović's work may not only be attributable to the fact that certain observers do not acknowledge its 'art frame'. Rather, I suggest that, under the influence of the increased integration of performance art into mass culture, the art frame *itself* has become instable and no longer precludes the sexualization of naked bodies. Thus, naked subjects also afford sexualized readings by members of a 'conventional' high-art audience, which *do* acknowledge the work's artistic frame.

I experienced instances of such eroticization of my naked body by audiences who are familiar with performance art, as well as performance theory scholars, in their perception of my work *SUIT* (2009–10). With *SUIT*, it was my intention to develop a digital performance interface that would thematize its own interaction with my body, rather than approach digital performance technologies as a more or less transparent medium for the transmission of the body's activity. In the performances, sound is generated using the signal of a Doppler heart monitor,[3] and humidity data, based on the sweating of my body. The project comprises a series of performance and installation works, in which my naked body is contained by a transparent PVC performance suit. I equipped a PVC go-kart rain suit with a humidity sensor, a Doppler heart monitor and a loudspeaker. When I wear the suit, I start to sweat, which causes the humidity registered by the sensor inside the suit to rise. Also, my heart rate, which is registered by the Doppler monitor, speeds up. The humidity and heart-rate data are then used to synthesize sound with a computer program. The sound is played through the loudspeaker in the back of the suit (Figure 7.1).

Since I envisaged the work as highlighting the interaction between my body and the technological PVC overall, I decided that it was important to be naked inside the suit. I felt that if I wore additional clothing, this would make the bi-directional interaction between my body and the performance technology somewhat opaque. At the same time, it was important that the suit was transparent, in order to show both my body and the technology surrounding it, and make the impact of the suit on my body (excessive sweating) visually perceptible.

However, despite my conceptualization of the work, it became apparent that for many audience members the visibility of my naked body was its most prominent aspect. A local Dutch TV channel titled its reportage about the work 'A nude man in a plastic suit making noise!' (TV Walcheren 2009), but quite to my surprise spectators who frequent the contemporary art scene, as well as performance scholars, in many instances also appeared to focus on the nakedness in the work. Although they would usually attempt to feign that their contemplation of my naked body was firmly confined within the art frame,

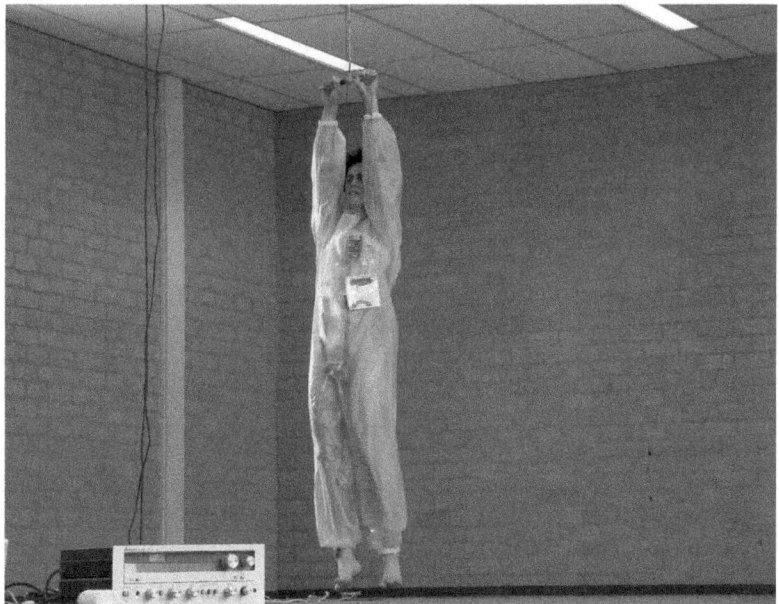

Figure 7.1 SUIT (2009–10) by Daniël Ploeger (Photo: Giel Louws)

there were several occasions on which it became rather obvious that the work had aroused voyeuristic and erotic interests that were based on a sexualized perception of my naked body. In addition to several suggestive invitations for nights out and sauna visits, one person told me in a conversation after a conference presentation that he could recommend 'a venue where you would get hundreds of phone numbers if you perform this'.

Thus, I realized that although my own objectives with the work were focused on discourses around the body and digital technology, audience members were often more concerned with the potential erotic and sexual connotations of my naked body and frequently perceived the interaction with the suit merely as a secondary aspect of the work. Reflecting on the performances, I also came to another realization though: although I had mostly been concerned with the way the suit would affect the involuntary behaviour of my body (and vice versa) in the conceptualization of the work, during the practical preparation of the work and my actual experience of the performances, a lot of my attention was directed towards the way the audience perceived my body: do I look good like this? Doesn't this position make me look too skinny? If the spectators watch me from over there, will the light make my skin appear pale? In other words, when it came to the actual experience of the performances, it became clear that even for me the fact that I was naked was not fully contained by Eck's art frame. In effect, it seemed that my concerns during the performances were more often directed at whether my appearance would adhere to normative notions of a desirable body.

Research on health behaviour of British men suggests that male concerns to have a healthy-looking, able body are often closely linked to their experience of being sexually desirable, which in turn strengthens their self-confidence (Robertson 2006: 11–13). Cultural theorist Mike Featherstone (2010) argues that these concerns can be traced back to the cultural prevalence of a concept of the body as an object that can be adjusted to correspond to an idealized form when the necessary effort and discipline are invested. This facilitates an understanding of a person's appearance as a reflection of this person's self. Consequently, people who do not adhere to the ideology of physical self-care are considered 'moral deviants' (Shilling 2003: 5). Thus, the idealized, disciplined and healthy physiques on the covers of magazines such as *Men's Health*, which are dominated by white, lean muscular bodies, act as generalized signifiers for beauty, success and moral superiority, and hence the pinnacle of sexual desirability. Taking this into account, I suggest that the concerns about the perception of my naked body which dominated my performance experiences of *SUIT* may be related to the potentially sexualized reading of my naked body by the audience.

Drawing from these three little case studies – Tunick's installations, Abramović's *Nude with Skeleton* and my own work *SUIT* – I would like to put forward the following suggestions. The collapse of the boundaries between 'high' and popular art, and the blurring of high-art and popular-art audiences and media representations, makes it problematic to conceptualize a so-called 'high-art audience' and make performance work with such a 'pure' audience in mind. Following Rob Cover's concept of the increased sexualization of nakedness as a consequence of the '"postmodern" destabilization of contexts' (2003: 55), naked bodies in performance art always afford a sexualized reading. This should be taken into consideration in the conceptualization of the work. In this context, performance artists should also ask themselves to what extent they read their own naked body (or the bodies of other participants in their work) from a sexual perspective. Are they genuine when they state that their work has 'nothing to do with sex or eroticism'? My own experience of the performances of *SUIT* shows that my actual experience of being naked in front of an audience was more profane than I had believed when I conceptualized the work.

It is not my intention here to argue that all performance art involving naked bodies will always only signify sex. What I do want to suggest, though, is that the belief that nakedness in certain performance-art practices has 'nothing to do with sex' at all, just because the artist has decided that this is not what the work 'is about', is somewhat naïve. In the following, I propose an approach to naked bodies in performance that takes into account its potential eroticization and seeks to address different aspects of the normative expectations that often accompany such readings of naked bodies, as well as artists' own complicity in the idealization of the eroticized normative body types represented in popular magazines, advertising and other mainstream media.

Complicating the sexualized nude

In my evaluation of the performances that formed part of *SUIT* and the subsequent conceptualization of my performance installation *ELECTRODE* (2011), I felt that if I was going to be naked in future work, I would need to acknowledge the potential sexualized reading of my body in the concept of the work. Consequently, it would also be necessary to engage with the normative desires and expectations frequently connected to such reading. More importantly, though, I realized that I would need to address the paradox between my critical theoretical perspectives on bodily disciplines in society and my simultaneous fascination with normative body types, which was all too apparent during the performances of *SUIT*; although I reject the idealization of mainstream body ideals in my critical thinking, I seem to adore the very body types I reject on a more intuitive level. Would it be possible to make performance work that engages with this issue, which appears to be beyond the grasp of critical theoretical inquiry?

Such work should strive for a confrontational ambiguity, where theoretical concerns are juxtaposed with these incompatible intuitive preferences. On one hand, the work would satisfy the audience's voyeuristic sexual gaze, as well as my concerns to 'look good' whilst displaying my naked body. However, this situation of indulgence would then be deliberately disturbed by means of a carefully constructed network of references to elements connected to the critical theoretical conceptualization of the work.

A possible realization of such an approach takes its cue from the four representational frames of naked bodies suggested by Beth Eck. As I suggested in my discussion of Eck's 'commodified frame' and Rob Cover's writing, the artistic, informational and pornographic frames seem to have become increasingly instable. However, this does not mean that they are not meaningful at all anymore; although a naked body (re)presented in a medical frame is not prevented from being read sexually, this doesn't mean that the perception of this body is likely to be sexualized to the same extent as it would be if it was presented in a pornographic frame. Thus, it is still possible to influence the way naked bodies are read by means of placing them in different contextual frames. Considering this, I propose an approach to nakedness in performance that seeks to heighten the sexualized perception of the body through a deliberate invocation of the 'pornographic frame', whilst simultaneously complicating and undermining this satisfaction of the audience's sexual gaze – and my own narcissist concerns to present my body as sexually desirable – through references to the three other frames: the informational, the commodified and the artistic. In my performance installation *ELECTRODE*, which might be regarded as a sequel to *SUIT*, I follow this approach.

In *ELECTRODE*, I am standing in the middle of a space, facing a projection of graphs on the wall. Electronically processed sound plays through two large loudspeakers, positioned on either side of the video projection surface. The activity of my sphincter muscle is registered with an *Anuform*® anal electrode connected to a *Peritone* EMG sensor. My naked body, with the electrode wire coming out of my anus, together with the packaging material and instruction manuals of the sensor and electrode, are lit by a spotlight from above. The sensor has been modified so that it can be connected to a computer, which uses the muscle data to synthesize the sound played through the loudspeakers and generate one of the graphs in the video projection.

The *Anuform®* anal electrode and *Peritone* EMG sensor are readily available and commonly used medical devices to monitor and treat problems related to a malfunctioning sphincter muscle. They are intended to monitor exercises that seek to strengthen the sphincter muscle of people who are experiencing weak muscle response, which manifests itself in faecal incontinence. In the exercises, the user performs sequences of voluntary sphincter muscle contractions at regular intervals, whilst the sensor device gives biofeedback by displaying the electric potential generated by the muscle. By means of keeping record of achievements registered during different practice sessions over time, the user seeks to improve performance. The use of EMG biofeedback for the treatment of faecal incontinence was first described in the 1970s (Engel, Nikoomanesh and Schuster 1974), but sensor technology for home use has only become affordable for the consumer market since the mid-1990s (Heymen et al. 1999). Previously, EMG sensors were very costly and primarily used for medical research. Because the male orgasm is accompanied by involuntary sphincter muscle contractions, EMG sensors to register sphincter muscle activity were first used in the 1970s in research into the nature of the male orgasm (Peterson and Stener 1970).

A graph of the sphincter contractions of an anonymous subject in a 1980s medical research project into the male orgasm is projected onto the wall I am facing. In this research project, which took place at the University of Minnesota, male subjects were asked to masturbate to orgasm whilst their sphincter muscle activity was registered with an anal probe (Bohlen, Held and Sanderson 1980). A second graph, representing the real-time contractions of my sphincter muscle during the performance, is projected below the first graph. Through voluntary contraction of my sphincter muscle, I try to imitate the contraction pattern of the top graph as closely as possible (Figure 7.2).

The EMG data is used to control different parameters of the GENDY (GENeration DYnamique) sound synthesis program, which was conceived by French-Greek composer Iannis Xenakis in the 1990s. GENDY is an implementation of Xenakis' stochastic dynamic synthesis method, which he developed from the 1950s. Stochastic methods are based on processing random values, limited by a probability distribution (see Luque 2009). A detailed description of this sound synthesis process is beyond the scope of this chapter, but what is of relevance here, is that

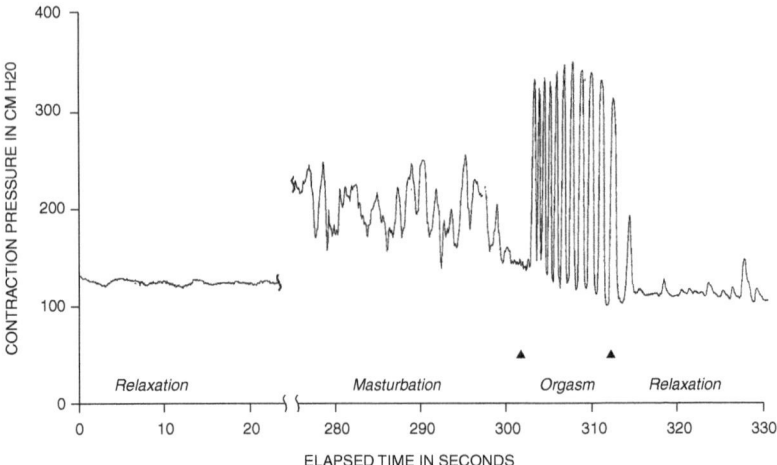

Figure 7.2 Sphincter muscle contraction pattern registered in an experimental subject during masturbation and orgasm (Bohlen, Held and Sanderson 1980), used in *ELECTRODE*

the GENDY algorithm is among the most famous digital synthesis processes, which can arguably be considered one of the archetypical sound synthesis methods of contemporary electronic music.

Throughout the performance, I am standing in the same position, taking a narcissistic pose reminiscent of an Action Man doll. I repetitiously perform the same orgasm sequence, interrupted by intervals of silence of approximately 30 seconds. The audience can move around freely within the space and enter and leave as they please.

In *ELECTRODE*, I seek to provoke an ambiguous experience of my bodily presence in the gallery, drawing from my approach to include references that suggest all four of Eck's frames of nakedness simultaneously. The different aspects of the work, which I described above, are conceived to evoke these different frames as follows:

Pornographic frame

The direct reference to sexuality in the performance's objective to *perform* an orgasm, combined with the macho pose taken by my white male body, and the erotic connotations of inserting an object into my anus, all seek to render the performance into a sex show in the most literal sense.

Furthermore, the repetitiveness of the attempts to reproduce one single graph from Bohlen's research as carefully as possible with my

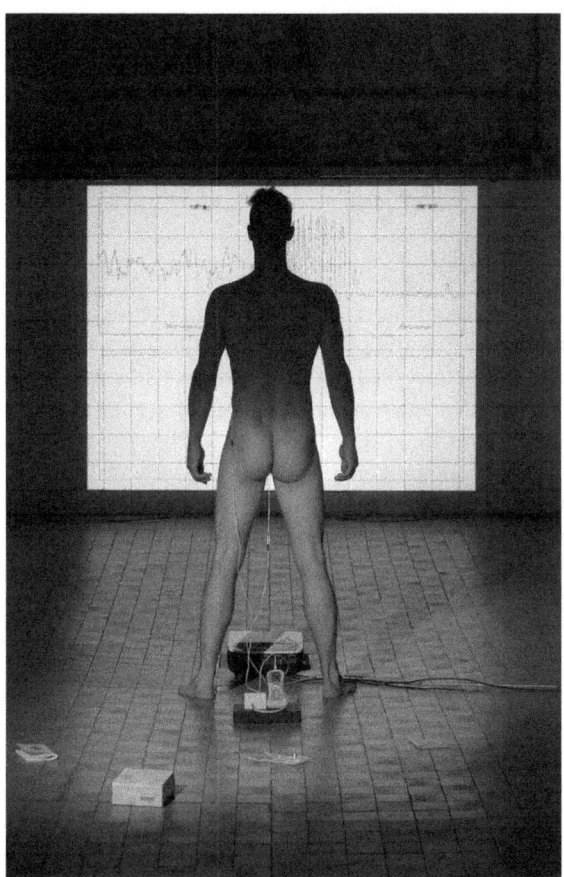

Figure 7.3 *ELECTRODE* performance by Daniël Ploeger in Ostrava, Czech Republic, August 2011 (Photo: OCNM Archive / Martin Popelář)

voluntary sphincter contractions is motivated by a desire to represent the sexual references of the work in a performance and skill-focused context, which is – in addition to its pornographic connotations – commonly associated with masculine perspectives on sexuality. In a research project on perceptions and experiences of heterosexual intercourse of both men and women, psychologists Roberts et al. found that most men in their research focus groups approached sexuality as a matter of 'technique and work' (1995: 525), where a 'good' sexual partner is defined by his ability to employ his physical skills to bring the female partner to orgasm.

In addition to this, the work was made sexually suggestive by the press release that preceded most shows, which announced the event as 'performance with anal electrode', rather than 'ELECTRODE'. As became clear in post-performance conversations, this description had indeed evoked the expectation of a homoerotic fetish show (or at least an arty stylized version of this) for many spectators.

Information frame

The use of medical data as source material in *ELECTRODE*, in conjunction with the representation of this data and the real-time contractions of my sphincter during the performance in the form of graphs projected onto the wall, was conceived to facilitate a perception of the work in the context of Eck's 'information frame'. A perception of my naked body in this frame is further heightened by the fact that the medical technologies used in the work are conspicuously presented as such. The packaging material of the electrode and the sensor, which show their purpose as medical technologies, are exhibited on the floor and illuminated by a spotlight. Also, the modification of the sensor was deliberately done in such way that the body of the device stayed intact and would still be recognizable as a medical device.

The fact that the medical technologies in the piece are intended for the treatment of faecal incontinence is of specific relevance here. Faecal incontinence concerns the unintentional loss of faeces from the rectum in people over three or four years old. It most frequently occurs with people over 60 years of age and children between seven and nine years of age. In the latter case, however, incontinence is mostly caused by psychological factors, rather than malfunctioning sphincter musculature (Whitehead and Drossmann 1996). Therefore, technologies such as the *Anuform®* and *Peritone* are generally associated with age-related bodily malfunctioning and thus fall outside the frame of reference of the sexually desirable young and healthy body. This complicates the work's references to the pornographic frame.

Commodified frame

When I first saw *Anuform®* and *Peritone*, and the accompanying manuals and packaging material, I was struck by its slick and appealing design. The appearance of the products, which reminded me more of the seductive commodities of companies like Apple or Nintendo, seems to be at odds with their image as 'taboo technologies': although they are widely used, it is highly uncommon to publicly talk about ownership of these technologies, let alone feature their appearance as a style accessory. I chose to conspicuously display the packaging material, product documentation, and the *Peritone* device itself, to heighten the technologies' commodity aspect.

Art frame

Although the fact that the work is always presented in galleries or other art venues already evokes Eck's 'art frame' in an obvious way, other aspects of the work seek to further heighten its framing as such. I chose to use the muscle data to synthesize sound by means of a stereotypical electronic sound synthesis process, so that my repetitious attempts to replicate the graph from Bohlen's research also affords to be perceived in the tradition of music performance with digital interfaces. I conceived this reference to formalist aesthetic approaches to sound synthesis with digital interfaces, which is prevalent in this performance culture,[4] to emphasize *ELECTRODE*'s art frame.

Thus, rather than downplaying or negating naked bodies' affordance of sexualization, as is arguably the case in Spencer Tunick's and some of Marina Abramović's work, and my own engagement with my exposed body in *SUIT*, I made an effort to give my concern to 'look sexy' a place in the conceptualization of *ELECTRODE*, whilst simultaneously undermining this desire through references to other framings of my naked body.

Audience responses to performances suggest that the work indeed triggers associations with different framings of my naked body. Two punters, who were interviewed by the Brighton-based radio station RadioReverb, described their experience of the show as follows:

> Coming at it as a gay man [...] and the idea of how that involves your ass during sex [...] it was quite interesting to see how it actually works [...] from a mechanical biological point of view. (First interviewee in Tuesday Live 2011)

> I thought it was interesting from a technical point of view. It reminded me almost of going to watch some sort of body building contest where you have people who have perfected certain muscles of the body and are [...] using them for us all to see [...] Scientifically, I thought it was interesting. Artistically, I don't really get it [...] Nice ass though. (Second interviewee in Tuesday Live 2011)

Apparently, they perceived my naked body primarily within Eck's informational frame, whilst there was also a hint at a sexual perspective in the second person's concluding remark about my 'nice ass'. A journalist for the Czech national newspaper *Lidové Noviny* also perceives my naked body in the informational frame of 'experimentation on human bodies', but emphasizes its contextualization in the (musical) art frame by the honorary title he awards me in the end of his review:

> one could see the silhouette of his naked body with a cable inserted from below. The tiles of the [performance space] completed the atmosphere of experimentation on human bodies that the performance evoked. The 'Jimi Hendrix of the sphincter' gave the sounds from the body's interior interesting timbres by means of electronic filters. (Klusák 2011)

Another interesting perspective is offered in a review by British contemporary music magazine *The WIRE*, which concludes with the statement that *'although* the [muscle data were] sonified with Xenakis' GenDy algorithm, this piece featured two assholes too many' (Hamilton 2011: 83; my emphasis). The reviewer recognizes that there are elements in the work that are at odds with a 'pure' artistic (and more specifically 'musical') frame, but seems offended by the fact that these aspects trouble the perception of the work's formalist musical element (Xenakis' algorithm).

These audience responses suggest that *ELECTRODE* does indeed afford the perception of my naked body in the context of several of Beth Eck's frames simultaneously. To a certain extent, the work also appears to provoke the experience of a conflict between these different frames; although the work's scientific/informational connotations render it 'un-artistic' to the second punter in the radio interview, he *does* seem to perceive my naked body from a potentially sexual perspective. Similarly, the *WIRE* reviewer frames the work as art, but is apparently put off by his perception of the – in his opinion – non-artistic connotations of my naked body.

Conclusion

In the first part of this chapter, I examined the conceptualization and perception of naked bodies in installation and performance work by Spencer Tunick and Marina Abramović, and in my own work *SUIT*. I drew from research in psychology on the relevance of contextual frameworks in the perception of naked bodies, the blurring of the boundaries between 'high art' and popular culture in performance art and its audiences, and a discussion of the likelihood of artists' sexualization of their own bodies. These perspectives lead to three propositions on engagement with nakedness in the conceptualization of performance artwork: (1) it is problematic to conceptualize performance work solely directed at a so-called 'high-art audience'; (2) work should take into account that – in postmodern culture – naked bodies in performance art always afford a sexualized reading; (3) artists should engage critically with their own potential tendencies to sexualized and voyeuristic readings of their naked body.

These three propositions formed the basis for my work *ELECTRODE*, which I discussed in the second part of this chapter. By means of deliberately juxtaposing elements that refer to three different contextual frameworks for the perception of naked bodies (art frame, information frame and pornographic frame), this work seeks to confront the paradox between my critical theoretical rejection of the idealization of mainstream body ideals, and my apparent more intuitive fascination with the very body types I reject in my critical thinking. Audience responses to the work suggest that the juxtaposition of references to different contextual frameworks indeed provokes an experience of ambiguity and conflict in terms of the reading of my naked body.

However, the question remains to what extent the diversity in the perception of nakedness in *ELECTRODE* does really facilitate a critical debate around the tensions between cultural critical perspectives, and intuitive associations and preferences concerning naked bodies. Do the audience reactions discussed not merely show that the work is a versatile object of entertainment that caters for the specific tastes and preferences of a broad range of audiences? Whilst this might to a certain extent be true, there is another relevant aspect of my approach to my naked body in *ELECTRODE*. Since my narcissistic concerns around the exhibition of my carefully shaped normative body are at the very core of *ELECTRODE*, my own experiences during the performances are now an integrated part of the work, rather than a largely overlooked and preferably hidden by-product, as was the case in *SUIT*. At the same time, the framing of this tendency in a web of conflicting references means that my attempts to look attractive will never be fully successful. Thus, performing *ELECTRODE* feels like an embodied confrontation with the difficulty of wanting to think critically, whilst trying to look sexy.

Notes

1. This was apparent in the public debate that was triggered when *Vanity Fair* published a naked photo of the highly pregnant actress Demi Moore on its cover in August 1991. Whilst some readers designated the photo as artistic, others experienced it as sexually explicit.
2. To illustrate this, Cover refers to the Seinfeld episode 'The Apology' (1997), in which Kramer's observation of different people's showering routines in the

gym changing room, in order to optimize his own showering ritual, is read as sexually offensive by the other gym visitors.
3. A Doppler heart monitor is a device that uses ultrasound to sonify the movements of the heart. Cheap monitors are marketed for pregnant women to listen to sonifications of their unborn baby's heartbeat.
4. The proceedings of the biannual conference of *New Interfaces of Musical Expression*, which is the main organization for practitioners and technologists in this field, are dominated by a focus on aesthetic and technological concerns, whilst cultural critical perspectives are largely ignored. I have discussed this issue elsewhere (Ploeger 2011).

Bibliography

Auslander, Philip (1989) 'Going with the flow: performance art and mass culture', *The Drama Review*, 33:2, 119–36.
Avalos, Steven (2010) 'Lady Gaga, celebs visit MoMA exhibit in NYC' www.popeater.com/2010/05/06/lady-gaga-moma (accessed 1 March 2012).
benkratschmer (2007) Marina Abramovic [video] www.youtube.com/watch?v=pno1gCrbeVk (accessed 5 March 2012).
Bohlen, Joseph G., James P. Held and Margaret O. Sanderson (1980) 'The male orgasm: pelvic contractions measured by anal probe', *Archives of Sexual Behaviour*, 9:6, 503–22.
Clark, Kenneth (1956) *The Nude: A Study in Ideal Form* (London: John Murray).
Cover, Rob (2003) 'The naked subject: nudity, context and sexualization in contemporary culture', *Body & Society*, 9:3, 53–72.
Dutch Amsterdam (2007) Amsterdam Nude. www.dutchamsterdam.nl/128-spencer-tunick-amsterdam (accessed 4 March 2012).
Eck, Beth (2001) 'Nudity and framing: classifying art, pornography, information, and ambiguity', *Sociological Forum*, 16:4, 603–32.
Engel, B.T., P. Nikoomanesh and M.M. Schuster (1974) 'Operant conditioning of rectosphincteric responses in the treatment of fecal incontinence', *New England Journal of Medicine*, 290, 646–9.
Featherstone, Mike (2010) 'Body, image and affect in consumer culture', *Body & Society*, 16:1, 193–221.
Hamilton, Andy (2011) 'Ostrava music days', *The WIRE*, November.
Heymen, Steve, et al. (1999) 'Prospective, randomized trial comparing four biofeedback techniques for patients with constipation', *Diseases of the Colon & Rectum*, 42:11, 1388–93.
insideoutXS (2011) Spencer Tunick-2010 [video] www.youtube.com/watch?v=BZPekrIgvsg&oref=http%3A%2F%2F (accessed 5 March 2012).
Klusák, Pavel (2011) 'Z Ostravy je džungle nových zvuku', *Lidové Noviny*, 29 August.
Luque, Sergio (2009) 'The stochastic synthesis of Iannis Xenakis', *Leonardo Music Journal*, 19, 77–84.
McNulty, Bernadette (2010) 'Spencer Tunick: bare with me', *The Telegraph*, 2 August.
MoMA Multimedia (n.d.) 'Marina Abramović: Nude with Skeleton' (2002/5/10) [audio] www.moma.org/explore/multimedia/audios/190/2016 (accessed 7 March 2012).

Owens, Craig (1984) 'The allegorical impulse: toward a theory of postmodernism', in Brian Wallis (ed.), *Art after Modernism* (Boston: David R. Godine), 203–35.
Peterson, I. and I. Stener (1970) 'An electromyographic study of the striated urethral sphincter, the striated anal sphincter, and the levator ani muscle during ejaculation', *Electromyography*, 1, 23–44.
Phillips, Rhodri (2010) 'Volunteers strip naked for sake of art', *The Sun*, 1 May.
Ploeger, Daniël (2011) 'Sounds like Superman? On the representation of bodies in biosignal performance', *Interference: A Journal of Audio Culture*, 1:1. www.interferencejournal.com/articles/an-ear-alone-is-not-a-being/sounds-like-superman (accessed 18 January 2015).
Roberts, Celia, et al. (1995) 'FAKING IT: the story of "Ohh!"', *Women's Studies International Forum*, 18:5/6, 523–32.
Robertson, Steve (2006) '"I've been like a coiled spring this last week": embodied masculinity and health', *Sociology of Health & Illness*, 28, 433–56.
Robinson, Georgina (2010) 'Thousands strip nude for Spencer Tunick photo in Sydney', *The Sydney Morning Herald*, 1 March.
Shilling, Chris (2003) *The Body and Social Theory*, 2nd edn (London: SAGE Publications).
Tuesday Live (2011) [radio programme] RadioReverb, 13 September, 17.00.
TV Walcheren (2009) Kipvis presents: 'A nude man in a plastic suit making noise!' [video] www.zeelandnet.nl/video/bekijk/video/4957/ (accessed 1 March 2012).
Vena, Jocelyn (2009) 'Lady Gaga tells fans "It's OK" to be a freak'. www.mtv.com/news/1627085/lady-gaga-tells-fans-its-ok-to-be-a-freak/ (accessed 19 January 2015).
Whitehead, W.E. and D.A. Drossmann (1996) 'Biofeedback for disorders of elimination: fecal incontinence and pelvic floor dyssynergia', *Professional Psychology: Research & Practice*, 7, 230–6.

8
Viewing the Pornographic Theatre: Explicit Voyeurism, Artaud and Ann Liv Young's *Cinderella*

Aaron C. Thomas

In a piece for the online *Examiner* in 2009, Jana Monji describes what she perceives as a trend towards increased onstage nudity in the offerings provided by Los Angeles-area theatres. Her piece is ostensibly a response to the premiere of *Hangin' Out: That Naked Musical*, and she asks many of the now-standard questions about nudity in the theatre: to wit, 'Is the amount of nudity on Los Angeles stages a good thing? Is it voyeuristic? Is it a sign of exhibitionism?' Martin Esslin asked a similar set of questions as long ago as 1968: 'Is [nudity] a good thing or a bad thing for art? Is it a symptom of declining morals? A sign of social decadence?' In the late 1960s, Esslin placed himself firmly on the side of what he saw as a new sexual ethics for the time period. Closer to the present, Monji proposes that while nudity 'can at times be entertaining', more often than not it 'detracts' from the show's actual topics. 'Then again', she allows, sometimes 'gratuitous nudity' is 'the whole point of the show'.

Leaving the notion of gratuitousness to the side for the present, we might do well to contrast the men and women in *Hangin' Out* – whose nudity apparently offended none of its West Hollywood audiences – with the 'warped', 'disturbing' and 'shocking' effects that the Royal Shakespeare Company's most recent production of Peter Weiss' *Marat/Sade* had on many of its audiences in Stratford. This 2011 revival of *Marat/Sade* (which had its English-language premiere at the RSC under the direction of Peter Brook in 1964) was helmed by New Brutalist playwright-director Anthony Neilson, and the new production contained a sequence with 'a gang rape and a character being tortured with a Taser'. While *BBC News* reported that 'at one preview show, 80 theatregoers left the show at the interval', a spokesperson for the RSC blithely reminded journalists and audiences that Weiss' play – now 50 years old – is an exploration of the philosophies of the Marquis de Sade, and that '[Sade's] philosophy is alive and well and streaming into our teenagers' phones in the form of pornography' (*BBC News* 2011).

Linking these two moments in twenty-first-century theatre is the concept of the pornographic. While scholars in film studies such as Linda Williams and Peter Lehman have been analysing pornography since the late 1980s, theatre studies has been slower to approach the pornographic – the obvious exception being Rebecca Schneider's *The Explicit Body in Performance* (1997). Yet there is no shortage of the pornographic on global performance scenes. Indeed, theatrical fare with sexually explicit content and so-called adult themes appears everywhere, from Cirque du Soleil's *Zumanity* in Las Vegas to Mark Ravenhill's 2001 play *Mother Clap's Molly House* in London to *Naked Boys Singing!* and its opening number 'Gratuitous Nudity' in New York City.

It has become commonplace to defend performances such as the RSC's *Marat/Sade* from the stigmatizing label 'pornography' through a citation of the performance's artistic merit. This chapter, however, asks what it might mean to say that a performance is pornographic but to insist simultaneously that pornographic theatre has a value of its own. How might we begin to rethink pornographic performances using the terms most often used to marginalize pornography (gratuitousness, utility, merit)? And how might such an analysis of the pornographic ask us to rethink the gratuitousness, utility or merit of the theatre itself? Subtending these questions is the always-present issue of the ethics of watching pornography, a question essentially linked to the ethics of spectatorship in the theatre.

This chapter approaches the pornographic in the theatre from three directions. First, we will attempt to translate into the language of the theatre analyses of pornography in film and video, retaining what we can from the work of these theorists when we look at theatrical performance. Second, in order to discuss how the pornographic theatre itself might function, we will turn to one of the most influential theatre theorists of the twentieth century, Antonin Artaud. Artaud's concept of the theatre of cruelty, focused as it is on the violent gesture, might seem an unlikely match with the pornographic, but it was Artaud, after all, who argued that 'the theatre is a passionate overflowing / a frightful transfer of forces / from body / to body' (Derrida 1978: 250).[1] He was, in the twentieth century, the theorist most intently focused on the possibilities of theatre to affect the human organism. Finally, this essay will examine *Cinderella*, a 2010 performance by the artist Ann Liv Young. The performance artist's work has been criticized as inept and without content, but I intend to locate Young's work as a direct heir to the Artaudian conception of cruelty. If Young's performance work is pornographic – and there seems little fear that such a descriptor is misplaced – its popularity and its effects on audiences not only testify to theatre's own pornographic nature, but also to what we might begin to call the value of the pornographic in the theatre, to what pornography itself might make possible.

The expense of spirit in a waste of shame

Walter Kendrick's seminal text on pornography, *The Secret Museum*, begins by investigating the history of the term itself. Though dictionaries routinely cite the word's origin as from the Greek *pornographos* (written material about prostitutes and prostitution), Kendrick finds that the concept of pornography originated in the mid-nineteenth century. He contrasts this historical concept with a more transhistorical one: obscenity. 'We have always had obscenity', Kendrick argues, 'at least as long as we have had a scene of public, reportable life that requires a zone of darkness to lend sense to it by contrast' (1987: 31). Pornography, on the other hand, has a genealogy, and rather than being simply an object at which one could turn one's gaze, pornography is better defined as *a way of looking* at an object.

Lynn Hunt's *The Invention of Pornography* finds, with Kendrick, that 'pornography did not constitute a wholly separate and distinct category of written or visual representation before the early nineteenth century' (1996: 9–10). In this way, Hunt joins Great Britain's famous Williams Report (1979) by defining this relatively new representational field as 'the explicit depiction of sexual organs and sexual practices with the aim of arousing sexual feelings', but she is careful to note that what is capable of being defined as pornographic is neither obvious nor has it remained constant over time (1996: 10).[2] In fact, far from being an easily definable taxonomic category, Hunt notes that 'pornography has always been defined in part by the efforts undertaken to regulate it' (1996: 11). As Kendrick argues, 'from the start, "pornography" named a battlefield, a place where no assertion could be made without at once summoning up its denial, where no one could distinguish value from danger because they were the same [...] "Pornography" names an argument, not a thing' (1987: 31).

The terms for arguments about pornography have often been set in the realm of the juridical, and it is understandable, therefore, that the descriptors used to define this or that object as pornographic have been fraught with the tactics either of defence or of damnation. In *Art and Pornography*, Morse Peckham argues – using the trial of Terry Southern and Mason Hoffenberg's *Candy* (1958) as his example – that 'if we wish to denigrate a work that includes sexual material, either a little or a lot, we call it "pornography"' (1969: 4). If we wish to defend a work, we might refer to that object, in Peckham's schema, as 'literature', since the designation 'literature' always maintains a value higher than any literary work on its own. Pornography and literary merit were the terms used either to damn or to praise *Candy*, and what Peckham's description of the trial makes clear is that art and pornography are often considered to be mutually exclusive categories.³ It is fundamental, however, to remember that in describing what pornography 'is' we remain firmly in the realm of discourse, not only within a way of looking at an object but also within a way of speaking about that object. If the ways in which we look at an object transform it into something that can be described as erotic, it is the words that we use in order to speak about an object that transport that something into the realm of the pornographic.

Morse Peckham, with his mocking nod towards the ability of so-called literariness to cleanse an object of its stigma as pornography, brings to light one of the measuring sticks frequently used to evaluate whether or not an object is pornographic. To speak of an object as literary or artistic is discursively to attach to that object a kind of worth: an object has literary *merit* or artistic *value*. But the phrase 'artistic value' is itself fraught with redundancy; an artistic object's value is the fact that it is artistic. It needs no other justification for its own value aside from its existence as art. This same tenuous logic holds for literary merit, as well: the 'merit' of a literary object is its 'literariness'. If these tautologies were long ago pointed out by cultural critics such as Pierre Bourdieu, the terms of value and merit have persisted in the evaluation of both art and literature.

An example in more recent history is the commotion over the incredibly popular novel *Fifty Shades of Grey* by E.L. James, which became, in 2012, the fastest-selling paperback of all time and has spawned two different stage spoofs, *50 Shades! The Musical* and *Spank! The Fifty Shades Parody*.⁴ This 'mummy porn sensation' has been roundly panned by every major Anglophone critic. The *Irish Daily Mail*'s Brenda Power, for example, calls *Fifty Shades* 'a shocking, shameful, offensive read. Not for the sex scenes – they're actually fairly tame – but for the incompetent, jaw-droppingly amateurish quality of the writing' (2012: 26). Power's disapproval echoes the majority of critical commentaries on this phenomenon. The novel is criticized for its lack of merit, and the evidence of the novel's lack of merit is its lack of 'literariness'. I do not wish to argue that *Fifty Shades of Grey* is good art, but rather that the terms with which it is evaluated are the same terms that are always used when discussing so-called literary pornography: an object deemed pornographic can be redeemable through a claim to literary merit or artistic value. Because *Fifty Shades*' author makes no such claims to artistic value, her book can easily be deemed 'mummy porn'.[5]

Questions of value or merit become slightly more confused when the medium under consideration is live performance. Debates over how much onstage sex or violence or nudity is necessary or gratuitous persist among playwrights, directors, critics, performers and audiences.[6] Gratuitousness and utility are at the heart of such a conversation in part because there is no tautology similar to 'literary merit' applicable to the medium of theatre. In other words, rarely does a critic judge a theatrical production to be worth more or less because of some ineffable 'theatricality' that might be comparable to the so-called literariness of a novel. Lynn Hunt's analysis makes clear that charges of gratuitousness – which claim that this or that presentation (of sex, nudity or violence) is unnecessary or lacks utility – work to regulate representation rather than to describe it. As Georges Bataille has said, 'Every time the meaning of a discussion depends on the fundamental value of the word *useful* [...] the debate is necessarily warped and the fundamental question is eluded' (1984: 62). Performances that are referred to as pornographic – and indeed pornography as a whole – exist within a paradox: 'pornographic' elements are accused of being gratuitous, of serving no function, while at the same time the very definition of pornography assumes a utility. To be pornographic can only ever also mean to *be used* as pornography, to serve, in fact, a *pornographic utility*. We might therefore modify Walter Kendrick, and with Georges Bataille say, that, like pornography itself, 'gratuitousness' names an argument, not a thing.

Artaud and the erotic

If, in the medium of literature, an accusation that a novel is pornographic can be combated through claims to literary merit, in the medium of the theatre there exists nothing akin to 'literariness'. Theatre artists have never been able to agree upon a definition of an ineffable or essential theatricality to which artists might have easy recourse in order to combat charges of gratuitousness. But what might such a theatricality resemble if we were to attempt to describe it? In other words, where might we look for terms by which we would be able to judge this or that theatrical production as useful or possessing value? This modernist question strikes at the heart of the work of Antonin Artaud and it is to his theories I wish now to turn in defence of the pornographic.

As early as 1922, Artaud was linking erotics and the theatre in his writing. Long before conceiving of his 'theatre of cruelty', he writes, in an essay about L'Atelier Theatre that:

> There are those who go to the theatre as they would go to a brothel. Furtive pleasure. For them the theatre is only momentary excitement. It is like the dumping-ground of their need to experience pleasure through all their physical and mental senses. The hypertrophy of the theatre of entertainment has created, alongside and above the classic idea of the theatre, a kind of game with easy rules which is now the norm in theatre and it masks the idea of theatre itself. So that one can say two theatres now exist: false theatre that is deceptive, easy, middle-class [...] But there is another sort of theatre that plays whenever it can, theatre conceived as the achievement of the purest human desires. (1971b: 130)

In this early essay, Artaud draws a distinction between the contemporary theatre's ability to give furtive pleasure, momentary excitement and deception to its audiences and the true theatre's attempt to achieve pure human desire.

As is commonly understood, Artaudian theory criticized the representational theatre in favour of what he would come to call an alchemical or metaphysical theatre (Artaud 2004b: 82–3). His metaphor for the difference between the two in this early piece is, notably, a sexual one: the brothel. He would later refer to the contemporary Parisian theatre using the metaphor of prostitution: 'the Comédie-Française', he declared in 1925, 'has been nothing but a sex house, and what sex! It has never had an inkling of an idea about theatre' (2004f: 17). But Artaud was against neither the physical nor the erotic *per se*. In fact, he considered his ideal theatre an 'achievement of the purest human desires'.

About his own Alfred Jarry Theatre he would say: 'audiences coming to our theatre know they are present at a real operation involving not only the mind but also the very senses and flesh [...;] they will not come out unscathed' (1971a: 17). In 1933 he wrote, further, that 'the principle [is not] to turn theatre again into art, an art of detachment, of *disinterest* but, on the contrary, to make the spectator *interested* through his organs, all his organs, deep down and whole' (2004c: 87). Rather than an eschewal of the physical or the erotic, then, Artaud actually turned his primary emphasis *towards* the physical, so that by the time of *Le théâtre et son double*, Artaud could write:

> To create art is to deprive a gesture of its reverberation in the organism, whereas this reverberation, if the gesture is made in the conditions and with the force required, incites the organism and, through it, the entire individuality, to take attitudes in harmony with the gesture.
> The theatre is the only place in the world, the last general means we still possess, of directly affecting the organism [...] and I propose to treat the spectators like the snakecharmer's subjects and conduct them *by means of their organisms* to an apprehension of the subtlest notions. (1958d: 81, Artaud's emphasis)

Far from avoiding physicality, Artaud proposes a theatre that affects his audiences in a profoundly material, even morphological way. If Artaud would have a metaphysical theatre, he would seek to achieve this metaphysics by means of the physical.

For Artaud, the boulevard theatre is anodyne, deadening; it is entertainment that tricks its audience, that 'repeats itself every night according to the same, ever the same old rituals' (1971a: 18). His idea of the popular theatre as useless – it 'fails to honour its *raison d'être*, its objective' (2004e: 88) – because it is repetitive and palliative is, perhaps, similar to Fredric Jameson's declaration in 1990 that 'the visual is *essentially* pornographic, which is to say that it has its end in rapt, mindless fascination' (1990: 1). What Jameson means here by pornographic is undoubtedly similar to what Artaud meant when he compared the Comédie-Française to a sex-house. For Jameson, the ultimate function of the visual is to dampen activity; for Artaud, the effect of the popular theatre – with its emphasis on the visual – is to do precisely the same.[7] And in order to critique this entertainment whose result is inactivity, both Jameson and Artaud adopt the metaphor of deviant, repetitive (and apparently unfulfilling) sexual activity.

I wish, however, to argue that Artaud's concept of the ideal theatre is not only distinctly physical but also a pornographic theatre, though certainly not in the monotonous, inactive sense in which Jameson uses the word. Artaud's ideal theatre is tied indissolubly to his concept of *cruelty*. For Artaud, cruelty is excessive, creative, and because he deems cruel any act that moves the human being out of its repetitive cycles, he finds cruelty to be life-giving. 'It is a mistake to give the word "cruelty" a meaning of merciless bloodshed and disinterested, gratuitous pursuit of suffering,' said Artaud in 1932 (1958a: 102). Instead, he finds cruelty 'in the flame of life, in love of life, life's irrational impulse. Erotic desire is cruel since it feeds on contingencies. Death is cruelty, resurrection is cruelty, transfiguration is cruelty' (2004d: 119–20). Cruelty is, in other words, anything that makes life *alive*. Artaud, therefore, pointedly locates cruelty in 'erotic desire' if not within sexual acts themselves.[8] This notion of cruelty is, like the popular notion of pornography, a paradoxical one. Cruelty, as Artaud defines it, is gratuitous, excessive, unnecessary, but he also sees acts of cruelty as serving a useful, creative – one is forced to say *productive* – function: flooding life with immediacy.

This Artaudian paradox is best explained by Georges Bataille, himself a studied reader of Artaud. Bataille notes, following Marcel Mauss, that 'so-called unproductive expenditures: luxury, mourning, war, cults, the construction of sumptuary monuments, games, spectacles, arts, perverse sexual activity (i.e., deflected from genital finality) – all these represent activities that, at least in primitive circumstances, have no end beyond themselves' (1984: 65). Pornography, too, might accurately be described as unproductive expenditure; indeed, as I argued earlier, pornography is often (tautologically) defined through an attribution of gratuitousness. Bataille argues, however, that 'unproductive expenditure' – loss without expectation of gain – possesses a 'positive property of loss' (1984: 70) or, as he phrases it elsewhere, 'creation by means of loss' (1984: 67). Bataille explains that gratuitous expenditures actively demonstrate an ability to bear the costs of loss, and in this way expenditure invests those who appear to be incurring a loss with 'nobility, honor, and rank in a hierarchy' (1984: 70). Bataille's category of unproductive or gratuitous expenditures includes the spectacular theatre proposed by Artaud as well as theatrical production in general. It is this creative ability that can make sense of Artaud's paradox. Artaudian cruelty is excessive, gratuitous, spectacular, and it is this very lack of utility that makes it productive, that invests the theatre of cruelty with the revitalizing power towards which Artaud aims.

The body of the viewer

I have so far been applying the term *pornographic* to Artaud's theatre because his theatre of cruelty shares with pornography the paradox of possessing both gratuitousness and utility; I want further to argue that Artaud's theatre is pornographic because of the way in which Artaud expects the viewer to be affected deeply on the level of the physical. Franklin Melendez, following Linda Williams,[9] asks us to 'regard pornography as a "body genre," a genre like the horror film and the melodrama, that strives to *move* the spectator – either to tears, terror, sexual arousal, or some mixture of all three. In effect, these genres subject their audience to these emotions, and pleasure consists in the viewer's passive reception, in being moved despite him- or herself' (2004: 415).

In Melendez's insightful analysis of pornographic videos, consumption of pornography entails two specific modes of viewing. The first is the type of viewing Artaud criticizes at the boulevard theatres, what Melendez calls 'a disembodied gazing predicated on consumption/visual possession' (2004: 404). Melendez stresses this gaze's structure: 'in which the world is displayed in/as objects. The aim of this gazing, in a psychoanalytic sense, is mastery, and in a material sense, it is possession [...] The absence of the body is key because it exempts the gazer from being looked back at (or being seen). Thus this visual mastery (active, even sadistic, in the psychoanalytic sense) may be read as predicated on its disembodiment' (2004: 422). It is this type of gaze that Peggy Phelan describes in *Unmarked*, when she warns us that 'the fetishized image of the female star serves as a deeply revealing screen for the construction of men's desire. The image of the woman displays not the subjectivity of the woman who is seen, but rather the constituent forces of desire of the man who wants to see her' (1993: 25–6). But Melendez argues that something different happens when we watch pornography, that, in fact, this disembodied gaze 'must be seen as operating in conjunction with corporealized vision', a mode of viewing that reminds the subject of his or her own corporeality (2004: 404). A viewer of pornography is a subject who believes him- or herself to possess the pornographic image, but that subject is also moved physically by that image. The distinction between subject/object is, in other words, blurred. This, Melendez says, 'accounts for the pleasure of pornography's physical effects on the body. In this way, experience comes to complement the facts of production, and pornographic viewership unfolds in the vacillation between two seemingly opposed poles, producing a visual pleasure that emerges as a function of both material production and physical consumption' (2004: 404). The pornographic, then, is produced between an object and the consumer of that object, and the consumer cannot be said truly to possess the object as he or she, on the contrary, comes to be manipulated by the object. The pornographic object affects the body of the subject on a physical level, changing that body, so that the subject him- or herself cannot be said to be distinct from the object of the pornographic gaze. Rather than considering pornography as a fixed (or even fluid) juridical designation, we might, then, think of pornography as a way of speaking about what happens when a member of an audience encounters a performance that, in its turn, *moves* him or her on the level of physiognomy.

Artaud does not contradict himself when he theorizes erotic desire as cruel and therefore productive at the same time that he uses the metaphor of the brothel in his description of the Comédie-Française. On the contrary, Artaud has disaggregated desire from sex in a way that (later) queer theorists would come to do.[10] Elizabeth Grosz, attempting to theorize a lesbian desire apart from Freudian psychology, offers, for example, that we might reformulate our notion of desire 'in terms of surfaces and surface effects' (1995: 175). 'Sexuality and desire', she argues, 'are not fantasies, wishes, hopes, aspirations (although no doubt these are some of its components), but are energies, excitations, impulses, actions, movements, practices, moments, pulses of feeling' (1995: 182). Arguing further – and echoing Artaud – Grosz posits that we might begin to 'see desire, sexuality as productive. Productive, though in no way reproductive, for this pleasure can serve no other purpose, have no other function, than its own augmentation and proliferation. A production, then, that makes, but that reproduces nothing' (1995: 183).

Grosz's theory moves away from sexuality considered only in terms of the genital or the hydraulic. She offers a vision of sexuality as non-reproductive, that is, *not useful*, as well as theorizing a sexuality of constant surface effects, pleasures that have no specific telos akin to the heterosexual male version of hydraulic – dare I say *kathartic* – sexuality of release, orgasm and ejaculation. As Artaud eschews the hydraulic, utilitarian sexuality of the brothel, Grosz's work imagines instead a productive desire of contact, surface effects and manifold pleasures, an erotics that, like Artaud's theatre, 'will become once more an authentic living operation' (Artaud 1958b: 111). For both Grosz and Artaud, this pleasure is gratuitous, non-reproductive, but both see this excess as fundamentally worthwhile to the very existence of the human organism: at once both wasteful and productive.

Productive pornography and Ann Liv Young's *Cinderella*

I wish to turn now to a concrete example of the pornographic in the theatre by examining the performance work of theatrical artist Ann Liv Young.[11] As Krista Miranda has reported in *Women and Performance*, Young's work 'pushes the boundaries of "propriety" to explore gender, sexuality and race via the female body [and] participates in the tradition of feminist explicit body work, a path paved by Karen Finley, Carolee Schneemann and Annie Sprinkle' (2011: 236).

Ann Liv Young's performances can easily be deemed pornographic. In *The Bagwell in Me* (2008), Young performed cunnilingus on her co-performer Isabel Lewis. The physical act of tongue coming into contact with vulva was projected in real time onto a screen so that the audience could watch – in Miranda's helpful phrase – 'oral sex as choreography'.[12] Later in *Bagwell*, Young vaginally penetrated Lewis with a strap-on, performing an explicit lesbian sex act on stage. Sexual activity, nudity, and explicit performance are frequent aspects of Young's artistic work. In *Cinderella* (2010), the artist, performing as a character she created named Sherry, urinates on stage and then announces she will defecate, only to find herself unable to 'perform'. And at a now-notorious event at the performance space P.S.1 in Long Island City, Young's character Sherry squatted to urinate in a large bowl as a part of the performance before removing her dress and masturbating for the audience while Mariah Carey's 'All I Want for Christmas Is You' blared in the background. 'Did you come?' one audience member asked. 'I did not,' Sherry answered (Young 2010).

To take another point of view, *The Bagwell in Me* was described by Andy Horwitz (2008) as 'spectacularly lazy and uninspired, [...] simplistic, unimaginative, obvious, completely lacking in insight, boring and, to be honest, not transgressive or shocking in the least'. Other critics have been similarly blasé about Young's work: the *New York Times'* Brian Seibert referred to *Sleeping Beauty Part I* (2012) as possessing an 'effrontery of dullness', noting that the artist performed with 'the professionalism of a reality show has-been making an appearance at a mall' (2012: C7). And performance artist Penny Arcade has been quoted in the *New York Daily News* as saying that Young's performances have neither content nor technique and that Young is a 'fake radical' (Griffith 2011). Audiences, too, have occasionally found Young's work unappealing, distasteful or boring – indeed, sometimes all of the above. Every review or personal account of an Ann Liv Young performance describes people walking out of the show; often this person is the reviewer himself.[13]

In short, hostile critics' complaints about Young's work have frequently adopted a condescending but decidedly unperturbed tone. It isn't that they dislike the work because it is 'pornographic'. They are averse to the work because it is somehow poorly done or inept or because it is derivative of – it couldn't possibly be a homage to – the true masters of this style of performance: Schneemann, Finley et al. Such criticism falls directly in line with ways in which the word 'pornography' has been mobilized in order alternately to champion or to censure. Young's work is defensible if the critic wishes to say it has 'merit' but gratuitous, lacking in technique, simply *pornographic* if he does not. I have been arguing, however, that pornography might be seen as productive, that we might use it as a critical perspective, as a way to speak about what happens when an audience member encounters a performance that affects him or her on a physiological level. Young's work is, from this point of view, undoubtedly pornographic, and productively so.

Cinderella begins with Young, sitting in a traditional helpless feminine pose, in the centre of a silver, glitter-covered paper heart surrounded by large knives. Orchestral fairytale-style music is followed by a voice-over announcing herself as a 'Disneyland storyteller', recounting 'the famous story of Cinderella'.[14] Young begins a monologue from Cinderella's point of view. She speaks into a microphone but can barely be heard. As the monologue finishes, Young begins singing along to a pre-recorded version of Air Supply's 1983 hit 'Making Love out of Nothing at All'. She sings off-key but at full volume, intoning every vapid lyric with vehemence. When the song ends, Young, as Sherry, finally rises from her position on the floor and asks the audience for its thoughts on the topic of Cinderella. The baffled audience understandably has nothing to say.

A second Cinderella monologue follows. This, too, is performed on the floor, at an impossibly low volume, and Young again reads directly from a piece of paper. The next song is a cover of Britney Spears' 1999 single '... Baby One More Time', after which Sherry, again, asks the audience if it is following along. The performance has begun to fail. The audience has no questions. 'I'm not even sure what to talk about with these people,' she mutters. 'Y'all don't have anything to say so far? Any questions about the character? About the motive? ... Nobody?' More difficult and uncomfortable conversation follows, with Sherry prodding her audience in a manner akin to a high-school teacher in a room full of students who haven't done the day's reading. During Sherry's next pop song, a rendition of the rapper T.I.'s 'Whatever You Like', the awkwardness begins to make more sense. A few seconds into the song, Sherry gestures to her assistant to stop the music. She explains to the audience that 'right now in the show, I'm pretending to be Cinderella's fairy godmother. OK? So I'm gon' grant her these wishes that we all have. OK?' The audience is restless. Some complain about being spoon-fed obvious information. She performs the song anyway, gesturing sexually and moving through the audience as though she were a bikinied dancer in a music video.

After the song, Sherry continues to fail. She keeps the audience waiting while she drinks a large quantity of water; she reads another nearly inaudible Cinderella monologue; she performs Aerosmith's 'Cryin", again at full volume. And this time when Sherry asks the audience for feedback people complain. The music is too loud. Not enough is happening. People walk out. Sherry banters with the audience – alternately sweet Southern charm and angry attack-dog. And then, after one last Cinderella monologue, Sherry places a bowl on the ground, squats, and begins to urinate. She adds soap to the urine, washes her wig with the soapy urine, and then reaches into a second bowl, this one containing faeces. Turning her back to the audience, Sherry bends over and wipes the faecal matter on her naked buttocks, taking time to rub it into every crevice. The act goes on just slightly too long. It is difficult not to feel uncomfortable. 'Really great. That was really fabulous,' Young tells the audience, but she reveals that this, too, has been a failure: 'I tried to poop in front of y'all tonight', she says, 'but I couldn't do it, because I did not have enough to eat, so I pooped prior to the show.' *Cinderella* appears to devolve further after this: Sherry sells bits of faeces, glitter, her Disney watch, her panties. The audience can buy pieces of the show to take home with them as souvenirs. Some people make purchases. Then, just like that, the show is over and Young exits the performance space.

When *New York Times* dance critic Alastair Macauley referred to *Cinderella*'s 'startling ineptitude' he got it mostly right (2010: C1). Macauley observes her inaudible monologues; he notes Sherry's arrogant expectation that everyone will know who she is. He found her singing 'off-pitch and her writing inadequate'. And he was irritated by having to wait ten minutes for Sherry to defecate on stage. As I've described the performance above, Macauley and I saw much the same thing in *Cinderella*, though the critic seems to believe that it is Young herself who is inept and not the character she is playing. Jeremy Barker reported a similar experience in the zine *Bellyflop*, finding Sherry's inability to defecate 'sweet in a very odd way' after she 'took advice from the audience' for half an hour and then behaved as though 'she'd let everyone down'. *Cinderella*, however, had been failing from the start, and Sherry's inability to produce the promised faeces on cue was not merely one moment of failure but, rather, a kind of ultimate false start in a performance that was, from the beginning, about expectations that would not ever be met.

Failure, as more perceptive critics have noticed, is a key component of what Young's current work, including *Cinderella*, explores. In *TDR* 56,

Anna Watkins Fisher finds that critical attention to Young's ineptitude completely misses the point: she focuses instead on Ann Liv Young's own 'shrewdness as an artist who cannot possibly fail because failing is exactly what she sets out to do in the first place'. In Fisher's reading, Young is a performer 'for whom failure is the condition of possibility for creating something unpredictable and surreal' (2012: 61). Fisher's point of view appears to be catching on. In 2011, when *New York Times* contributor Claudia La Rocco reviewed Young's piece *Mermaid Solo* and asked her readers 'Is there any performer doing more interesting work with the art of failure right now?' the answer was obvious.

Discussion of *Cinderella*, then, as well as of Young's other recent performances, has circulated around the concepts of both failure and pornography. Young's *Cinderella* is undoubtedly pornographic: in addition to her foul-mouthed character Sherry, the artist has included nudity, masturbation, defecation and urination in the performance. The audience, in fact, comes expecting these things; we arrive *in anticipation of* pornography. It is precisely this disappointed anticipation that Macauley articulates when he complains that Young 'failed to defecate on cue, despite having given an advance interview advertising her ability to do so' (2010: C1). The artist is not pornographic enough: she has advertised access to her explicit body but has failed to provide it. Young's failure to give the audience the (pornographic) show it appears to want – a polished, clean, payoff – echoes a question asked by scholar/artist Tim Etchells in *Certain Fragments* when he describes work that 'turn[s] on its audience', that stares at the audience and asks it 'What was it that you wanted to see?' 'What did you demand?' 'What was it that you wished for when you came inside tonight?' (1999: 64). Young's work tries to answer that question. The audience literally asks for more, even tries to help her finish.

(Not) finishing

Young's juxtaposition of objects in *Cinderella* is complex. Beside the explicitly pornographic content of *Cinderella*, Young has placed silver glitter, a Disney princess, a famous fairy tale, the consumerist kitsch of souvenir sales and an absurd collection of USAmerican pop music – T.I., Britney Spears and Air Supply. This assortment of popular entertainments, most of which are originally aimed at young female consumers, in turn creates a set of questions about their identity with one another. And Young's juxtaposition of these forms necessarily colours them all with the taint of the pornographic. *Cinderella* accuses Disney's princesses of pornography, of turning a sexualized gaze towards the lives and bodies of young girls. The disparate popular music Young has chosen, with lyrics such as 'show me / how you want it to be' and 'late night sex, so wet and so tight', is even more obviously pornographic. If Ann Liv Young sells her faeces, her wristwatch and her pantyhose, the artist makes clear that the entertainments her performance cites are busy selling sex. As Artaud complained about the work of the Comédie-Française, we might now say of Young's motley crew of pop musicians: 'nothing but a sex house, and what sex!'

In this way, Young's work makes evident the pornographic content of work by people like Britney Spears, T.I. and Walt Disney. *Cinderella* is aimed squarely at producers of sexualized images of women. As Fisher has insightfully argued, Young's work 'critiques the limited spectrum of representational models available to young women who do not accept the paucity of positions on offer by the mass media and by feminism'; instead, she sees Young as one of a group of artists utilizing irony, 'who instead undertake to contradict themselves through performance' (2012: 71). In short, Young understands pornography in the way that I am arguing Artaud's work both criticizes and utilizes the pornographic. *Cinderella* understands popular music as pornographic and it *simultaneously performs the pornographic*, with Sherry as the pornographic object manipulating the viewer/consumer.

I have argued that we might conceive of pornography as a way of naming what happens when a viewer encounters a performance that affects him or her on a physiological level. Young's work is unquestionably having this effect. Audiences and critics have reported deep anger, frustration and horror, as well as embarrassed fascination and lingering unsettlement. Young's work is, in an Artaudian sense, unremittingly cruel. And as I argued above, for Artaud cruelty is, paradoxically, gratuitous at the same time as it is productive. Audiences at *Cinderella* felt as though they were wasting time, as though what they were watching was unnecessary, obvious, excessive, but this is precisely the work that Young was doing with *Cinderella*. This gratuitousness, this pornography, produces something else. What exactly it is that Young's performances produce is both impossible to categorize and beside the point, but by denying her audiences the release of the traditional theatre, the release of pornographic utility, Young draws attention to the pornography that is always already present in the traditional theatre and uses her own pornographic performance to produce something that has the possibility of having a profound effect on the physical body of the spectator.

Finally, the major strand of this chapter has been to interrogate the purpose of pornography in the theatre and place the contemporary viewer within it. Running beside this, however, has also been the question of the theatre's own purpose. Artaud's theory calls explicitly for a type of performance that cannot be watched passively, a theatre that does not produce only the rapt, mindless fascination that Fredric Jameson deplored. He called for a theatre that instead remakes the body of each audience member. As artists and those who write about art continue to work to remake the theatre, to re-envision the possibilities of theatrical performance, Artaud's call still resounds deeply.

It is my argument that accusations of pornography always demand that the theatre define itself *against* the pornographic in order to differentiate and legitimate itself. I have claimed, to the contrary, that pornographic performance has the ability to do what Artaud wanted his true theatre to do in the early part of the twentieth century, to physically affect an audience at the level of the organism. While the pornographic theatre understands its own explicitly voyeuristic aim, shamelessly refusing to hide its own pornographic utility, the legitimate theatre, as Brecht noted in 1926, cannot always say what is wanted of it (1964: 7). The traditional theatre ideologically covers over its own pornographic aims, the *katharsis* of the tragedy, the payoff of an evening's entertainment, the tidy wrap-up of the bourgeois Realist problem play. The work of Ann Liv Young would seem to argue that the most effective way for the theatre to defend itself from Artaud's accusation that it is nothing more than a brothel, offering only momentary excitement, is, paradoxically, to move ever closer towards the pornographic.

Notes

1. US American spellings from this and other English translations of Artaud have been silently altered in this essay.
2. The Williams Report is more properly known as the *Report of the Committee on Obscenity and Film Censorship*. For more on the Williams Report see Ellis (2006: 31–4).
3. Peckham's own opinion is exactly the opposite of this point of view; he argues that art and pornography are independent categories for the remainder of his book.
4. My gratitude to Meghan Hawkins Digneit for drawing my attention to *Spank!* and for meticulously copy-editing this essay.
5. The phrase *mummy porn* is explicitly misogynist, intended to denigrate this particular form of pornography as 'not even good porn' because it is directed towards heterosexual female consumers. Pornography, as Lynn Hunt has

pointed out, has always been a boys' club, and the idea that women might have their own fantasy lives demands, at the very least, an insulting name with which to describe it. See Hunt (1996: 44). On women writing pornography for women, see Brown (2012).
6. See Lee (2006: 36). Lee's use of the word *gratuitous* in her review of the stage version of *Midnight Cowboy* sparked a response from the playwright; see Fountain (2006: 21).
7. Artaud was increasingly impatient with the visual even in his early writings. 'The strictly showy side of the show must be abolished', he said in 1924. His idea was that 'people would come not so much to see as to participate. The audience must have the feeling that they can, without any special skill, do what the actors are doing' (Artaud 2004a: 13).
8. He says precisely this later in 1932: 'I have therefore said "cruelty" as I might have said "life" or "necessity," because I want to indicate especially that for me the theatre is an act and perpetual emanation, that there is nothing congealed about it, that I turn it into a true act, hence living, hence magical' (Artaud 1958c: 114).
9. See Williams (1991) for the formulation of this concept.
10. I am consciously naming Artaud as a queer theorist here. To my mind, the appellation works for him, as well as for many of his co-conspirators and contemporaries in the Parisian avant-garde – I am thinking of Jarry, Péladan, Eluard, Tzara, Picabia, Cravan, Duchamp and the Baroness Elsa von Freytag-Loringhoven, to name only a few.
11. My deep gratitude to George McConnell for turning my attention to Ann Liv Young, as well as for helping me think through her work and finding language to describe some of her projects.
12. Miranda (2011: 238). In a talk given at the annual meeting of the American Society for Theatre Research in 2010, Miranda pointed out that if the video used in *Bagwell* is video of *actual* penetration, the very presence of the medium calls into question rather than proves the veracity of the explicit sex act. It ought to be obvious, in other words, that the video might easily have been pre-recorded.
13. Unsurprisingly, these critics are often male.
14. This performance is available on DVD via Young's website.

Bibliography

Artaud, Antonin (1958a) 'Letter to Jean Paulhan, 13 September 1932', in Mary Caroline Richards (ed.), *The Theatre and Its Double* (New York: Grove).
Artaud, Antonin (1958b) 'Letter to Jean Paulhan, 28 September 1932', in Mary Caroline Richards (ed.), *The Theatre and Its Double* (New York: Grove).
Artaud, Antonin (1958c) 'Letter to Jean Paulhan, 9 November 1932', in Mary Caroline Richards (ed.), *The Theatre and Its Double* (New York: Grove).
Artaud, Antonin (1958d) 'No more masterpieces', in Mary Caroline Richards (ed.), *The Theatre and Its Double* (New York: Grove). Originally published 1938.
Artaud, Antonin (1971a) 'The Alfred Jarry Theatre', in Victor Corti (ed.), *Collected Works II* (London: Calder & Boyers). Originally published 1926.
Artaud, Antonin (1971b) 'L'Atelier theatre', in Victor Corti (ed.), *Collected Works II* (London: Calder & Boyers). Originally published 1922.

Artaud, Antonin (2004a) 'The evolution of set design', in Claude Schumacher and Brian Singleton (eds), *Artaud on Theatre* (Chicago: Ivan R. Dee). Originally published 1924.
Artaud, Antonin (2004b) 'Letter to Jean Paulhan, 29 August 1932', in Claude Schumacher and Brian Singleton (eds), *Artaud on Theatre* (Chicago: Ivan R. Dee).
Artaud, Antonin (2004c) 'To a friend, 4 March 1933', in Claude Schumacher and Brian Singleton (eds), *Artaud on Theatre* (Chicago: Ivan R. Dee).
Artaud, Antonin (2004d) 'To M. Roland de Renéville, 16 November 1932', in Claude Schumacher and Brian Singleton (eds), *Artaud on Theatre* (Chicago: Ivan R. Dee).
Artaud, Antonin (2004e) 'To Natalie Clifford Barney, 12 August 1933', in Claude Schumacher and Brian Singleton (eds), *Artaud on Theatre* (Chicago: Ivan R. Dee).
Artaud, Antonin (2004f) 'To the director of the Comédie-Française, 21 February 1925', in Claude Schumacher and Brian Singleton (eds), *Artaud on Theatre* (Chicago: Ivan R. Dee).
Barker, Jeremy (2010) Review: *Cinderella, Bellyflop Magazine*, 5 September, http://bellyflopmag.com/reviews/ann-liv-young-cinderella (accessed 15 November 2013).
Bataille, Georges (1984) 'The notion of expenditure', *Raritan*, 3:3, 62–79. Originally published 1933.
BBC News (2011) 'Marat/Sade: audiences walk out of "perverse" RSC show', *BBC News*, 24 October, www.bbc.co.uk/news/entertainment-arts-15428711 (accessed 25 October 2011).
Brecht, Bertolt (1964) 'Emphasis on sport', in John Willett (ed.), *Brecht on Theatre: The Development of an Aesthetic* (New York: Hill and Wang). Originally published 1926.
Brown, Craig (2012) 'Are middle aged mums really suddenly being seduced?', *Daily Mail (London)*, 30 June.
Derrida, Jacques (1978) *Writing and Difference* (University of Chicago Press). Originally published 1967.
Ellis, John (2006) 'On pornography', in Peter Lehman (ed.), *Pornography: Film and Culture* (New Brunswick, NJ: Rutgers University Press), 31–4.
Esslin, Martin (1968) 'Nudity: barely the beginning?', *New York Times*, 15 December.
Etchells, Tim (1999) *Certain Fragments: Contemporary Performance and Forced Entertainment* (New York: Routledge).
Fisher, Anna Watkins (2012) 'Like a girl's name: the adolescent drag of Amber Hawk Swanson, Kate Gilmore, and Ann Liv Young', *TDR*, 56:1, 48–76.
Fountain, Tim (2006) 'Mary Whitehouse is alive and well', *Guardian*, 24 August.
Griffith, Carson (2011) 'Hipster warfare breaks out during performanc artist Ann Liv Young's show at Delancey Lounge', *New York Daily News*, 12 January.
Grosz, Elizabeth (1995) *Space, Time, and Perversion: Essays on the Politics of Bodies* (New York: Routledge).
Horwitz, Andy (2008) 'Bill T. Jones and other dance-y discontents', *Culturebot*, 4 October. www.culturebot.org/2008/10/1742/bill-t-jones-and-other-dance-y-discontents (accessed 14 November 2013).
Hunt, Lynn (1996) *The Invention of Pornography: Obscenity and the Origins of Modernity, 1500–1800* (New York: Zone Books).

Jameson, Fredric (1990) *Signatures of the Visible* (London: Routledge).
Kendrick, Walter (1987) *The Secret Museum: Pornography in Modern Culture* (New York: Viking).
La Rocco, Claudia (2011) 'Body shop', *Artforum*, 14 January, http://artforum.com/diary/id=27347 (accessed 16 November 2013).
Lee, Veronica (2006) 'Dustin off a classic: avoight at all costs ...', *Evening Standard (London)*, 8 August.
Macauley, Alastair (2010) 'This time the trouble isn't wicked stepsisters', *New York Times*, 6 September.
Melendez, Franklin (2004) 'Video pornography, visual pleasure, and the return of the sublime', in Linda Williams (ed.), *Porn Studies* (Durham, NC: Duke University Press), 401–27.
Miranda, Krista (2011) 'Staring at the (clitoral) sun: arousing abjection in Ann Liv Young's *The Bagwell in Me*', *Women and Performance*, 21:2, 235–48.
Monji, Jana (2009) 'Things you're more likely to see on stage: full frontal nudity', *Examiner*, 25 March, www.examiner.com/theater-reviews-in-los-angeles/things-you-re-more-likely-to-see-on-stage-full-frontal-nudity (accessed 5 March 2012).
Peckham, Morse (1969) *Art and Pornography: An Experiment in Explanation* (New York: Basic Books).
Phelan, Peggy (1993) *Unmarked: The Politics of Performance* (New York: Routledge).
Power, Brenda (2012) 'Fifty shades of tosh', *Irish Daily Mail*, 30 June.
Seibert, Brian (2012) 'A fairy tale princess who takes bathroom breaks', *New York Times*, 14 January.
Williams, Linda (1991) 'Film bodies: gender, genre, and excess', *Film Quarterly*, 44:4, 2–13.
Young, Ann Liv (2010) *Sherry vs PS 1*, DVD.

Part V
Voyeurism and Naked Bodies

9
'Music for the Eyes' in *Hair*: Tracing the History of the Naked Singing Body on Stage

Tim Stephenson

Hair is *the* musical that has come to symbolize the turbulent interaction of politics, commercial entertainment, sexual liberation and protest of the late 1960s. It rapidly became 'a mood picture of a generation – a generation dominated by drugs, sex, and the two wars, the one about color and the one about Vietnam' (Barnes 1967). As a pre-Lloyd Webber West End looked enviously across the Atlantic for its next musical hit, who would have thought that the happy coincidence of the collapse of theatre censorship and the arrival of the carefully manufactured Broadway success of Rado and Ragni's 'freaked-out mish-mash of psychedelic-babble' (Miller 2001: 66) would facilitate *Hair*'s explosion onto the musical scene? Although *Hair*'s off-Broadway gestation was initially panned by the critics, its popularity continued to grow. By the start of the 1970s it was established on Broadway and in the West End, and had played in 18 other countries worldwide. *Hair* had undeniably become 'the *zeitgeist* of the times' (Horn 1991: xiii), generating a proliferation of contemporary opinion which provides the material for the examination of audience and performers' reactions in both the US and the UK. But how was the naked singing body perceived on stage once freed from the socialization, ornament, disguise or concealment of costume, and what 'signalling function' (Pavis 1998: 81) does it relay to the viewer?

Does *Hair* really merit its pivotal position as one of Broadway's 'groundbreaking musicals' (Miller 2001: 66) or is it more, as Horn satirizes, 'inherently insignificant' (1991: xiii)? If it was such a genre-breaking experience, can it still justify this label? And why is it still primarily remembered for its infamous nude scene? How has a simple tableau described at the time as 'leav[ing] most playgoers open-mouthed with yawns' (Time Magazine 1968) have achieved such notoriety? Was the theatrical representation of a 'Human Be-in' really so shocking, or does the apparent obsession with this brief moment of theatrical disrobing reveal more about society's voyeuristic attitude to staged nudity? *Hair* might have opened the door for the overt inclusion of sexual themes and naked bodies in musical theatre, but would anyone be brave enough to walk through? This chapter will therefore examine the historical precedents that established patriarchal dominance and the objectification of women at the centre of the historical canon of the musical. It will explore the subversion and reinforcement of these ideals in the musical *Hair*, see how we view those objectified bodies on stage and start to identify the resultant complexity of the osmosis of male hegemonies and gender representations within the modern musical. It will also trace the history of the naked singing body in musical theatre as a sexualized object of desire.

Pavis explains the fundamental difference and the inevitable sexualization of the performative nude: '[u]nlike nudity in painting [...] in theatre there is really a flesh-and-blood person that the spectator is seeing. Hence its [sic] "inevitable" eroticism, but also discomfort, as the pleasure is attenuated by the fear of being caught in the act of voyeurism' (Pavis 1998: 238). It is the way the naked performer renegotiates the dynamic with the audience that causes this discomfort, and with a publicity campaign extolling the nude scene *Hair* clearly attracted audiences fully aware of their own voyeuristic intentions. Nevertheless, witnessing the scene itself would have made them aware of both their individual and their collective voyeurism. According to Rodosthenous, this creates, 'a psychological awakening for the viewers, as they become increasingly self-aware that they are committing the culturally taboo act of "watching" another body within the legalized framework of the theatrical act' (2012: 63). Thus, the 'innocent and endearing tableau' (Brien 1968), although not conceived as a sexualized act, would have been hard to perceive in any other way. This is partly because of the calculated process of the teaser campaign that preceded it, but more because of the interpretation of the process of disrobing which is hard for most spectators to perceive in any other way. 'There is no motive for being at such performances other than to indulge in a fascination with the sexuality that clothing conceals' (Danesi 2004: 185). This reminds us that 'a naked body on stage reintroduces the spectator's gaze and private body as he or she is wrested from the fiction into the reality of exhibition and desire' (Pavis 1998: 238).

Voyeurism, validation and objectification in the early musical

The late Victorian origins of the musical reinforced the objectification of women from the heterosexual male perspective. The British music hall and the American vaudeville traditions featured numerous female performers; dancers, circus performers and other novelty acts which gave the opportunity for the legitimized display of the female body in costumes that breached the normal etiquettes of the time. 'Female performers were commodified as the wearers of revealing costumes, but, it was the revealed parts, not the costumes themselves that were the real spectacle' (Davis 1989: 322).

Some female singers became big stars: non-challenging idealized theatrical representations of emancipation within an era where female rights were minimal. Narrative-based theatrical forms reinforced this patriarchy. For example, the light-hearted satire of Gilbert and Sullivan's operettas are full of air-headed 'maidens' and 'wards' destined to swoon, instantly fall in love and collapse helplessly at the feet of older, heroic or titled men. *Patience*, Phyllis in *Iolanthe*, Rose Maybud in *Ruddigore* and Mabel in *Pirates of Penzance* all exhibit such stereotypical traits, and little needs to be said for the symbolism of the names Peep-Bo and Yum-Yum, two of the 'three little maids from school' in *The Mikado*.

By the 'roaring' twenties musical theatre in America was an established form of commercial entertainment built around star actors and actresses. Most Broadway shows were structured as musical revues which popularized new songs and gave a platform for the public to see the stars they read about in the fledgling celebrity media. At the heart of this was a high-class production line of revues created and controlled for almost 25 years by Florenz Ziegfeld. Situated in the heart of Broadway, the Ziegfeld Follies engaged composers and lyricists like Irving Berlin, Oscar Hammerstein and Jerome Kern during the pre-war era. However, its origins lay in Europe in the Folies Bergère, and central to both shows were alluring female stars (like Josephine Baker and Louise Brooks), dancing girls, suggestive costumes and burlesque-inspired routines. '*Ziegfeld*'s displays of feminine beauty were bold and daring and became more bold with each edition. He went from the suggestive to the explicit over time however never quite crossing the line to full nudity' (Parlor Songs 2004).

Ziegfeld described himself as the 'glorifier of the American girl' (Associated Press 1932) and his talent-spotting prowess along with his numerous dalliances with his showgirls became legendary. 'He auditioned girls for his shows by first watching them walk in high heels. "Before I see their faces, I want to see how they walk. There's more sex in a walk than in a face or even in a figure"' (Padgett 2013). He made stars of some of the female leads, with Barbara Stanwyck, Rose Louise Hovick (Gypsy Rose Lee), Lana Turner, Lillian Roth, Paulette Goddard, Ruby Keeler and Vivienne Segal all starting their careers as 'Follies girls' and subsequently gaining fame or notoriety on the stage or silver screen. In so doing he established a glamorized mythology around the showgirl, even going on to produce the 1929 film *Glorifying the American Girl* for Paramount where the 'static tableaux of chorus girls [are] "glorified" by being clothed in feathers and lamé, standing around in the middles of huge sets and doing little or nothing while turntables revolve them and essentially do their dancing for them' (Conlan 2011).

The success of Ziegfeld's formulaic musical revues was fuelled by the sexual freedoms of the jazz era, and they spawned numerous copycat revues. The most famous of these were George White's Scandals which, along with Ziegfeld, established the musical at the epicentre of the early Broadway mediatization of popular culture. They also started the flow of shows around the country, across the Atlantic, onto radio and into Hollywood. These musicals reinforced the stereotype of sexualized, objectified women: pretty, young, slim, white and conforming to male-generated notions of idealized beauty.[1] Davis notes, 'theatre-making and performance are gendered processes, full of significations that have meaning for men and that reinforce male cultural hegemony' (1989: 321), and the early musical was central to the reinforcement of this patriarchy.

Hollywood was quick to capitalize on the formula with early film musicals transferring the patriarchal stage etiquettes to the silver screen with plots that provided vacuous rationales for the exposure of the female body through the development of narratives confirming the subjugation of women. The 1920s saw the start of the symbiotic flow of musicals from the Broadway stage to film which continues to the present day. Whilst some stage musicals were more or less directly translated onto film, such as *Desert Song* (1929), *Showboat* (1929) and *Anything Goes* (1936), others capitalized on the voyeuristic Broadway reputation for dancing girls, suggestive routines and minimal costumes with new spectacular dance routines. The male audience's voyeuristic tendencies were further titillated through a plethora of backstage musicals. Thus, films such as the *Fox Movietone Follies* (1929), *Broadway Scandals* (1929), *George White's Scandals* (1935) and even the dubiously myopic biopic *The Great Ziegfeld* (1936) confirmed Hollywood's, and by implication Broadway's, hegemonic masculinity for middle America and middle England.

Championing these attitudes was the six-times-married Busby Berkeley, a Broadway dance director with over 20 shows to his credit, who in 1930 was persuaded to forge a career as a choreographer and film director whose lavish dance routines 'glorified', or objectified, women. He achieved this by choreographing 'surreal musical sequences – interludes of imaginative and often highly subversive sexual fantasies' (DeFreitas 2006). His kaleidoscopic patterning within these sequences depended on the exposure of as much female flesh as possible, and the formula was repeated over and over again, with his trademark production numbers acting as 'a showcase of the female anatomy that were both lyrical and lewd' (Vieira 1999: 177). His dancers were usually dressed in see-through diaphanous dresses or bikinis intended to leave little to the imagination, whilst remaining just on the right side of the regional censors.[2]

Many of the dancers Berkeley persuaded to perform in Hollywood had worked with him before as 'Ziegfeld Girls' on the Broadway stage, although by the time they performed on the West Coast they had transformed into 'Goldwyn Girls'. Perhaps more than any other film he directed, *Roman Scandals* (1933) epitomizes the attitude towards the acquiescent objectified female performer prevalent at the time. In this film, slave girls in bikinis are forced to dance for the goggle-eyed gratification of the overtly voyeuristic and lecherous male slave owners. The central 'sales' platform is surrounded by fully nude and manacled female slaves whose modesty is only protected by the profusion of their long blonde wigs.

In a later scene, Eddy Cantor, the dreaming male lead,[3] wanders through a harem of partially naked bathing women singing, 'Keep young and beautiful'. The song's lyrics parallel the cinematographic objectification entreating women to engage in various forms of beautification to gratify and ensnare men, and stave off the threat of rejection. 'Take care of all those charms, And you'll always be in someone's arms' (Warren and Dubin 1933). The following year, Berkeley directed the Warner Brothers film *Dames*, which facilitated more gratuitous objectification and partial nudity. He even outlined his hegemonic philosophy in the eponymous title song, 'As I was telling all those gentlemen a while ago, What do we go for? To see a show for? Tell the truth we go to see you beautiful dames' (Warren and Dubin 1934). This was a common trend in musicals of the time.

At the same time, across the Atlantic, the steady influx of American shows into the West End supplemented the home-grown musical talent led by the plays and musical revues of Noël Coward. It was clear that his sage comedic advice, 'Don't put your daughter on the stage, Mrs Worthington',[4] was not being heeded. The 'Gaiety Girls' of the Edwardian era had given way to more provocatively dressed troupes of synchronized female dancers, like the 'Tiller Girls' at the London Palladium and 'Cochrane's Young Ladies' at the London Pavilion. Meanwhile, a none-too-successful theatre in the heart of Soho performing a loss-inducing vaudeville-esque diet of comedy, popular songs and novelty acts was about to turn its fortunes around through the overt objectification of naked women. That theatre was the Windmill.

The tableau vivant, the staging of a 'living picture' depicting scenes from literature, art, history or everyday life, was an established and respectable form of both private and public entertainment throughout the Victorian era.[5] Music hall and variety had adopted the form for more salacious purposes, but it was their inclusion in Ziegfeld's revues which reinforced idealized representations of feminine beauty through displays of scantily clad women in artistically inspired poses. Despite the careful arrangements of Ziegfeld's resident stage designer Ben Ali Haggin,[6] who choreographed the stage shows from 1917 to 1925, the purported justification for such displays as being inspired by the nude in fine art remains dubious at best. This was the era of the nude bodystocking or less, with choruses of dancing girls introducing the eroticized central tableaux in all of the Broadway Follies extravaganzas, the Revues and the Midnight Frolics which dominated Ziegfeld's output. The format was also transcribed directly onto film.

In the 1929 film *Ziegfeld Midnight Frolic* there is a central Tableau of Jewels. Here, three rotating tiers of chiffon-draped women act as a prelude to the appearance of a giant clam shell which disgorges a dancing girl in micro-shorts and nipple pasties. Whilst the allusion to Botticelli's *Birth of Venus* may have been the initial inspiration, I rather doubt the subsequent dance routine had much to do with Renaissance art. By the time a similar Botticelli-inspired tableau graced the stage at the Windmill Theatre some six years later in Revudeville, the women were completely naked and full-frontal nudity had arrived on the London stage.

At that time all forms of stage performance in Britain were controlled by the Lord Chamberlain in his role as theatrical censor. He had the right to refuse a licence to material deemed offensive to public decency and morality, but in a self-censoring theatrical world that had been regulated for more than two hundred years, no one seemed to question who defined what was 'decent' or whose 'morals' were being applied. His role not only 'degraded the theatre but represented audiences as too witless to protect themselves' (Shellard and Nicholson 2004: 3). But the system was not there to protect audiences, or even the major offices of state, it was a tool to reinforce male hegemony. It confirmed the role of the virtuous, obedient wife, objectified and castigated the stereotype of the fallen woman, abhorred the concept of extramarital sex and eradicated any references to non-heterosexual relationships.

Historically, the perceived direct equation between sexual desire, nudity and promiscuity effectively removed all nudity and partial nudity from the theatrical stage, although music hall, burlesque and other staged but less-scripted forms of entertainment continued to push at the boundaries. The enforcement of regulation was also uneven and porous, and the script-based methodology allowed considerable leeway for producers and directors as 'many playwrights and performers were adept at deploying extra-textual references, subtexts, inter-theatrical resonances, unscripted tones, gestures and expressions in order to deliver meanings and implications not made in the submitted text' (Eltis 2013: 4). Nevertheless, the proposal to put full-frontal nudity on stage as part of the Revudeville show was sufficient to gain the immediate attention of an archaic and anachronistic London-centric theatrical censorship system that required 'that plays at least paid lip-service to social and moral orthodoxies' (Eltis 2013: 3).

Mrs Henderson, the owner of the Windmill, was far from the usual theatrical impresario. As a rich widow with society status and a pre-existing friendship with Lord Cromer (the incumbent Lord Chamberlain between 1922 and 1937), it obviously helped forward the argument that the static tableaux she proposed should not be considered 'indecent'. Her persuasive powers were considerable and led to the famous ruling, 'If it moves it's rude' (Goldsmith 2005), and from 1932 onwards the objectified female nude on stage, whilst not officially endorsed, was at least unofficially condoned. 'Lord Cromer's office played ball with the Windmill. They used to telephone to say when their senior official – the aptly-named George Titman – was on the way to watch a show, allowing plenty of time for the girls to put on a few more wisps of chiffon' (Goldsmith 2005).

There was obviously a contradiction between the purported artistic rationale for stage nudity and the voyeuristic intentions of an almost exclusively male audience 'who flocked to the tiny 300-seat theatre' (Goldsmith 2005). The audiences were not seeking artistic enlightenment but sexual validation through the legitimized voyeurism of nude women on stage. The tableaux vivants appeared at the conclusion of carefully choreographed musical numbers with 'the people in the favoured first six rows well-placed to ogle, and almost touch, the girls' (Goldsmith 2005). The exposed naked female body might not have been singing quite yet but it certainly accompanied the musical valediction of the revue.[7]

This overt objectification brought into focus the differences between nakedness and nudity in performance. As Pavis explains, 'a naked body on stage reintroduces the spectator's gaze and private body as he or she is wrested from the fiction into the reality of exhibition and desire' (1998: 238). The use of static nude poses at this time was the logical conclusion of the increasing exposure of the performative female body as an object for male gratification that can be traced back into the previous century. Britain remained steeped in Victorian sexual mores and attitudes which equated female sexual power with pubic hair. The Lord Chamberlain ensured this was disguised or removed from the tableaux as surely as it had been edited from the history of fine art from the ancient Greeks onwards (Walker 2012). As Goldsmith observes, 'anyone who balked at the idea of raw sexual nudity could buy into this more ethereal artistic concept and take what seems to us now a rather hypocritical stance' (Goldsmith 2005).

In the West End, as had happened with Ziegfeld's shows on Broadway, other mainstream revues competed by adopting similar approaches, such as the Streamline Revue promoted by C.B. Cochran at the Palace Theatre in 1934. Here Cochran's Young Ladies, 'a troupe of handpicked beauties' (Harding 2004), performed numbers in a satirical Gilbert and Sullivan-inspired pastiche of *Patience*, entitled *Perseverance*. Ellis and Herbert's show ran for 178 performances and included a dance routine where the 'young ladies' effectively danced naked wearing top hats, spats and a few strategically glued-on beads replacing their usual bikinis. Stage nudity had emerged from the underground confines of the Windmill's masculine environment into pre-war middle-class theatrical respectability.

Meanwhile, in America, the pre-war prurient voyeuristic excesses of some musical films had been partially curtailed by the introduction of the Hays Code in 1930. The Great Depression also had a major impact on Broadway, closing shows, limiting the number of new shows and drastically shrinking the scale and scope of most productions. Broadway was in decline; the Wall Street crash may have destroyed Ziegfeld's reputation and career as quickly as his fortune but the opulent excesses of rows of chorus girls continued to fuel voyeuristic cinematic productions and remained synonymous with the film musical for many years to come. 'Fifty chorus girls prancing on the wing of an aeroplane in *Flying Down to Rio* (1933) epitomised the film musical' (Young 2002: 228).

The post-war eras in the US and the UK saw a return to more constrained approaches to stage nudity. A slow moral backlash started to gain a hold, fuelled by a combination of conservative values and cautious challenges to traditional gender roles. In the UK the cracks within the censor's role were becoming evident. His authority was challenged on a regular basis by those who knew the fare they wished to put on would not escape his attention and simply staged their performances within private clubs. This once again effectively removed staged nudity from public view, although by driving it underground it opened the door for the increased exploitation in the strip clubs and burlesque revues of a rapidly expanding Soho sex industry. 'The distinction between nudity, which is "decorative, titillating or silly", and nakedness which "exposes skin to expose much more"' (Brantley 2013), would have to wait until *Hair* arrived on the musical stage to be further explored.

On both sides of the Atlantic the patriarchal narratives of the early musical continued to stereotype performative female roles with bohemian simplicity: lorette or grisette, Madonna or whore, virtuous virgin or femme fatale. The dichotomies of these archetypes of femininity were reinforced through productions which were 'male-dominated, male-identified and male-centred [...] and organized around an obsession with control and the oppression of women' (Johnson in Ravari 2010: 153). Both archetypes were sexualized and objectified, but one offered the societal conformity of the heterosexual utopian dream, whereas the other offered the voyeuristic promise of loose morals and the redolent eroticism of illusory nudity. Thus, these theatrical representations served to reinforce the hegemony that 'women exist as potential sexual objects for men' and to 'provide heterosexual men with sexual validation' (Donaldson 1993).

Patriarchal paradox or the commercialization of nudity?

Was *Hair* really 'the revolution they [Broadway] had been waiting for' (Miller 2001: 66)? There is no doubt that it had a big impact on the staid formulas of Golden Age musicals,[8] and was unusual in making entertainment out of portraying nonconformity and the behaviour and attitudes of a youthful counterculture. The rock-music score reflected the sound of the younger generation, but who was it being written for, and why? At first glance *Hair* seems to be an idealistic 'poster of the sixties' and an 'agit-prop musical' (Horn 1991: 135), but was the narrative the anti-establishment issue-based protest it appears to be? Was *Hair* really the first musical to foreground the issues of drugs, sexual freedom and racism, and to adopt an anti-war stance? And was it the first to put nude performers on the New York stage? The answer to all of these questions is no. It is my contention that the apparent 'revolution' symbolized by *Hair* is the construct of a retrospective 'rose-tinted' historicized approach to cultural analysis.

Hair's almost mythical countercultural status needs to be challenged. Despite the apparent anti-establishment politics, it was no more or less commercially driven, patriarchally motivated and opportunistic than any of its predecessors. Rado and Ragni's genius was to construct the right product, for the place at the right time, and then to have sufficient acumen to allow experienced Broadway professionals to adapt, improve and exploit their product. To do that they needed to capitalize on the off-Broadway sensationalism generated by the media and gain even more notoriety. What better way to do that than by publicizing their inclusion of full-frontal nudity as the show moved onto Broadway.

Rado and Ragni were not trying to change the world: they and their backers wanted to make money. Whilst *Hair* undoubtedly 'took aim at war, racism, sexual repression, and other societal evils' (Horn 1991: 1), was the foregrounding of these themes and the libidinous virtues of drug use really as radical as has been claimed? Despite extolling sexual freedoms, the acceptance of sexual difference and the liberties of 'free love', it is clear that much of this material was included simply to shock. The language of songs like 'Sodomy'[9] may have jarred, and 'Black Boys' and 'White Boys' may have satirically highlighted the delights of miscegeny, but none of this really challenged heterosexual conformity other than by destabilizing the Golden Age sanctity of marriage. Špiljak claims that 'an important part in the process of naturalisation of patriarchal gaze is played by the production of representations of hegemonic femininity and masculinity' (2010), and there is nothing in *Hair* to upset those patriarchal stereotypes.

The objectified Sheila is the virtuous grisette in a love triangle with Berger and Claude. The promiscuous pregnant Jeannie is the loose-moralled lorette. The objectified Sheila is controlled and abused by Berger. Claude, on the other hand, is obsessed with Sheila and fetishizes her but doesn't want to destroy his relationship with Berger. 'Berger wants Sheila only for the physical pleasures of sex, nothing more, while

Claude wants her for the spiritual pleasures of pure love' (Miller 2001: 80). Berger considers Sheila a sexual object and thinks so little of her he even suggests she sleep with Claude to change his mind over the draft. Other female characters are equally sexualized and objectified. '[In] one touchingly funny song [...] a girl asks in an innocent voice that an obviously insensitive brief acquaintance return and take advantage of her and her girl friend again [...] the lovely "Good Morning Starshine" captures the wonderful feeling a young girl experiences when she stays up all night with a young man' (Hewes 1968a). So much for the theatrical representation of the purported equalities of 'free love'!

The sensation and notoriety claimed for *Hair*'s introduction of nudity onto the Broadway stage was also far from revolutionary. The voluntary disrobing by the cast in the 'Be-In' which closed Act I, was described by Brien as 'an innocent and endearing tableau', adding that, 'the New York theatre has been on the bare buff kick for most of this season' (1968). Partial and full nudity had been appearing on and off the Broadway stage since the early 1960s, eliciting varied responses from the authorities, but always gaining significant media attention for the perpetrators. The off-Broadway production of *Hair* was fully clothed, so what prompted O'Horgan to introduce the nude tableau for the show's Broadway debut? Was it coincidence that the sensation of that season was Anna Halprin's *Parades and Changes*, where the performers 'calmly undress and dress, parade about the space and finally out of it' (La Rocco 2009). Halprin's choreography also alluded to the prevalent hippy culture including improvised non-linear narrative performances based on 'happenings' (Isaacson 2012).

Wollman explains that 'due in large part to the sexual revolution, stage nudity became increasingly fashionable in the experimental realm through the mid to late 1960s' (Wollman 2013: 13). Rado and Ragni's erstwhile mentors and colleagues in the experimental theatre scene had been peeling off their clothing with alacrity in recent years. In addition to Halprin's work, the same year saw Living Theatre's *Paradise Now* gain notoriety for a scene where actors critiqued various social taboos whilst undressing on stage. Richard Schechner's *Dionysus in 69* by the Performance Group further explored the audience–performer relationship in a largely nude reworking of the Euripidean drama *The Bacchae*. All of these performances attracted significant media attention and led to arrests (or the threat of arrest) for indecent exposure (Marsh 2013).

The financial necessity for the backers of *Hair* was to raise at least $34,000 per week to cover the cost of their move to the Biltmore Theatre (Zolotrow 1968). Gaining publicity would be key, and what better way to do this than by capitalizing on the vogue for staged nudity by starting a campaign based on 'previewers' word of mouth and skilfully planted gossip-column items' (Bender 1968), and leaking this to the press. If O'Horgan's inclusion of nudity was influenced more by the necessity for publicity than for its artistic merit, it worked, although maybe it didn't have quite the impact he expected. Despite the inclusion of male and female full-frontal nudity, Hair failed to incur the wrath of the authorities. The audience may have been attracted by the thrill of seeing naked people on stage, but to what extent was the brief tableau perceived as sexual in nature, and was this the authors' intent? 'In the last ten seconds of the "Be-In" scene, five boys and three girls appear naked on the dimly lit stage. It is genuine, it is natural, and in my opinion is neither lewd nor obscene (which is what a jury would have to judge it, if [...] some puritanical official should try to censor it)' (Hewes 1968b). Hair had successfully transferred to its new Broadway home and nudity was the key that unlocked its commercial success. And yet, despite the idealism of the show's politics and the purported illusion of sexual freedom and equality, it arguably continued to patriarchally objectify and sexualize its female performers. It also challenged the traditional Broadway audience who were, perhaps for the first time, overtly confronted by the 'breaking of the fourth wall' (Wollman 2006: 48) and the implications of their own prurient voyeurism.

So does *Hair* justify O'Horgan's claim to have created a 'theatre form (that) reflects a social epoch in full explosion' (Miller 2001: 67)? The form may have 'paved the way for the non-linear concept musical' (2001: 66), but the narrative treatment was traditional. The cornucopian idealism of the plot may have been highly satirical but it was not revolutionary. 'Gerome Ragni and James Rado's book and lyrics, with their quick-sketch comic routines and satiric musical pastiches, suggest good old American vaudeville filtered through a mescaline haze' (Brantley 2008). *Hair* may be dressed with terminology and profanities designed to shock, and liberally decorated with sexual (Hewes 1968b) and drug-taking references, but the storyline is completely conventional: a hero narration story with a love triangle. Finally, the brashness of the commercial exploitation, including the media-hyped notoriety of the nude scene, contradicts the idealism of the political themes woven into the narrative. It was seen as casuistic at best and unconscionable at worst by critics at the time. '*Hair* is bald opportunism. It exploits every obvious up-to-date issue – the draft, the war, even negritude – in a crass effort to be both timely and tidy [...] the structure is weak, the plot ridiculous, the point of view vague and finicky, the writing mediocre

[...] *Hair*, like the hero's beloved blond tresses, is a gauche wig. Let it be forgotten' (Smith 1967).

Sexual protest or voyeuristic exchange?

Whether commercial exploitation, or a defiant representation of political protest, the symbolic importance of the nude scene in *Hair* has grown out of all proportion to the impact it had at the time. 'The tableau is such a dimly lit still life that it will leave most playgoers open-mouthed with yawns' (Time Magazine 1968). And yet its symbolic significance arises from the seminal manner in which it reinterpreted the traditional relationship between audience and performer.

Danesi reminds us that the act of removing clothes in front of an audience 'constitute[s] a hedonistic performance' (2004: 185). The performer is both exposed and indulgent at the same time. The optional nature of the performers' engagement in the *Hair* tableau emphasizes this 'hedonism', although it remained a courageous act in which they were 'looking to one another for approval of their exhibitionism' and 'draw[ing] their strength from being part of a crowd' (Brantley 2008). The redolent sexuality of the objectified Sheila, and to a lesser degree the roles of Jeanie, Crissy and Dionne, reinforces the promise of nudity throughout the production. Thus, whether or not those individuals chose to engage in the tableau or not, the effect was still to consummate that promise for the audience. The semantic difference between nakedness and nudity so clearly defined in the tableau vivant is reinterpreted in *Hair*. The 'Be-In' was not just a nude tableau but a naked engagement with the audience where the performer was exposed, unprotected and vulnerable, although Kountouriotis notes that 'nakedness is doomed never to be truly naked but clothed at least by the bewildering and disconcerting effect of choosing nakedness' (2009: 3).

So, in *Hair*, a paradox of interpretation remains between the original asexual intent – 'The nudity is not done for shock. It's not done vulgarly or out of an ugly moment. It's a beautiful comment about the young generation' (Ragni in Ward 2002) – and the audience's sexualized perception of the performative experience as described by Alan Brien. Previewing *Hair*'s arrival on Broadway in 1968 he wrote, 'Three or four (my eyes were too busy to count) beautifully sculptured young girls also appear, proudly bare to the navel, while another stands, uncovered, from head to heel, in half profile' (Brien 1968). The reason for this sexualized perception is because 'nudity in theatre treads on the very liminality of what society believes constitutes an acceptable reason for undressing' (Rodosthenous 2012: 76).

In its transfer from off-Broadway to the Biltmore Theatre, the director Tom O'Horgan had to confront the transition from the intimacy of a small-scale thrust performance to the traditional proscenium arch. His decision to change the expected audience dynamic was driven by a desire to challenge the traditional staging of the musical. 'You felt you had to break through [...] it was an emotional reaction to something the body didn't want to do' (O'Horgan in Wollman 2006: 48). He did this through the inclusion of scenes where the cast wandered through and performed with the audience. Although this may now seem passé, at the time it was revolutionary. The director is 'turning his audience from passive viewers into unwitting voyeurs' (Rodosthenous 2012: 63), but when there is nudity involved within this new dynamic, is it inevitable that the visual impact overrides the meaning? Does the medium become the message? 'Nudity is above all a matter of showing and seeing; it assumes that the body, the thing made naked, is an entirely visual phenomenon' (Toepfer 1996: 76). If so, the dramatic impact of performative nudity challenges the accepted processes of theatre turning around the primacy of the narrative where the 'performative aspect [is a] necessary subordinate to the text' (Pavis 1998: 388) and elevating the visual spectacle above the narrative into a 'voyeuristic interaction' (Rodosthenous 2012: 76).

It was this interaction, rather than the nudity itself, that caused such a reaction. Oliver Tobias, who played Berger in the West End in 1968, described his actions. 'When the opening night came [...] the proscenium arch was broken. The role I played (Berger) climbed over the audience, kissed a bald man. I took my jeans off and handed them to a woman in the front row. This kind of broke the barriers between the audience and the performers' (BBC 2010). Nevertheless, 'nudity, conceived as performative nakedness, remains *still difficult* to accept in our western culture, *still* controversial and unsettling' (Kountouriotis 2009: 6), and there were a range of opinions amongst the performers about the effectiveness of this voyeuristic twofold exchange.

Robert Stigwood, the impresario behind the success of *Jesus Christ Superstar*, claimed that the nude scene in *Hair* 'was much ado about nothing [...] except for selling tickets' (*The Story of Musicals* 1, 2012). If, as Wanburger claims, 'theatre is voyeurism, [then] theatre audiences should not be allowed to escape into a piece, but rather they should be constantly reminded that they were watching' (2009). O'Horgan's Brechtian approach to direction broke the traditional relationship between audience and performer, and then re-emphasized the renegotiation of this dynamic through the nude scene where the audience could not escape the reality of its individual and collective voyeurism. This voyeurism sexualized the defiant and proud performers who, fully aware of the impact of their nudity, were looking back.

Opting to perform nude

The 1960s heralded a radical change in attitudes towards performative nudity with resultant challenges to the societal taboos and hegemonic authority. Increasing use of nudity in theatre was only part of a wider reinforcement of female objectification which swept across a range of media, becoming almost *de rigueur* during the 1970s, further blurring the distinctions between nakedness, nudity, glamour and pornography. Arguably this sea change in attitudes stemmed back to 1964 where the ever-popular burlesque shows throughout America were redefined largely by the performances of one dancer, Carol Doda. She became instantly famous for performing topless in a monokini in the Condor Club in San Francisco.

By taking the 'tease' out of striptease she changed the landscape for the nude performer; 'what was happening now was about nakedness – and not undressing' (Shcteir 2004: 319). Shcteir argues that it did not take long for the impact to cross over into other performative genres, and in particular into experimental theatre, attracted by the symbolic politicization of her dancing. 'Doda sometimes said she took her bra off to overturn the sexual oppression of the McCarthy years' (Shcteir 2004: 320) as she became more and more immersed in student protest, supporting students at UC Berkeley in 1966 and the anti-war movement through the movie *Head* in 1968. 'Doda set off a trend. By the end of June [1968] toplessness had turned into a nationwide craze: topless restaurants, shoeshine parlors, ice cream stands, and girl bands proliferated' (Shcteir 2004: 321).

The performative nudity of *Hair* therefore appeared with all the consequent pressures for performers to equate their radicalism and anti-establishment protest with public display of their nude bodies. And yet the obsession with nudity was still largely a patriarchal fetish. Men may have been taking their clothes off on the New York stage with equal abandon to women, but other than Alan O'Brien's comment that the male cast members of *Hair* were 'noticeably virile and well endowed' (Brien 1968) their impact was largely ignored as the mainstream male-dominated media pursued its obsession with female nudity.[10] Nude male performers were seen as semiotically robust and narratively justified, whereas nude female performers were usually sexualized and eroticized regardless of the performative context. Nevertheless, the Madonna/whore dichotomy was starting to be challenged as commentators struggled to get to grips with how 'nice girls' could be persuaded to perform nude.

In 1968 *Esquire Magazine* interviewed a number of the female performers from *Hair* in an attempt to sensationalize this dichotomy. The interview rather backfired as it simply ended up reinforcing the normality of their decisions whether or not to perform in the nude scene. Some of the performers had no moral qualms but admitted to a lack of courage. 'I don't have the nerve; it's such a personal thing' (Diane Keaton). Whereas others still felt the societal pressure for conformity, 'I don't feel the world is ready to approve. And I very much want to be approved of' (Lynn Kellog). Countering these opinions was the collective 'tribal' pressure of being surrounded by other performers who were disrobing, normalizing this otherwise taboo act. 'I've lost a few inhibitions in this show. At first I just stripped to the waist, but people complained that I was copping out' (Emmaretta Marks).

Many of the performers' explanations provide confirmation of patriarchal societal attitudes, such as Melba Moore's comment:

> 'I don't join the nude scene onstage. For three reasons: a) I want to be a singer, and it might hurt my career, b) I'm too fat, c) My husband would object vehemently,' and Leata Galloway, 'Even if I wanted to, my manager wouldn't let me. Anyway, I have enough hassles with the stagehands as it is.'

Yet others seemed to have bought into the 'normality of nakedness' that was arguably being promoted to capitalize on their naivety. 'Now I do it every performance. It took getting rid of a few hang-ups' (Shelley Plimpton). The performers clearly understood the sexualized audience interpretation of the tableau and the importance of their interaction with them. Lorri Davis explained, 'the audience is important though; if they're responsive and with it, I take my clothes off. If they're deadheads, I don't bother,' whereas Suzzanah Norstrand, when asked whether the audience intimidated her, replied, 'Are you kidding? The front rows are always full of fags, and they just look at the boys.'[11] Whatever the rationale, the cultural significance of the scene had by now progressed way beyond the initial innocence of a simple musical tableau.

Pavis clarifies the different forms of nudity on stage and the manner in which the audience reacts to that nudity. 'A distinction must be drawn between erotic theatre or shows that systematically use nudity – chiefly of women – as a voyeuristic genre, and fictional theatre where the act of disrobing is required by the dramatic situation' (Pavis 1998: 238). But the spate of adult musicals spawned by the success of *Hair* would work to deliberately blur these distinctions. In many ways, these revues were a return to the vacuous sketch-format musicals of the 1930s, with a satirical emphasis placed on lampooning all aspects of sexual behaviour. However, there was one major difference, and this was the manner in which the 'new nudity' created performances that actively confronted the audience, making them foreground their voyeurism in an active two-way exchange that cast off inhibitions and exploded traditional middle-class values. 'The new nudity needs an "artistic conscience", complained one writer. But the downtown gurus of the avant-garde did not care about critics, or humor. They cared about getting the bourgeois audience to shed its inhibitions' (Shcteir 2004: 326).

Whilst theatre explored the 'new freedom allotted by *Hair*, [with] a slew of boundary-pushing plays' (Ward 2002), musical theatre remained resolutely silent. Then, in June 1969 Kenneth Tynan's *Oh! Calcutta!* opened off-Broadway. Tynan explained that he'd put the show together because 'I realized there was no place for a civilized man to take a civilized woman for an evening of civilized erotic entertainment' (Shcteir 2004: 326). This loosely constructed series of sexual skits would become 'a Broadway monolith with the longest number of shows in history'[12] (Ward 2002).

The early 1970s saw a string of off-Broadway erotic musicals 'that attempted to honestly examine sexual mores, trends and myths with all-encompassing good humor' (Ward 2002). Many of these appeared and disappeared as rapidly as the actors' clothing on stage. In 1971 Newburge and Urbont's *Stag Movie* opened, starring Adrienne Barbeau who had come from *Fiddler on the Roof* to disrobe in a rather disappointing 11-week run at the Gate Theatre. It was slated by the critics, uncomfortable at its explicit plot centred on the making of a porn movie in a motel room. 'When a musical concludes with the principals proclaiming in song "We came together," you know the term "dramatic climax" has been abused forever' (Hischak 2011: 134).

Despite lashings of gratuitous nudity, the erotic musical was not destined to last. As sexual attitudes changed, the explicit nature of the sketches and the lewdness of the lyrics could not maintain the shock value required for commercial success. Maybe there was more truth in

Hair performer Lorri Davis' comment, 'When you've seen one body you've seen them all' (Esquire Magazine 1968), than she realized at the time. Although performative nudity had to operate within legal constraints, critics complained that many of these revues were too pornographic. Yet few got into trouble with the authorities because of the tacit understanding of the boundaries between lampooning and simulating sexual activity.[13]

By the end of the 1970s the spate of adult musicals had all but disappeared, partially because they were just not very good, but primarily because the ability of stage nudity to shock had dissipated. As societal attitudes to sex and nudity evolved, these musicals failed to fulfil their voyeuristic promise, fell down on artistic integrity and, with one or two notable exceptions, were commercial disasters. So why, despite a surfeit of pubic hair and genitalia on display, did these musicals largely fail to attract sufficient audiences? If theatre is voyeurism, as Pavis contends, and voyeurism is 'an intense curiosity which generates a compulsive desire to observe people (un)aware in natural states or performed primal acts and leads to a heightening of pleasure for the viewer' (see Rodosthenous, p. 6, above), then these musicals made their audiences viscerally aware of their own voyeurism which, by implication, interfered with their pleasure. This increased self-awareness eroded the personal 'twofold' fetishized gaze challenging the illusion of the objectified female. With the collapse of the fourth wall, the intimacy of many of the performance venues and the in-built audience interaction it became difficult for the voyeur in the audience to seek sexual validation.

Furthermore, this validation was challenged by the dilution of the eroticism of the 'nudity/nakedness' dichotomy because of the protagonist's interaction with other sexualized or nude performers. Thus, there arises a contradiction between the construct of a nude show specifically designed with voyeuristic intent, and the audience's increased self-awareness which consequently erodes the intimacy of the voyeuristic dialogue by the sheer quantity of overt nudity made available.

Contemporary tantalizing nudity in musicals: some conclusions

'Musical theatre [...] has always been a middlebrow, commercial art form' (Wollman and Sternfeld 2011: 8), and was, and continues to be, patriarchal: primarily feeding the male gaze that is obsessed with looking at, objectifying and defining women in relation to male stereotypes. Gratuitous nudity in musicals is scarce and contemporary instances usually comply with Pavis' 'fictional theatre' definition (1998: 238), where nudity is a requirement of the narrative (*Spring Awakening*). Sexual themes continue to be discussed, explored and satirized (*Jerry Springer: The Opera*, *The Book of Mormon*), and overt performative sexuality and promissory nudity is engendered within many female roles and narratives (Satine in *Moulin Rouge* or Velma in *Chicago*). 'If desire is the subtext of narrative, sexuality and gender are equally motivating forces in representation' (Dolan 2012: 63).

Further recent additions to the contemporary mix of 'tantalizing nudity' on the musical stage is the inclusion of nudity through directorial interpretation[14] (*Cabaret*), our media-hyped obsession with glamorous female celebrity performers (Martine McCutcheon in *My Fair Lady*, Amanda Holden in *Shrek the Musical*), the overt foregrounding of queer politics (*La cage aux folles*, *Kiss of the Spiderwoman*) and the paradoxical emergence of musicals claimed to be developed for a 'female gaze' (*Wicked*, *Legally Blonde* and *Mamma Mia*).

Director Rufus Norris' inclusion of full-frontal male and female nudity in the 'gas chamber tableau' in the 2012 London revival of Kander and Ebb's *Cabaret* was designed to have an impact. 'It is the ending that will stay with you. This time the nudity is not to titillate but to shock in the most terrible way with the Emcee disrobing to join them' (Smith 2013). Yet, it is precisely their nakedness, their exposure and vulnerability, that elicits this response. There is nothing sexual in this scene, although as the production was built around the celebrity of Will Young as the Emcee, one might argue that he was nude, whilst the rest of the cast were naked. Contemporary society is obsessed with celebrity, and if one adds objectification, sexualization and the potential for nudity, then you have the perfect commercialized asset.

Despite the prevalence of full and partial nudity in the media, it remains rare in musical theatre. Musicals like *Naked Boys Singing* are the exception rather than the rule. 'Full-on nudity isn't something audiences will encounter very often in the theatre. As a result [...] they seem to absorb much of the performer's discomfort' (Butler 2009). This is because the dialogue between audience and performer changes the second they start to disrobe on stage. The relationship changes from passive to active, the fourth wall is broken and each individual member of the audience is confronted by their sexualized, objectifying voyeurism. Ironically this can be to the benefit of the performer: 'Instead of us, it's them worrying: "Am I looking too closely? What if they catch me sneaking a peek southwards? Am I enjoying this a little too much?"' (Butler 2009).

Clearly things have changed since *Hair*. 'In the old days it [nudity] used to throw an uneasy frost across an auditorium, but these days I think people really enjoy it and we got a lot more bums on seats because of the nudity – bums on seats and bums on stage' (Rupert Everett quoted in Masters 2013). But this still begs the question, who is the audience for musicals nowadays? Given the patriarchal history of the musical, it might be surprising to hear producer James Nederlander[15] state: 'Men do not want to go to shows, their wives want to go to shows. So we got to give something the men like, they gotta see some ass' (Stephen Fry quoting James Neelander on *The Story of Musicals* 2012). In our visually overloaded mediatized society, are we really motivated by something as simple as 'seeing some ass'?

As the musical is both 'heavily representational (drawing on the audience's concrete experience of the world), and heavily non-representational and "unreal" (pointing to how things could be better)' (Dyer 2002: 27), then the voyeuristic engagement of the audience with performative nudity probably retains some impact because these contradictions can be 'rendered as one' (2002: 27). Should we not be allowed to indulge our media-fed obsession with celebrity, promissory nudity and gendered objectification free from concerns as to whether the 'seven flaccid penises taking part in a naked cancan' (Butler 2009) in *Naked Boys Singing* signify anything at a metaphysical level, or whether the 'naked female bodies are an expression of emancipation, rather than the consequence of patriarchal gaze control' (Špiljak 2010)?

According to Dolan, 'Sexual desire has long been a motivating narrative factor in plays and performances' (2010: 3). This links to Dyer's observation that 'the cultural and historical specificity of entertainment' (2002: 19) suggests that the function of the musical is to provide the audience with a sense of 'escapism' and 'wish fulfilment'. Furthermore, Mulvey suggests that 'a society's collective consciousness includes its sexuality' (1996: xiii). The logical endorsement of both these positions is that the audience for the musical needs to park its collective sense of guilt at the box office, enjoy the multifarious forms which have developed, revel in the simplicity of the narrative stereotypes, and wallow in the intimacy of the performer–audience relationship fully complicit in the glorious 'deceit' manifest in front of them.

Notes

1. For example, the Gershwin musicals *Oh, Kay* (1926) made a star of Gertrude Lawrence, *Rosalie* (1928) starred Marilyn Miller, *Showgirl* (1929) starred Ruby Keeler and *Girl Crazy* (1930) Ethel Merman and Ginger Rogers. Both

Rosalie and *Showgirl* were produced by Ziegfeld. The pit orchestra on the opening night of *Girl Crazy* at the Alvin Theatre on Broadway included the 'aspiring' young jazz musicians Benny Goodman, Jimmy Dorsey and Glen Miller!
2. Even if this meant shooting alternate scenes for distribution in different US States.
3. Cantor had also performed in the *Ziegfeld Follies* on Broadway from 1917 to 1927.
4. According to Sheridan Morley, who wrote Noël Coward's biography entitled *A Talent to Amuse*, the song was written in 1933 as an answer to the hundreds of requests he received to find parts for daughters in his next production. Meant as a warning, it had the opposite effect as most women took it as a joke.
5. There is even a programme for the Tableaux Vivants performed by members of the royal family at Osborne House in 1891 in the royal collection.
6. He was an accomplished portait painter and also designed for the Metropolitan Opera Ballet.
7. After a while the Lord Chamberlain's office ceased visiting the Windmill to check on the monthly revisions to the Revudeville tableaux, preferring instead to receive a photograph for approval.
8. *Hair* ran for four years on Broadway and had 19 international productions within two years.
9. For example, 'Sodomy' not only questions conventional attitudes to sex but also attacks Catholic hypocrisy towards sex and the pederastic tendencies of its priests.
10. In 1969 *The Sun* newspaper started to include daily glamour photographs and in 1970 the final remnants of clothing were discarded and Page 3 became synonymous with topless objectification.
11. Is this perhaps a liberated reinterpretation of the male gaze?
12. It had 5959 performances. It was subsequently overtaken by *Les Miserables*, *Cats* and *Phantom of the Opera*, amongst others.
13. Some shows, like *Le Bellybutton*, attempted to blur these boundaries further by casting Marilyn Chambers, a hardcore pornstar from *Behind the Green Door* (1972), in the principal role.
14. Often in revivals of works not previously associated with performative nudity.
15. Producer of over one hundred of the most acclaimed Broadway musicals and plays of all time, including *Annie*, *Applause*, *La cage aux folles*, *Me and My Girl*, *Nine*, *Noises Off*, *Peter Pan*, *Sweet Charity*, *The Will Rogers Follies*, *Woman of the Year* and many others.

Bibliography

Associated Press (1932) 'Florenz Ziegfeld dies in Hollywood after long illness', Obituary, 23 July 1932 in *New York Times: On This Day In History* www.nytimes.com/learning/general/onthisday/bday/0321.html (accessed 18 September 2013).

Barnes, Clive (1967) 'The theater: *HAIR*, a love-rock musical, inaugurates Shakespeare Festival's Anspacher Playhouse', *New York Times*, 30 October.

BBC (2010) *Witness Programme for the World Service*. First broadcast 28 September. www.bbc.co.uk/learningzone/clips/musical-hair-premieres-in-london-1968-audio/11148.html (accessed 18 September 2013).

Bender, Marilyn (1968) 'Hair – topless, and no bottoms, either', *New York Times*, 28 April.

Brantley, Ben (2008) 'Let the sunshine in, and the shadows', *New York Times*, 8 August.

Brantley, Ben (2013) 'Showing it all, revealing nothing', *New York Times*, 6 June.

Brien, Alan (1968) 'Alan Brien takes an advance look at a frontal attack on Broadway', *The London Sunday Times*, 28 April, Hair Articles Index, www.michaelbutler.com (accessed 18 September 2013).

Butler, Steven (2009) 'The joy of nude musicals', *The Guardian* www.theguardian.com/stage/theatreblog/2009/jul/28/nude-musicals (accessed 18 September 2013).

Conlan, Mark Gabrish (2011) *Glorifying the American Girl (Paramount) 1929*, MovieMagg http://moviemagg.blogspot.co.uk/2011/01/glorifying-american-girl-paramount-1929.html (accessed 15 November 2013).

Danesi, Marcel (2004) *Messages, Signs, and Meanings: A Basic Textbook in Semiotics and Communication Theory*, 3rd edn (Toronto: Canadian Scholars' Press).

Davis, Tracy C. (1989) 'The spectacle of absent costume: nudity on the Victorian stage', *New Theatre Quarterly*, 5:20, 321–33.

DeFreitas, Justin (2006) *The Surreal and Subversive World of Busby Berkeley*, 21 April, The Berkeley Daily Planet www.berkeleydailyplanet.com/issue/2006-04-21/ (accessed 18 September 2013).

Dolan, Jill (2010) *Theatre and Sexuality* (Basingstoke: Palgrave Macmillan).

Dolan, Jill (2012) *The Feminist Spectator as Critic* (Ann Arbor: University of Michigan Press).

Donaldson, Mike (1993) *What Is Hegemonic Masculinity?* Research online University of Wollongong, 22:5 http://ro.uow.edu.au/cgi/viewcontent.cgi?article=1149&context=artspapers (accessed 18 September 2013).

Dyer, Richard (2002) *Only Entertainment*, 2nd edn (London: Routledge).

Eltis, Sos (2013) *Acts of Desire: Women and Sex on Stage 1800–1930* (Oxford University Press).

Esquire Magazine (1968) 'Optional nudity in *Hair*', September edition, Hair Articles Index www.michaelbutler.com/ (accessed 18 September 2013).

Goldsmith, Vivien (2005) 'Windmill: always nude but never rude', *Daily Telegraph*, 24 November.

Harding, James (2004) 'Sir Charles Blake Cochran', *Oxford Dictionary of National Biography*, Oxford University Press www.oxforddnb.com/templates/article.jsp?articleid=32471&back= (accessed 18 September 2013).

Hewes, Henry (1968a) 'The theater of shattered focus', Saturday Review, 13 January, Hair Articles Index www.michaelbutler.com/ (accessed 18 September 2013).

Hewes, Henry (1968b) 'Blow', Hair Articles Index www.michaelbutler.com/ (accessed 18 October 2013).

Hischak, Thomas (2011) *Off-Broadway Musicals since 1919: From Greenwich Village Follies to The Toxic Avenger* (Lanham, MD: Scarecrow Press).

Horn, Barbara L. (1991) *The Age of Hair: Evolution and Impact of Broadway's First Rock Musical* (New York: Greenwood Press).

Isaacson, Elisa (2012) *Q & A: Anna Halprin on Parades and Changes*. Beta Blook (Blog) Posted 14 November, 11:22 AM, http://blook.bampfa.berkeley.edu/2012/11/q-a-anna-halprin.html (accessed 29 November 2013).

Kountouriotis, Pavlos (2009) 'Nudity, nakedness, otherness and a still difficult spectator', *Movement Performance Research Journal*, 34, 1–10.

La Rocco, Claudia (2009) 'Flashback to the '60s: with clothes and without', *New York Times*, 20 November.

Marsh, Natalie (2013) 'Mira i Konflikta (Dance Blog.)', 20 January http://nataliepmarsh.blogspot.co.uk/ (accessed 18 September 2013).

Masters, Tim (2013) 'Actors reveal challenges of stage nudity', BBC, 6 March, www.bbc.co.uk/news/entertainment-arts-21654036 (accessed 23 September 2013).

Miller, Scott (2001) *Rebels with Applause: Broadway's Groundbreaking Musicals* (Portsmouth, NH: Heinemann).

Mulvey, Laura (1996) *Fetishism and Curiosity* (Bloomington: Indiana University Press).

Padgett, Ken (2013) 'Florenz Ziegfeld: impresario extraordinaire' http://agilewriter.com/Biography/Ziegfeld.htm (accessed 15 November 2013).

Parlor Songs (2004) *Florenz Ziegfeld and the Ziegfeld Follies: The Parlor Songs Academy* http://parlorsongs.com/issues/2004-1/thismonth/feature.php (accessed 19 October 2013).

Pavis, Patrice (1998) *Dictionary of the Theatre: Terms, Concepts and Analysis* (University of Toronto Press).

Rado, James and Gerome Ragni (1967) *Hair*. Lyrics accessed from www.stlyrics.com/h/hair.htm (accessed 6 August 2013).

Ravari, Zahra Khozaei (2010) '*Vinegar Tom*: women's oppression through patriarchal–capitalist domination', *Review of European Studies*, 2:2, 153–63.

Rodosthenous, George (2012) '*Outlying Islands* as theatre of voyeurism: ornithologists, naked bodies and the "pleasure of peeping"', *Studies in Theatre & Performance*, 32:1, 62–77.

Shcteir, R. (2004) *Striptease: The Untold History of the Girlie Show* (Oxford University Press).

Shellard, Dominic, Steve Nicholson and Miriam Handley (2004) *The Lord Chamberlain Regrets: A History of British Theatre Censorship* (London: The British Library).

Smith, Jeanette (2013) 'Review: Will Young stars in *Cabaret*', Liverpool Empire Theatre, 3 September, www.clickliverpool.com/culture/reviews/1219726-will-young-brilliant-in-cabaret.html (accessed 3 September 2013).

Smith, Michael (1967) '*Hair* – Off Broadway review', *The Village Voice*, 2 November, Hair Articles Index www.michaelbutler.com/ (accessed 18 October 2013).

Špiljak, Karmen (2010) 'Gaze and gender, construction of female identity in popular culture with special focus on comical genres', www.academia.edu/2628844/ (accessed 10 September 2013).

The Story of Musicals (2012) Episode 1, BBC 4 by TwoFour, Tuesday 3 January, 21:00, executive produced by Juliet Rice and series produced by Stephen Franklin.

Time Magazine (1968) 'Review of *Hair*', 10 May, Hair Articles Index www.michaelbutler.com/hair/holding/articles/ (accessed 6 June 2011).

Toepfer, Karl (1996) 'Nudity and textuality in postmodern performance', *Performing Arts Journal*, 18:3. 76–91.
Vieira, Mark A. (1999) *Sin in Soft Focus: Pre-Code Hollywood* (New York: Harry N. Abrams).
Walker, Paige (2012) 'Genital depilation and power in classical Greece', *Berkeley Undergraduate Journal of Classics*, 1:1, 1–11.
Wanburger, Casey (2009) *Theatre is Voyeurism*, Ka-tet Theatre Company Blog, 28 July, www.katettheatre.org/blog/theatre-is-voyeurism/ (accessed 23 September 2013).
Ward, Jonathan (2002) 'Come in my mouth: the story of the adult musicals of the '70's', *Perfect Sound Forever* (Online music magazine) www.furious.com/perfect/adultmusicals.html (accessed 14 September 2013).
Warren, Harry and Al Dubin (1933) *Keep Young and Beautiful*, Roman Scandals http://lyricsplayground.com/alpha/songs/ (accessed 12 November 2013).
Warren, H. and A. Dubin (1934) *Dames*, Dames http://lyricsplayground.com/alpha/songs/ (accessed 12 November 2013).
Wollman, Elizabeth (2006) *The Theatre Will Rock: A History of the Rock Musical from Hair to Hedwig* (Ann Arbor: University of Michigan Press).
Wollman, Elizabeth (2013) *Hard Times: The Adult Musical in the 1970s* (Oxford University Press).
Wollman, Elizabeth and Jessica Sternfeld (2011) 'Musical theatre and the almighty dollar: what a tangled web they weave', *Studies in Musical Theatre*, 5:1, 3–12.
Young, William H. (2002) *The 1930s* (Westport, CT: Greenwood Press).
Zolotrow, S. (1968) 'Producer of *Hair* to attack scalpers and aide charities', *New York Times*, 16 May.

10
Outlying Islands as Theatre of Voyeurism: Ornithologists, Naked Bodies and the 'Pleasure of Peeping'

George Rodosthenous

David Greig's fascinating study of bird-watchers, *Outlying Islands* (2002),[1] at first glance seems to be a play about the loss of innocence. As the story unfolds, one gets a clearer idea of the underlying subtexts where the act of 'watching' develops a predominant role and upstages the other themes of the play. Following its first version as a radio play broadcast on BBC Radio 3 (5 May 2002), *Outlying Islands* took the Edinburgh Fringe Festival by storm in the Traverse Theatre Company's production (August 2002, dir. Philip Howard), winning several major awards and having a sold-out run at the Traverse Theatre. Later that year, the original production transferred for another sold-out run at a much more intimate auditorium in the Jerwood Theatre Upstairs at the Royal Court Theatre in London (5–28 September 2002) and subsequently toured Scotland and Canada.

Throughout the work of Greig, there are scenes that seem to exploit voyeurism in theatre and the act of watching (semi-)naked bodies. For this chapter, I will select a number of key scenes from the play and consider Greig's theatrical dramaturgical skill of turning his audience from passive viewers into unwitting voyeurs. Also, I will look in depth into the literary text and the contribution of the stage directions in order to examine the writer's original intentions, which are sometimes not evident in the performance itself. Alongside this textual analysis, there will be explicit links to Philip Howard's original Traverse Theatre Company production of *Outlying Islands* (2002) and its critical reception. Finally, I will argue that the dramatic use of naked bodies on stage creates a psychological awakening for the viewer, as they become increasingly self-aware that they are committing the culturally taboo act of 'watching' another body within the legalized framework of the theatrical act.

In order to propose that theatre has the ability to function as an act of voyeurism, we need to contextualize the pleasure(s) of watching within a theatrical framework. For the purpose of this chapter, I will discuss theatre in its most traditional form, that is, in a proscenium-arch space: a form of theatre that still assumes the invisible 'fourth wall' that separates the actor from the audience. So, let us make a series of adjustments before applying this theory to the theatrical act. Voyeurism is, indeed, the action of watching 'unaware' bodies involved in private (or sexual) actions to derive (sexual) pleasure. In redefining pleasure, and removing the sexual connotations from pleasure, can we still encounter a naked body (of the performer or even a character) without embracing the sexual politics of our gaze?

I would like to suggest that, in *Outlying Islands*, theatre involves such a voyeuristic exchange between the performer and the audience, where the performer (either as exhibitionist or 'unaware' of the audience's gaze) and the audience (the voyeur of this exchange) are placed in a legalized environment for that interaction. Of course, this provokes a series of new questions: Does the fact that the audience is paying to watch the bodies upset this relationship? Can the performer ever be unaware of the audience's gaze? If the performer is presented (for this discussion) as an exhibitionist, does the 'act of paying' negate and denude the audience from its voyeuristic rights?

Intimacy in theatre suggests that the kind of voyeurism that theatre permits underpins the writer's ability to convey powerfully intense scenes. I will attempt to analyse Greig's dramatic techniques with connection to intimacy and nudity. Can we distance ourselves from watching an 'object of desire' to watching the fuller image as part of the whole *mise-en-scène*? And what happens when the 'fourth wall' is violated, when the character talks to the audience directly, breaking the secret agreement of the unacknowledgement of the audience?

The play deals with the visit of two ornithologists, John (played in the original production by Sam Heughan) and Robert (Laurence Mitchell), on an outlying island of Scotland just before World War II and their encounters with the island's keeper Kirk (Robert Carr), and his young niece, Ellen (Lesley Hart). After the uncle's accidental death, the young trio is forced to face the painful realities of desire, enforced limitations of closed social environments and their first sexual awakening, surrounded by birds, a pagan chapel and water. Greig states that '[t]hey're supposed to be there to watch birds, but really they watch each other' (Greig in Rimmer 2002). The remote setting provides explicitly voyeuristic opportunities, and the protagonists' own personal tendencies towards voyeurism and exhibitionism allow the audience to explore issues of voyeurism in theatre, the 'pleasure of peeping' and the pleasure(s) of watching naked bodies on stage. According to Joyce McMillan, the play raises

> a whole range of huge questions about [...] how we see ourselves as a species; tensions between social obligation and individualism [...] morality and desire [...] the knowing voyeurism of modern media culture and the relative innocence of life without the watching eye. (McMillan 2002)

Naked bodies in *Outlying Islands*: 'observation [...] appreciation and general perverted staring' (Greig 2002: 30)

> Nudity in performance refers to the exposure of the most erotically exciting and excitable sexual identifiers of the body, with exposed genitals being the most complete 'proof' of the body's vulnerability to desire and the appropriating gaze of the Other. (Toepfer 1996: 76)[2]

I will further explore the notion that nudity on stage offers an awakening of sorts for the audience. Looking at a selection of critical responses to the play *Outlying Islands*, I will show how Greig's use of the naked body forces the viewer to confront the voyeuristic element in the actor/audience exchange. I will then argue that this dramatic technique highlights the theatre as a space where it is 'legal' to become a voyeur of the naked form away from other legalized contexts such as the medical or the sporting.

Greig had used full-frontal nudity as a recurring motif in his earlier plays (*The Architect* (1996), *The Cosmonaut's Last Message to the Woman He Once Loved in the Former Soviet Union* (1999), *The Speculator* (1999) and *Victoria* (2000)). It usually has a natural, ritualistic quality (Toepfer 1996: 87) which emerges organically from the narrative of his scenes. Whilst nudity in public is still a taboo in our society, in theatre it has been tolerated as part of the whole narrative and theatrical storytelling. However, it can cause problems in smaller, or less tolerant, communities even today, evidenced when '[a] regular venue on the Traverse Highland tour did not take the show because of the nudity and predicted backlash from more conservative elements within the community' (Hamilton and Scullion 2005: 72).

The presence of a live, clothed audience and a naked performer creates an edgy dynamic because of all the sexual politics it carries:

> Nakedness in contemporary culture is a solo affair, or else it is sexual by virtue of the presence of a gazing second party. For nakedness to occur among the gaze of others *without sexuality* for the very practical reasons of bathing, changing clothes, artistic representation, examinations for purity or health, sporting events or other practicalities, discrete frames or contexts need to be established which permit the signification of that nakedness to elude sexuality.[3] (Cover 2003: 56)

Nudity in theatre treads on the very liminality of what society believes constitutes an acceptable reason for undressing. Artistic representations of the naked body often come with an implied sexual gaze (as directed in the text or as added by the director during rehearsals) which set them apart from other more permissible situations where the naked body is 'gazed' upon for medical, sporting or other practical reasons. *Outlying Islands* includes a sensitive, but rather explicit, erotic scene where John and Ellen make love on the table of the chapel for the first time. In his poetic stage directions, Greig offers the director (*auteur*-voyeur) the opportunity to decide, together and in agreement with his performers, the explicitness of the scene. The script reads as follows:

> *She undresses.*
> *Her clothes fall to the floor.*
> *She laughs [...]*
> **Ellen** Take off your clothes [...]
> I'm cold.
> Warm me.
> *They move to the table.*
> *Ellen guides John down onto it.*
> *She above him [...]*
> *A moment of touching.*
> *Kissing [...]*
> **Ellen** Let me take you in [...]
> *A moment.*
> *Their bodies perfect.* (Greig 2002: 104–7)

What is useful to this discussion is to try and penetrate the actor's psyche at this very 'exposed' moment. The characters are supposed to be rather young, and indeed the actors themselves were during this production: Sam Heughan, who played John, was still studying at the Royal

Scottish Academy of Music and Drama at the time. In the original production, Howard's blocking and Chahine Yavroyan's atmospheric lighting might have helped put the actors at ease for this scene, but there was still a need to be confidently naked, simulating a sex scene (as an actor) and 'pretending' to be shy and nervous at the same time (as the character): all this under the eager stare of the audience. Even though this must have been challenging for the actors, it made me feel edgy, and perhaps some of the rest of the audience. This is possibly because it is difficult 'to see any nude body (especially one which desires to be seen) without considering the implication that an invitation to see the body entails an invitation to desire the body' (Toepfer 1996: 77). One of the reviewers of *Outlying Islands* commented on this compulsive watching and whether it was regarded as decent in the 'legalized' transfer to the theatrical space, noting that keeping your eyes to yourself is a 'lesson[] we're all taught early on [...] but it's advice that [...] theater patrons pay to violate' (Tarter 2004).

In order to contextualize this discussion, I will look further at the critical reception of that scene in the original production. Many (re)viewers felt the need to comment extensively on this scene. In Edinburgh, Mark Brown (2002) wrote that '[f]or all this, however, one suspects there will be those who become somewhat fixated by the moment of nudity in the play'. Robert Dawson-Scott (2002) noted that in the earlier radio version of the play, the scene in question was merely suggested by 'a few whispered endearments, a rustle of clothing perhaps [...] the pictures were in your head'. But this reductionist approach is not possible in the visual context of the stage play and there was an overall sense from reviewers that the implicitness of the radio version was somehow more decent than the nudity presented by Philip Howard. Dawson-Scott also noted Howard's adverse reaction to the warnings often found on theatre posters for shows that contain nudity, quoting, 'I was damned if I was going to have a sign saying "This show contains nudity"', and arguing himself that the sex in *Outlying Islands* was 'touching and beautiful' (Dawson-Scott 2002).

It soon became evident that the reviewers disagreed on the presentation of the naked bodies on stage. The range of responses to such an explicit scene varied widely, possibly caused by cultural upbringing, social constraints, gender, sexual preferences and personal tastes. Watching the same production in Canada, Regan Danly (2006) claimed that the nudity was more 'distracting than affective' and commented that it only served to 'remind us that it [was] merely a simulation', concluding that the 'nudity amounted to a gimmick, taking us entirely off the island and back into the theatre'.

For my part, I found it a highly effective, genuinely theatrical use of human nakedness. Greig wrote a scene where it was permissible to watch those bodies in a 'legalized environment' and explored the boundaries of voyeurism in the theatre. Charles Spencer (2002) also agreed by commenting that '[t]he show's comic, touching, powerful erotic sex scene is one of the finest I have ever seen in a theatre – or anywhere else, come to that', and perhaps that was Greig's main intention from the start. In an interview with him he confirmed that 'Theatre is our chance to look at people and watch how they behave. It is scientific. It is also basic instinct [...] It is a consensual exchange [...] Watcher and watched require each other' (Greig 2011: 12).

The audience has an expressed need to watch (the semiotics of possibly repressed expression) and the performers have an inherent need to exhibit (as part of their psychology of exhibitionism). The audience, by its very construction, has a fascination with observing the human body. The overwhelming popularity of voyeuristic television programmes such as *Big Brother* and the sensationalism of paparazzi photos of celebrities now play a large part in contemporary culture and seem to have tapped into an innate desire to 'watch' other bodies. But can all these media tricks and devices really compete with the adrenaline of watching a theatrical performance? Does this exchange work only for the ones who watch? Els Deceukelier (one of Jan Fabre's actresses) believes that this voyeuristic interaction is a twofold exchange:

> I need a public. I suspect that actors who pretend they don't need a public are liars. I believe that all actors like to be seen, but at the same time they must have something of the *voyeur*, for [they] also look at the public. Therefore, who is looking at whom? (Deceukelier in Van den Dries 2005: 393)

Overt voyeurism and exhibitionism: 'decency' and bird's-eye view(s) in *Outlying Islands*

Ellen He watches me.
John I know. I know.
     He does the same to me. (Greig 2002: 95)

I have argued that the modern Western stage play offers the audience the opportunity to experience the culturally 'forbidden' pleasures of watching bodies (naked or otherwise) within a safe and 'legal' environment, although as the very mixed reviews of *Outlying Islands* suggest, the idea of becoming unwitting voyeurs of a sexual act does not always sit well with some. I chose Greig's *Outlying Islands* as the focus for this chapter as I believe his use of language and dramatic technique eloquently explores the licentious pleasures of voyeurism. In this next section, I will explore these techniques further and highlight how they allow the audience to become 'aware' that they, too, are always complicit in the act of 'watching' bodies within the Western theatrical framework.

For the second half of the play (scene four onwards), the three young characters are left on the island entirely on their own and this encourages a further exploration of the surroundings as they 'become[] a metaphor for human experience as the three younger characters confront the furthest reaches of self-knowledge and sexual desire' (Allfree 2002). But even in this microcosmical society of three, social constraints still bear down upon the characters. Philip Culbertson (1998) disseminates this social constructionist argument, stating that

> [H]uman identity, both individual and interpersonal, is the product of the social contexts within which we have spent our lives. A social context teaches us what we are allowed to feel or not feel and how to express our feelings; which relationships are mandatory, preferred, obligatory, optional, or undesirable; what we can dream and what we must never dream. (Culbertson 1998: 1)

And it is at this point within the play that their definitions of morality, what is socially accepted and 'the limits of decency' (Greig 2002: 100) are all challenged and redefined. Greig explores a series of dualities between the freedom of the flying birds and the limitations of the social constraints placed upon the characters. There is clearly a fascination of the young men to watch birds: they are ornithologists by profession. This enables them to escape from their inner troubled worlds and the remoteness of the island. The only other place they find escapism is in their dreams. The young men's personal association with birds and the act of flying is further developed thematically: John desires to become a (human) bird, to be a flyer – he considered applying for the air force. Robert is fascinated and at ease with the birds, so much that Ellen describes him, when he is with them, to be 'laughing and shrieking like he's found his own family' (Greig 2002: 56). Unfortunately, at the end of the play, he actually attempts to fly, with tragic consequences.

Ellen also has her own fascination with watching films in the evenings: she saw the same film 'thirty-seven times' (Greig 2002: 56).

During the day, though, in her dream-like states, which become more frequent after her uncle's death, she begins to feel like she is in a film with one of her favourite film characters – Stan Laurel. This dream-like state also begins to extend to watching the two young ornithologists clothed (watching birds) or naked (bathing in the sea). These images are Ellen's only escape from the remote environment of the island. She even describes the two young men as Laurel and Laurel. Together with the young ornithologists, she is exploring the new boundaries of society without other people and their judgements; she is redefining what she 'can dream' and what she 'must never dream'.

The audience's positioning in the darkened space on the other side of the fourth wall allows them a privileged bird's-eye view of the situation: yet another link to the theme of ornithology. In her 2002 article, 'Dirty devils, dead playwrights and dodgy pedagogues', Kate Bassett criticized Greig's 'analogies – not least the bird-watching, feathered and otherwise' as being 'schematic'. However, I am inclined to disagree with Bassett as these analogies are integrated in the storyline and are organically developed in the overall dramaturgical motifs of the piece. The freedom of the birds in flight serves as a strong contrast to the feelings of shame surrounding sexual desire that have been culturally imposed on the characters, and this allows the idea of being a voyeur (and it being an acceptable act) to be explored amongst the young, impressionable protagonists, as well as confronting the audience with the uncomfortable fact that they, too, are voyeurs gaining pleasure from watching the (semi-)naked bodies on stage.

Ellen as the voyeur: watching bo(d)ies

In possibly one of the most lyrical moments in Greig's entire body of work, there is an unexpected moment where Ellen describes directly to the audience an experience; her first experience of watching a naked male body:

> **Ellen** I remain watching and the boy starts to stripping his shirt and trousers from him his body white and skinny and he strips it all, he strips off all his clothes and they lie in the puddle of hot sun about him and I watch him and he doesn't know and he closes his eyes and his hands fall to touching himself to the giving himself pleasure and there in the hot sun on the rock like a young gull preening I watch him and I'm thinking this is the thing of the most beauty I have ever seen this badness this fallen thought and I want to drink it this

moment like a draught of whisky [...] and I think I think I think what is this feeling I'm having here this feeling of affection that's rising in me. (Greig 2002: 56)

This loss of innocence is presented like a piece of music with repetitions, flourishes and with little punctuation to reflect the freedom of that moment: 'the thing of the most beauty I have ever seen' (Greig 2002: 56). Robert's *actual* sexual pleasure becomes Ellen's *visual* sexual pleasure. Without any moral or social limitations and without a single trace of guilt, Ellen's account is a device that allows the audience to watch the same scene in their imagination and indirectly involves them in implicit voyeurism.

Ellen as the exhibitionist: her body being watched

Ellen shows clear signs not only of voyeuristic but also of explicit exhibitionistic behaviour:

> **Ellen** I rose, he watched me rising, the morning was warm,
> I went to bathe.
> At the stream.
> As I was washing my body –
> I looked up the hill towards the village.
> And he was still watching me. (Greig 2002: 96)

According to Robert, 'She moves with an acute awareness of being watched [...] every movement of hers is arranged into a small performance for the spectator' (Greig 2002: 29). She is happy to be watched because that erases the deformation of her claw-hands and makes her worth looking at. When Robert photographs her naked while she is bathing in the river, she feels like a film star being photographed and further demonstrates her exhibitionistic side, and when John suggests that they burn her naked picture, Ellen rebels, asking, 'Am I so monstrous you'd rather it burned than look at it?' It is clear she wants John to look at her picture and see her in her natural state, in her natural habitat, as she laments, 'I've never seen myself. Look at it [...] Look at the picture he's [Robert] made of me. This is how he sees me' (Greig 2002: 29).

It is important to see how the voyeur, Robert, is not guilty of any crime in Ellen's eyes. Even if Robert watches her without permission, she is still not disturbed by that activity and actively encourages it. For

Robert, this is an opportunity to continue his pleasurable watching of the forbidden and is perhaps Greig's way of helping the audience to reconcile their own grievances at becoming voyeurs of taboo acts. John helps provide the moral antithesis for the audience when he expresses distaste at the explicit voyeuristic happenings on the island when he retorts to Robert, 'It's a damn fine line between that kind of talk and perversion' (Greig 2002: 29).

When John finds out about the function of these pleasurable 'watching' activities, a rivalry develops between the two young men, and this competition encourages them to act in a way which removes all moral and social barriers or taboos. In a monologue by John,[4] he admits his desire for Ellen, in a way which creates symmetrical connections, both thematically and grammatically, with Ellen's monologue earlier in the play (as discussed above).

> **John** I swim. I lie on the rocks like a white seal in the hope that she will see me the way she saw him. I lie beside her in the chapel and listen to her breathing [...] I am no longer confidently aware of whether a memory of her is real or something I wish were real and in the hours of the early morning when I am at my weakest I feel only a thin wall separates me from rising and going to her bed and [...] (Greig 2002: 92)

This passage gives further understanding of the fine line that John is treading: he is constantly in an excited state of desire and cannot distinguish between reality and his memory. At this point, it would be interesting to note Greig's fascination with writing characters who adore listening to other people's breathing while they are asleep (there are examples in *The Cosmonaut's Last Message to the Woman He Once Loved in the Former Soviet Union*, *The Architect* and *The Speculator*). Greig himself admits that '[a]ll my characters are me, I just imagine myself in different situations. Ellen yearns for a different world. That taps with my psyche and I give it a practical reality' (Greig in Rimmer 2002).

Homosociality and Robert's gull eyes: male bonding, 'a chap's first time' and the consequences

Earlier in the chapter I posed the question: can we encounter a naked body (of the performer or even a character) without embracing the sexual politics of our gaze? Through an exploration of the critical framework of homosocial relationships as explored by Flood (2003, 2008), Kiesling (2005) and Culbertson (1998), I will finally highlight that perhaps it is not possible to completely remove the 'sexual' from the act of watching. Flood writes that,

> Homosociality organises men's sociosexual relations [...] sexual activity is a key path to masculine status, and other men are the audience, always imagined and sometimes real, for one's sexual activities. Heterosexual sex itself can be the medium through which male bonding is enacted. (Flood 2008: 339)

Greig organically sets up an ideal environment for homosocial activity to flourish: two young men obsessed with birds and watching in a closed remote social environment. Even if John is the shyer of the two, it is he who is the first to strip off his clothes, in Robert's presence (who is actually watching him), whilst being unaware that Ellen (who is standing by the door) is watching him as well. The stage directions in this case are explicit: 'He takes off his underpants and puts the shorts and vest on' (Greig 2002: 88). Flood (2003: 7) suggests that men want to have an imagined audience whose gaze would inform the meaning of their sexual relations, but this claim is reversed in the erotic love encounter between John and Ellen as John finds it embarrassing to continue the sexual encounter in Robert's presence, commenting, 'It's just a bit – off-putting – having a spectator. On a chap's first time' (Greig 2002: 106).

In this case, it is Ellen who wants to have an audience, to be watched during the sexual encounter so that she can be elevated from being an 'ordinary mortal' to become what she desires so much: a 'watched' iconic image of a film star. With the absence of social constraints on the island, the young impressionable characters are allowed to transcend merely dreaming about breaking social taboos and are given the freedom of the birds and celebrities they idolize and watch. This transformation from ordinary mortals to film stars is facilitated by 'gull-eyed' Robert watching their first sexual encounter and is beautifully described by Ellen:

Ellen Let me see him seeing us [...]
      We are caught in his gaze, boy.
      The bird's look.
      Gull Robert-watching.
      Drawing us unto his gull eyes.

> Into his gull mind till.
> I'm watching myself.
> Watching me and you.
> Like film stars we are boy,
> Made film stars by his gull eyes. (Greig 2002: 106–7)

But this causes serious distress to Robert, who feels excluded from the triangle and cannot find ways to change his status as 'third wheel'. His homosocial relationship to John is threatened and this becomes problematic for their friendship. Scott Fabius Kiesling (2005: 721) explains this behaviour by stating, 'if [...] heterosexual desire overrides [...] homosocial desire [...] it can threaten the status of [...] homosocial connections'. This classic staple of dramatic texts – the love triangle – and the power struggle that it creates, makes for compelling viewing/reading. The poetic language of Greig pushes the limits of accepted social behaviour, and with the permission of Ellen, allows Robert to watch and Ellen to exhibit and gain visual pleasure, in the same way that a voyeur/exhibitionist would in real life. But Robert is not only hurt because he is attracted to Ellen, but because he is also attracted to John. This attraction is not necessarily homosexual. Culbertson writes about the unerotic attraction between males which is often found in conventional love triangles:

> In the triangle of two men and a woman, the attraction between the two men must be taken at least as seriously as the attraction between each man and the woman [...] This desire to unite powers with another man is one possible non-genital form of Eros, this desire and attraction creating the exaggerated impulse to homosociality [...] The male gaze not only objectifies, but must objectify for homosociality to work. Ironically, the homosocial system can be maintained only when men avert their gaze from each other; the gaze, however figuratively, must remain focused on a woman. (Culbertson 1998: 2)

Culbertson's dissemination of the homosocial framework highlights a need for 'non-erotic' attraction between men and this type of relationship is clear between Robert and John. However, the tragic end of Robert shows that his behaviour, under the mask of homosociality, was hiding a much more passionate inner world of frustration and possibly even 'unspoken love'. In a conversation between the two young men, John expresses that Robert always gets what he wants, to which Robert emphatically replies, 'How could you possibly know what I want?' (Greig 2002: 88).

There is an ambiguous air to this conversation. Perhaps Robert is confused as to what he really truly desires? Maybe he is mistaking his homosocial attraction to John as a hidden homosexual attraction? Or maybe it is the other way around? Whatever the true reason, it seems that he is punished at the end of the play for his desires. His tragic end as 'he ran at the cliff edge and spread his arms out [...] and flew' (Greig 2002: 112), reminds us of an Icarus-like figure who miscalculates his moves in a moment of desperation and increased emotional frustration resulting from rejection and betrayal caused by the breakdown of the homosocial framework.

Conclusion

> Our wish to watch the other, our voyeurism, dictates conditions of the performance. Its role is certainly cathartic and in this way maybe even positive, but it is also a reflection of one's unpreparedness for the direct facing with oneself. We could almost talk about the relation actor–spectator as a pair voyeur–exhibitionist in which narcissism mediates as well as transfers. (Filipovic 2003: 76)

Filipovic's statement reminds us of the positive power of theatre to act as a platform for our personal fantasies to be explored and exploited on stage, but the following questions are still prominent: Is there a correlation between voyeurs and the act of theatre-going? Can the psychologies of exhibitionism be applied to the needs of a performer performing on stage? Can the traits of narcissism be traced in the performer's behaviour? Could 'theatre as voyeurism' function as a medical treatment for voyeurism itself?

The ultimate voyeur – the *auteur* director – makes most of the decisions related to the visual nature of the performance. And the audience receives and shares (with possibly the same fascination) the end result. The relationship between the performer and spectator can be re-read as a two-way exchange: bodies for paid exposure/display in a legalized environment. Thus, the act of watching acquires a new role which surpasses the simple function of pleasure which is associated with it. It enables the viewer to engage further with the 'theatre's mediation to comment, justify, explain and promote a better understanding of the complexities of human nature' (Rodosthenous in Greig 2011: 3). In *Outlying Islands*, the two ornithologists are watching what they desire to be themselves, while young Ellen decides to live the moment and immerse herself in a dream world where she is the leading film star amongst a tragic love triangle with no future. Voyeurism can be 're-read as a new freedom of the gaze, and its fetishistic attributes re-evaluated as an emancipation of restrained energy, testing the boundaries of taboo' (Rodosthenous in Greig 2011: 3).

Notes

This chapter was published in an earlier longer version as George Rodosthenous (2012) '*Outlying Islands* as theatre of voyeurism: ornithologists, naked bodies and the "pleasure of peeping"', *Studies in Theatre & Performance*, 32:1, 62–77.

1. *Outlying Islands* was first produced in August 2002 at the Edinburgh Fringe Festival. Performers: Robert Carr, Lesley Hart, Sam Heughan, Laurence Mitchell. Director: Philip Howard.
2. Karl Toepfer divides up the different kinds of nudity in performance into mythic, ritual, therapeutic, model, balletic, uninscribed, inscribed, obscene and pornographic in Toepfer (1996: 76).
3. Also see John Berger's discussion of the naked and the nude in Berger (1972).
4. This monologue was cut from the 2002 production and from the second edition of the script.

Bibliography

Allfree, Claire (2002) 'Distance no object', *Metro*, 9 August.
Bassett, Kate (2002) 'Dirty devils, dead playwrights and dodgy pedagogues', *The Independent*, 11 August.
Ben Chaim, Daphna (1984) *Distance in the Theatre: The Aesthetics of Audience Response* (Ann Arbor, MI: UMI Research Press).
Bentley, Eric (1991) *The Life of the Drama* (New York: First Applause Printing), 156–7.
Berger, John (1972) *Ways of Seeing* (London: BBC and Penguin Books).
Big Brother UK (2000–present) [TV Series] Endemol UK, Channel 4/Channel 5.
Billington, Michael (2004) 'Bone', *The Guardian*, 14 September.
Blank, Leonard (1973) 'Nakedness and nudity: a Darwinian explanation for looking and showing behaviour', *Leonardo*, 6:1, 23–7.
Brown, Mark (2002) 'Elegant island drama a little too caught up in its sense of time and place', *Scotland on Sunday*, 4 August.
Cover, Rob (2003) 'The naked subject: nudity, context and sexualization in contemporary culture', *Body & Society*, 9:3, 53–72.
Culbertson, Philip (1998) 'Designing men: reading the male body as text', *Textual Reasoning: The E-Journal of Post-Modern Jewish Philosophy*, 7 (June).
Danly, Regan (2006) www.canadianactor.com/info/r-islands.html (accessed 23 August 2006).
Dawson-Scott, Robert (2002) 'It's a shocking conundrum', *The Herald*, 3 August.

Filipovic, Ljiljana (2003) 'Theatre of the unconscious', *Literature and Psychology: A Journal of Psychoanalytic and Cultural Criticism*, 49:1/2, 65–76.

Flood, Michael (2003) 'Men, sex and mateship: how homosociality shapes men's heterosexual relations', Paper presented to *(Other) Feminisms: An International Women's Gender Studies Conference*, University of Queensland, 12–16 July.

Flood, Michael (2008) 'Men, sex and homosociality: how bonds between men shape their sexual relations with women', *Men and Masculinities*, 10:3, 339.

Greig, David (2002) *Outlying Islands* (London: Faber and Faber), 29–112.

Greig, David (2011) '"I let the language lead the dance": politics, musicality, and voyeurism: David Greig in conversation with George Rodosthenous', *New Theatre Quarterly*, 27:1, 3–14.

Hamilton, Christine and Adrienne Scullion (2005) '"Picture it if yous will": theatre and theatregoing in rural Scotland', *NTQ*, 21:1, 61–76.

Kiesling, Scott Fabius (2005) 'Homosociality in men's talk: balancing and recreating cultural discourses of masculinity', *Language in Society*, 34, 721.

McMillan, Joyce (2002) 'A question of value', *The Scotsman*, 5 August.

Rimmer, Louise (2002) 'I'm shocked by what my plays end up saying', interview with David Greig in *Scotland on Sunday*, 11 August.

Schneider, Rebecca (2000) 'On taking the blind in hand', *Contemporary Theatre Review*, 10:3, 24–6.

Spencer, Charles (2002) 'Munro returns to her peak', *The Daily Telegraph*, 5 August.

Tarter, Alice (2004) 'Shocking ending punctuates City Theatre's "Outlying Islands"' *Pittsburgh Tribune-Review*, 15 October.

Toepfer, Karl (1996) 'Nudity and textuality in postmodern performance', *Performing Arts Journal*, 54, 18:3, 76–87.

Van den Dries, Luk (2005) *Corpus Jan Fabre*, trans. Arthur Pritchard (Paris: L'Arche).

Index

Abramović, Marina, 149–51, 155, 161
accidental voyeurism, 6
Actaeon, 20, 112–15,
affective relations, 129, 141
Agamben, Giorgio, 126
Alston, Adam, 13, 83, 86
Artaud, Antonin, 35, 47, 59, 62, 167–8, 170–5
   Theatre of Cruelty, 33, 42, 47, 167, 171, 173
Augoyard, Jean-François, 75
aural simulation, 73
Auslander, Philip, 150–1
auteur, 1, 214, 223
aversion, 5, 121

The Bacchae, 1, 197
Bach fugue, 3
Bacon, Francis, 58
Barthes, Roland, 95–6
Bataille, Georges, 21, 114, 122
Beckett, Samuel, 10, 43
Bel, Jerôme, 122
Ben Chaim, Daphna, 12
Bennett, Susan, 11
Bentley, Eric, 13
Berger, John, 126, 224
Berkeley, Busby, 191
Berleant, Arnold, 136
Bieito, Calixto, 2
Big Brother, 3, 216
Billington, Michael, 14–15, 17
binaural recording, 73
binoculars, 15, 22, 137–8
Blank, Leonard, 13
Bleeker, Maaike, 10
Bloomfield, Arthur, 135
The Blue Room, 2, 6, 14
Bohlen, Joseph G., 158, 161
Bonenfant, Yvon, 76–8, 81
The Book of Mormon, 205
Bosch, Hieronymus, 48
Bouchard, Gianna, 11

Brandstetter, Gabriele, 123
Brantley, Ben, 14, 195, 198–9
Brecht, Bertolt, 90, 113–14, 116
Brook, Peter, 166
Brown, Ross, 75
burlesque, 5, 15, 189, 193, 195, 201
Butler, Steven, 205–6

cage aux folles, La, 205
Calendar Girls, 1
Calvert, Clay, 6
cam4.com, 3
Castellucci, Romeo, 2, 7, 50–65
   Divine Comedy, The, 19, 57
   Genesi, 59, 62
   Julius Caesar, 7, 19, 51, 53
   On the Concept of the Face Regarding the Son of God, 60, 62–3
   Paradise, 19, 57
   Purgatory, 58, 60
castration, 5, 36–7, 39, 42
celebrity voyeurism, 6
Chicago, 205
chirurgeon, 35, 37, 48
Cirque du Soleil
   Zumanity, 167
Clark, Kenneth, 148–9
collective voyeurism, 7, 188, 201
Comédie-Française, La, 171
commercial exploitation, 198–9
complicit voyeurism, 7
compulsive voyeurism, 7
concentric bubbles of spatial distance, 81
Conrad, Joseph, 58
Cover, Rob, 151–2, 155–6
curiosity, 6, 22, 53, 74, 91, 103, 204

'Dance of the Seven Veils', 1, 7
Danesi, Marcel, 188, 199
Davis, Lorri, 189–90, 202, 204
Debord, Guy 50
Deceukelier, Els, 43, 48, 216

deconstruction, 90
Derrida, Jacques, 18, 42, 82, 167
deviance, 4, 6
Dewey, John, 133
Diamond, Elin, 97
Diana, goddess, 112–15, 122
Dionysus in 69, 116
directional spectatorships, 85
Disney, Walt, 150, 177–80
disrobing, 1, 5, 118, 135, 188, 197, 202–3, 205
Dolan, Jill, 206
Doyle, Maxine, 72
dreamthinkspeak
   The Rest is Silence, 14
Dubois, Olivier, 130
   Tragédie, 140–1, 142
Duchamp, Marcel, 18, 30–1, 48, 130
The Duchess of Malfi, 14
Dyer, Richard, 206
Dyson, Clare, 130, 137, 142

Eck, Beth, 20, 148–51, 154, 156, 158, 160–2
Eiko & Koma, 133
Electric Hotel, 71–7, 79–80, 85–6
emotional voyeurism, 7
endoscope, 51–2
epopteia, 57
Equus, 1, 6, 14
erotic, 9, 17, 44, 73, 78, 81, 83, 96, 188, 195, 202–4, 213–14, 216, 221–2
exchange, 3, 7–8, 11, 16–17, 31, 33, 85–6, 93, 112, 135, 199, 200, 203, 212–13, 216, 223
exhibitionism, 16, 22, 29, 53, 166, 199, 213, 216
explicit voyeurism, 7, 21, 166

Fabre, Jan, 2, 18, 20, 29, 32–48, 111, 116–22, 125, 216
   As Long as the World Needs a Warrior's Soul, 35, 39
   History of Tears, 35–7
   Je suis sang (I am Blood), 29, 33–9
   Orgy of Tolerance, 34, 44
   The Power of Theatrical Madness, 43
   Quando l'uomo principale è una donna, 39

The Scheldt, 43
This is Theatre like it Was to be Expected and Foreseen, 116
Featherstone, Mike, 154
Fenichel, Otto, 5
fetishism, 10, 12
Fifty Shades of Grey, 169
Filipovic, Ljiljana 223
forbiddenness, 5
Foucault, Michel, 30–1, 126
framing, 93, 96, 147, 161, 163
Freud, Sigmund, 9, 12, 29, 35, 37, 39, 46, 175
Frisch, Max, 19, 88, 92–7, 105–6
full-frontal nudity, 21, 192–3, 196, 198, 205, 213
The Full Monty, 1
Fura dels Baus, La
   XXX, 17
furtive voyeurism, 7

Gardner, Lyn, 14, 89
gay, 15, 161
gaze, 2–3, 8–9, 11, 14, 16, 18–19, 22, 30–2, 45–6, 38, 50–2, 54, 56–8, 60–4, 73, 80, 82, 85, 88–9, 92, 96–7, 101–2, 104–6, 112–13, 125, 128, 130, 141, 143, 152, 156, 168, 174, 180, 188, 194, 196, 204–6, 212–14, 220–4
Gendlin, Eugene, 128–9
Gordon, Colette, 83
Gounaridou, Kiki, 9
The Graduate, 1, 6
gratification, 4, 5, 8, 13, 191, 194
gratuitousness, 21, 166–7, 170, 173, 180
Green, André, 95
Greig, David, 21–2, 211–24
   The Architect, 213, 220
   The Cosmonaut's Last Message to the Woman He Once Loved in the Former Soviet Union, 213, 220
   Outlying Islands, 18, 21–2, 211–24
   The Speculator, 220
Grosz, Elizabeth, 175
guilt, 1, 3, 7, 8, 11, 13–15, 95, 97, 206, 219

Hair, 187, 195–206
Halprin, Anna, 130, 131, 134–5, 197
　Parades and Changes, 20, 131, 134, 197
Haring-Smith, Tori, 9
Hart, Lesley, 212
headphones, 19, 72–3, 75–6, 124, 137–8
Henderson, Mrs (Laura), 193
Heughan, Sam, 212, 214
Hitchcock, Alfred, 73
Hoffman, Barbara, 15
homosociality, 220–2
Howard, Philip, 211, 215
Hrvatin, Emil, 34
Hunt, Lynn, 168, 170
Hydrocracker, 88, 97, 101, 104
　The New World Order, 88–9, 97, 101, 104

immersive, 8, 13–14, 71–2, 82–3, 86–7
implicit voyeurism, 7, 219
inspectionalism, 5
intellectual voyeurism, 7
intimacy, 9, 13, 19, 71, 73–4, 76, 78–87
intimate voyeurism, 7

Jameson, Fredric, 172, 181
Jarry, Alfred, 171
Jerry Springer: The Opera, 205
Johnson, Dominic, 10
jouissance, 42, 44–6
The Judas Kiss, 1

Kamper, Dietmar, 42
Kantor, Tadeusz, 88, 97–106
katharsis, 181
Keaton, Diane, 202
Kellog, Lynn 202
Kendrick, Walter, 168, 170
keyhole, 2, 10, 30, 32–3, 39, 45, 51, 58
Kidman, Nicole, 6

La Rocco, Claudia, 179
Lacan, Jacques, 9, 12, 32, 36, 42, 44
Laws, Richard, 4–5, 8
Leach, Robert, 8
Lefebvre, Henri, 133

Lepecki, Andre, 134
Leppert, Richard, 111
LeRoy, Xavier, 111, 121–4
　Low Pieces, 123–5, 134–6
Longhurst, Michael, 15
Lord Chamberlain, 192–4
Lulu, 1, 14

Machon, Josephine, 11
MacKendrick, Karen, 132
Marks, Emmaretta, 202
Marks, Laura, 11
masculine hegemony, 21
Mauss, Marcel, 173
McCarthy, Paul, 150, 201
McMillan, Joyce, 213
Melendez, Franklin, 173–4
Merleau-Ponty, Maurice, 74–5
Metz, Christian, 9
Metzl, Jonathan, 5
mise-en-scène, 10, 54, 212
Mitchell, Laurence, 212
mixoscopia, 4
Money, John, 4, 16
Monji, Jana, 166
Moore, Melba, 202
Mother Clap's Molly House, 167
Moulin Rouge, 205
Mulvey, Laura, 9, 206
Muybridge, Eadweard, 141

nachträglich, 37
Naked Boys Singing, 2, 7, 167, 205–6
Naked Brunch, 8
naked voyeurism, 8
Neilson, Anthony, 166
Nield, Sophia, 82
Nietzsche, Friedrich, 39
Norstrand, Suzzanah, 202

O'Donohue, William, 4–5, 8
O'Horgan, Tom, 197–8, 200
Oddey, Alison, 10
off-Broadway, 187, 196–7, 200, 203
Oh! Calcutta!, 2, 116
Olle, Alex, 17
optical revelations, 54
Ovid, 112, 115
Owens, Craig, 150

Pallasmaa, Juhani, 76, 78–9
Palmer, Scott, 79–80
Panopticon, 18, 30–1
Papaioannou, Dimitris, 2–3
    Inside, 2–3
Papaioannou, Spyros, 9
Paradise Now, 116
The Pass, 1, 14
pathological voyeurism, 8
patriarchal, 188, 190, 195–6, 198, 201–2, 204, 206
Pavis, Patrice, 8, 187–8, 194, 200, 203–5
Peckham, Morse, 169
peepers, 5
Pentheus, 1
Phelan, Peggy, 174
phenomenological and affective experience, 89
Piaf, 7
pictophilia, 5
Pinter, Harold, 89–90, 97, 101, 104
Plimpton, Shelley, 202
Ploeger, Daniël, 147–64
    ELECTRODE, 147, 155–63
    SUIT, 152–6, 161–3
pornographic theatre, 167, 172, 181
pornography, 5, 21, 45–6, 148, 152, 167–70, 173–7, 179–81, 201
postdramatic theatre, 29
pre-oedipal state, 37, 39
primal acts, 6, 74, 204
Privates on Parade, 1
prosthetic, 17
proxemics, 79, 81, 90
proximity, 7, 78, 86, 128, 130, 137, 141
psychoanalysis, 6
Punchdrunk, 7, 10, 14, 19, 71–2, 82–7
    The Drowned Man, 14, 19, 71–2, 82–6
    Sleep No More, 7, 14
purification, 35, 38

Radcliffe, Daniel, 6
Rado and Ragni, 187, 196–7
Rancière, Jacques, 129
Read, Alan, 9

Renaissance, 60, 113, 192
Rimmer, Louise, 212, 220
Robertson, Steve, 154
The Romans in Britain, 1
Rose, Jacqueline, 12–13
Roy, Sanjoy, 139–40
Royal Court Theatre, 14, 211
Royal Shakespeare Company, 166
Ruckert, Felix, 130, 137

Sade, Marquis de, 44–5, 166–7
St-Pierre, Dave, 20, 130, 138–9
    Un peu de tendresse bordel de merde, 138–40, 142
Salome, 1, 7
Sartre, Jean-Paul, 18, 30
Scarpetta, Guy, 88, 97–105
scenographic, 72, 82, 85
Schneider, Rebecca, 11–12, 167
scopophilia, 5, 9, 29
scopophilic voyeurism, 8
scoptolagnia, 5
sexualized objectification of women, 188–9
Shepherd, Simon, 12
Shilling, Chris, 154
Sidiropoulou, Avra, 10
site-specific, 71, 88–92, 96–102, 104–6
Sloterdijk, Peter, 42
Smith, Spencer, 4
Sociètas Raffaello Sanzio, 50–5, 62, 64–5
sociosexual relations, 221
solicitation, 4, 16
spectating, 10, 74, 79, 82
spectatorship, 8, 10, 71, 73, 85–6, 167
Spencer, Charles, 6, 14, 216
Spring Awakening, 205
Stanislavsky, Konstantin, 51–2
Stockhausen, Karlheinz, 22

tableaux vivants, 40, 194
taboo, 12–13, 15, 17, 23, 35, 38–9, 61, 74, 160, 188, 197, 201–2, 211, 213, 220–1, 224
Take Me Out, 1, 6–7, 14–15
tangible corporeality, 116–17

technology, 73, 75, 77, 80, 153–4, 157
theatron, 12, 22, 51, 58
third image, 19, 51, 54
'Tis Pity She's a Whore, 15
Titian, 112–17, 123, 125
Toepfer, Karl, 20, 116, 131, 200, 213, 215
Torgue, Henry, 75
transcendence, 10, 22, 31, 33, 42, 48
troilism, 5
Tunick, Spencer, 147–50, 152, 155, 161–2

Übersfeld, Anne, 11, 126

vaudeville, 189, 192
Vergara, Camilo José, 91
violence, 64, 112–13
visuality, 9, 10–11, 76

Warburg, Aby, 56
What the Butler Saw, 9
White, Christine, 10
Whitehead, Jay, 15
Wiles, David, 22
Windmill Theatre, 192–4
Wollman, Elizabeth, 197–8, 200, 204
Woyzeck, 14, 72

Xenakis, Iannis, 157

Yalom, Irvin, 5
Yeats, W.B., 128
You Me Bum Bum Train, 7
Young, Ann Liv, 167, 176–81
   Cinderella, 167, 175–80
   Mermaid Solo, 179

Ziegfeld, Florenz, 189–94
Žižek, Slavoj, 45–6

Printed and bound in Great Britain by
CPI Group (UK) Ltd, Croydon, CR0 4YY